FROM APOSTASY TO RESTORATION

FROM APOSTASY TO RESTORATION

KENT P. JACKSON

Deseret Book Company
Salt Lake City, Utah

Appreciation is expressed for photographs and artwork on the pages listed: Art Resource, New York, 43 and 60; The Church of Jesus Christ of Latter-day Saints, 2, 63, 69, 84, 87, 106, 125, 128, 130, 133, 138, 173, and 249; Richard Neitzel Holzapfel, 131; Kent P. Jackson, 38, 49, 73, 119, 136, 138, 142, 154, 157, 164, 185, 189, and 227; Harold B. Lee Library, Brigham Young University, 142 and 243; Library-Archives, Reorganized Church of Jesus Christ of Latter Day Saints, Independence, Missouri, 124, 137, 196, 198, and 232; Library of Congress, 221; Missouri Historical Society, 236; Al Rounds, 94. All pictures © by the sources indicated and used with permission.

Library of Congress Cataloging-in-Publication Data

Jackson, Kent P.
From Apostasy to Restoration / Kent P. Jackson
p. cm.
Includes bibliographical references and indexes.
ISBN 1-57345-218-1
1. Great Apostasy (Mormon doctrine) 2. Restoration of the gospel (Mormon doctrine) 3. Church of Jesus Christ of Latter-day Saints—Apologetic works. 4. Mormon Church—Apologetic works. 5. Church history—Miscellanea. I. Title.
BX8643.G74J33 1996
230'.9332—dc20 96-40989
CIP

Printed in the United States of America

10 9 8 7 6 5 4 3 2 1

Contents

Illustrations

Preface

The defining event of the Latter-day Saint faith is the restoration of the gospel—the process that reestablished on earth, through the ministry of the Prophet Joseph Smith, the Church of Jesus Christ and all the blessings that accompany it. Those blessings include the Lord's priesthood—the authority to act in his name and speak his words in his behalf. They also include his doctrine, restored anew in pristine purity, to teach us what we need to know to serve him and return to his presence. Among other things, the doctrine of the Restoration teaches us the answers to life's greatest questions, including who we are, why we exist, and what lies beyond death for us.

This book is an introduction to the Restoration during the days of the Prophet Joseph Smith and to the events by which it was accomplished. It begins with chapters that summarize the Apostasy, the process by which the ancient Church of Jesus Christ was lost from the earth along with the pure doctrine of God that was taught in it. Then it follows in sequence the principal events and contributions of the Restoration, beginning with the circumstances that led to the First Vision and culminating in the great doctrinal teachings from the last years of Joseph Smith's life. Although this is not a history book, it chronicles the major milestones of the Restoration within the context of events in the earliest days of the Church.

Each topic in this book deserves an entire volume, but I hope this survey will provide a useful summary that will lead to greater study and greater appreciation for the marvelous blessings of the restored Church of Jesus Christ and the gospel message that it proclaims to the world. I present this book as an expression of my own testimony of the truth of the Restoration, of the divine origin of the mission of the Prophet Joseph Smith, and of the divinity of The Church of Jesus Christ of Latter-day Saints.

I would like to thank faithful assistants who have checked sources, edited, and proofed the pages of this book: Lisa M. Kurki, Jason O. Roberts, Ana N. Shaw, and LeGrande W. Smith. To Suzanne Brady and her colleagues at Deseret Book I am also thankful. I would also like to express my appreciation to honored colleagues at Brigham Young University who have read portions of the manuscript and have offered invaluable suggestions: Richard L. Anderson, Alexander L. Baugh, Dong Sull Choi, Richard O. Cowan, Larry E. Dahl, Richard D. Draper, H. Dean Garrett, Leon R. Hartshorn, Dennis L. Largey, Robert J. Matthews, Paul H. Peterson, Larry C. Porter, Stephen E. Robinson, and Bruce A. Van Orden.

Chapter 1

What Do We Mean by "True Church"?

Individuals who are not members of The Church of Jesus Christ of Latter-day Saints are often puzzled when they hear us say that ours is the "true church." Because the Lord has declared such to be the case (D&C 1:30), we need not apologize for this assertion, nor should we think ourselves bold for believing it. But we do need to know what it means.

Obviously, if there is a true church, it is not because the people in it are "truer" than others or because they try harder to please God. A church can only be the church of Jesus Christ if the Lord himself establishes it, authorizes it, and recognizes its works as valid and binding. The question, then, is not one of good intent but one of divine authorization.

The scriptures teach us that this divine authorization is to be manifested in two fundamental ways: in the authority for God's earthly servants to act in his name, and in teachings that are revealed from him and are acknowledged by him to be correct. Thus the true church must possess true authority and true doctrine, and both of these must be revealed from God. We believe that The Church of Jesus Christ of Latter-day Saints meets these necessary requirements.

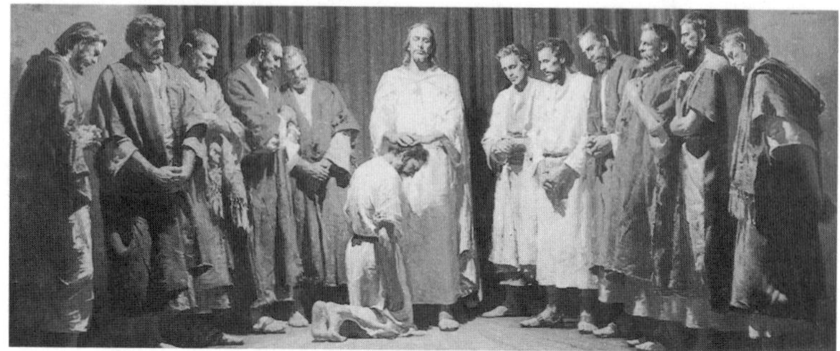

Jesus ordaining the Twelve

True Authority

When the Lord taught his ancient apostles, whom he had called to be ministers of the gospel, he said, "Ye have not chosen me, but I have chosen you, and ordained you" (John 15:16). Most readers of the New Testament overlook the importance of this short sentence, but it carries a message that is a fundamental principle of true religion. People do not have the right to call themselves to act in God's name. Nowhere in the scriptures do we have examples of the Lord's true servants designating themselves to his work. Neither a desire to serve, nor a sense of mission, nor a love of God and fellowmen—however heartfelt and sincere these may be—authorizes one to enter the Lord's ministry. The scriptural precedent shows that the call must be from God. And where God already has true servants on earth, the call comes through them, his representatives.

This principle is taught in the New Testament in a discussion of priesthood authority: "No man taketh this honour unto himself, but he that is called of God, as was Aaron" (Heb. 5:4). The Old Testament tells us how Aaron was called. The Lord's authorized servant, Moses, learned by revelation that it was God's will that Aaron serve (Ex. 28:1). Accordingly, the prophet called and ordained him (Ex. 40:12–16). Jesus called the apostles (Matt. 4:19–22; 10:1–8) and seventy others (Luke 10:1–2) to minister in his name. After his resurrection, the apostles, who served as his representatives on earth, called another to replace Judas and join them in their apostolic work (Acts 1:15–26). They also called seven others to important assignments (Acts 6:3–6), as well as elders and bishops to preside in local congregations (e.g., Acts 14:23; Titus 1:5). This pattern is always followed when authorized servants of God are found.

The book of Acts provides an interesting account from the history of the Early Church that illustrates some of these fundamentals. When Philip preached the gospel in Samaria, he met with success and converted many. Having been authorized to do so, he baptized his converts in the name of Jesus (Acts 8:5–12). But it appears that his authority did not extend to the laying on of hands to give the gift of the Holy Ghost; for this, the apostles were called from Jerusalem (Acts 8:14–17). However sincere, worthy, or desirous Philip may have been, his assignment had limitations, and he knew he could not call himself to prerogatives that were not his. When the apostles gave the new believers the gift of the Holy Ghost, a convert named Simon, recognizing that the apostles had authority from God, sought to purchase it (Acts 8:18–19). Even with his confused understanding of the nature of priesthood, he realized that he could not call himself to it but must receive it from God's servants who already possessed it.

Many honorable persons with the purest of motives have devoted their lives to the service of Christ and their fellowmen. It is safe to suppose that they will be rewarded abundantly in the eternities for their devoted efforts. But with respect to priesthood authority—the power to minister in Christ's name as his authorized representatives—the principles seen in New Testament times are as valid today as they were then. As the Prophet Joseph Smith taught, "We believe that a man must be called of God by prophecy, and by the laying on of hands by those who are in authority, to preach the Gospel and administer in the ordinances thereof" (Article of Faith 5; see also D&C 42:11).

The Church of Jesus Christ of Latter-day Saints could not assert that it is the Lord's church unless its own claim to authority were consistent with these principles. Our testimony is that in every way it meets the scriptural standard. Joseph Smith was called of God in the most literal way. Initially, God the Father and Jesus Christ appeared to him—the First Vision. Subsequently, he was ordained and given authority by the ministry of heavenly messengers. John the Baptist ordained him to the Aaronic Priesthood, which includes the authority to baptize. The ancient apostles Peter, James, and John ordained him to the holy apostleship, conferring on him the keys of the kingdom—the authority for mortals to preside on earth in Christ's name as his earthly representatives.

This apostolic power has continued in the Church from Joseph Smith's time to our own. It is the authority by which modern apostles and prophets lead the Church today. All who have held priesthood in the Church of Jesus Christ have received it through a chain that links them back to Joseph Smith's ordinations under the hands of resurrected men from ancient times. Individuals are called through the spirit of revelation by those already possessing authority, and they are ordained or set apart by them. Thus they, in turn, become the Lord's authorized servants, and their works are valid and acknowledged of God.

True Doctrine

As with priesthood, doctrine can only be recognized as true and authoritative if it is revealed from God. Otherwise, it represents—at best—an honorable attempt to understand the mind of God without any way to know it.

True doctrine flows from true priesthood authority. Joseph Smith taught that the Melchizedek Priesthood "is the channel through which all knowledge, doctrine, the plan of salvation and every important matter is revealed from heaven."[1] It is "the channel through which the Almighty commenced revealing his glory at the beginning of the creation of this earth and through which he has continued to reveal himself to the children of men to the present time and through which he will make known his purposes to the end of time."[2] Thus, where the keys of the priesthood are found, the windows of heaven will be open. Where true authority is not found, revelation sufficient to guide individuals to salvation is lacking.

Knowing that the Bible contains the word of God, many Christians have learned to rely on it as the source of their doctrinal knowledge. In this they are to be commended, because they recognize that the truth of God can only be known by what has been revealed from him to his servants. This understanding is far superior to the idea that divine truth can be ascertained through human reasoning or through the philosophies of men. Were it not for the Restoration, a belief that the Holy Bible is the sole repository of revealed sacred knowledge might be the best option available for honest seekers of the truth.

But the restoration of the gospel changes the situation dramatically. Through Joseph Smith, a modern prophet, we learn that the Bible does not contain all that God revealed anciently, nor did it arrive in our day without inaccuracies. He taught that "many important points, touching the salvation of man, had been taken from the Bible, or lost before it was compiled."[3] He said that he believed in the Bible "as it came from the pen of the original writers,"[4] or "as far as it is translated correctly" (Article of Faith 8), with "translated" seemingly referring to the entire process of transmission from the original manuscripts to modern-language translations. But "ignorant translators, careless transcribers, or designing and corrupt priests have committed many errors."[5]

These are not new ideas to serious students of the Bible, who have long recognized imperfections in its transmission. What is remarkable, however, is what the Lord did to reveal anew the fulness of his gospel—by opening the heavens again. The restoration of doctrinal truth through Joseph Smith is what one latter-day apostle has called a "wonderful flood of light."[6] And indeed it is both wonderful and luminous.

The doctrinal restoration involves the revelation of new books of scripture, which Latter-day Saints view as authoritative alongside the Bible. Joseph Smith added more to the canon than any other known individual in history. The Book of Mormon, which was revealed through him, is a sacred record similar to the Bible. But its teachings of Christ and his plan of redemption are not surpassed in any other book. The Doctrine and Covenants contains more than one hundred divine communications from God to his modern Prophet, in which he gave from heaven an abundance of truth concerning his will for us. The Pearl of Great Price, a collection of doctrinal revelations reserved to come forth in our day, reveals things that are not found in any other source. Through the Joseph Smith Translation of the Bible, the Prophet restored truth that had become lost through the corruption of ancient revealed texts, giving us the scriptures "even as they are in [God's] own bosom, to the salvation of [his] own elect" (D&C 35:20).

The Prophet's sermons and writings are another source of divine revelation. By the power of the Holy Ghost, he had a clear understanding of truth and knew how to teach it. And because he had that power, we have been blessed with a doctrinal outpouring that is perhaps unsurpassed at any time in history except when Jesus himself taught on earth. Because we know that Jesus was the source of the Prophet's revelations, we can trust his teachings to be the mind and will of the Lord for our time. They are true because they pass the only valid test of doctrinal authenticity: they were revealed from God.

The True Church

Because this modern-day revelation of priesthood and doctrine brings back authority and truth that had existed in earlier times, we call this process the Restoration. We proclaim that the gospel of Jesus Christ has been restored and that the Church of Jesus Christ, long absent from the earth, is again to be found and is acknowledged as the Lord's Church. Christ directs his Church through apostles and prophets, whose authority continues that which was restored to Joseph Smith by Peter, James, and John. "For thus shall my church be called in the last days," the Lord said, "even The Church of Jesus Christ of Latter-day Saints" (D&C 115:4). It is "the only true and living church upon the face of the whole earth" (D&C 1:30).

Why is it the true church? Because the Lord established it, revealed its teachings, revealed the authority under which it is governed, continues to direct its affairs, and recognizes its works as valid and binding.

Notes

1. Andrew F. Ehat and Lyndon W. Cook, eds., *The Words of Joseph Smith: The Contemporary Accounts of the Nauvoo Discourses of the Prophet Joseph* (Provo, Utah: Religious Studies Center, Brigham Young University, 1980), 38.

2. Ibid., 39.

3. Dean C. Jessee, ed., *The Papers of Joseph Smith,* 3 vols. (Salt Lake City: Deseret Book, 1989–97), 1:372.

4. Ehat and Cook, *Words of Joseph Smith,* 256.

5. Joseph Smith, *History of The Church of Jesus Christ of Latter-day Saints,* ed. B. H. Roberts, 2d ed. rev., 7 vols. (Salt Lake City: Deseret Book, 1957), 6:57.

6. Neal A. Maxwell, *A Wonderful Flood of Light* (Salt Lake City: Bookcraft, 1990), 15.

Chapter 2

The Apostasy

The Church of Jesus Christ of Latter-day Saints has taught since its beginning that there was an apostasy of the Church that was founded by Jesus during his earthly ministry and led by the apostles after his ascension. This is a fundamental belief of our religion: if there had not been an apostasy, there would have been no need for a restoration.

To understand the Apostasy, we must first understand that Jesus established a church. We Latter-day Saints take this fact for granted, because we see evidence of church organization in the New Testament (e.g., Acts 1:12–16; 4:32–37; 6:1–7). But even more important, it is a matter of doctrinal principle that wherever the gospel, the keys of the priesthood, and the saving ordinances exist, there will be found the Church of Jesus Christ. These circumstances existed from the very beginning of the Savior's ministry.

The book of Acts and the New Testament epistles contain a wealth of information about the ancient Church in its early years. After Jesus' resurrection it was presided over by apostles whom he had called (Matt. 4:19–22; 10:1–8) and to whom he had given the authority and the inspiration to call others when vacancies in the Twelve occurred (Acts 1:15–26). Local Church leaders served under the direction of the Twelve, from whom they received their authority and their message (e.g., Acts 14:22–23; Titus 1:5). Spiritual gifts were common in the Church (Acts 2:1–4; 3:1–7), and the power of Christ was at work as the message of salvation spread into many lands (Acts 14:3–10). The vitality of the Church was evidence of its divinity. Its leaders possessed the authority of God, and its message was the pure doctrine of Christ.

A century later, things had changed dramatically. The original apostles were gone, but others were no longer being called to take their places. Christians spoke with longing of the old days when the Lord's servants were among them.[1] The doctrinal unity of which the Twelve were guardians had dissolved, and groups with very diverse teachings had come into existence and were competing for power in the Christian community.[2]

Rebellion, Mutiny, Revolution

In seeking a definition of *apostasy,* Church members frequently turn to 2 Thessalonians 2:3 and cite the phrase in the King James Version, "a falling away." Unfortunately, the translation of this verse is both inadequate and misleading, and it has been the cause of some historical misinformation in the Church that has made it difficult to understand the nature of the Apostasy and how it happened. The intent of the original word is much more dramatic and points to something much more profound than "a falling away."

The Greek word used by Paul in 2 Thessalonians 2:3 is *apostasía,* from which we have the English word *apostasy.* It is constructed from two Greek roots: the verb *hístēmi,* "to stand," and the preposition *apō,* "away from." The word means "rebellion," "mutiny," "revolt," or "revolution," and it is used in ancient contexts with reference to uprisings against established authority. The idea of a gentle drifting that comes to mind with the phrase "a falling away" is not one of its meanings.

In a revolution or rebellion, the objective is to remove the leaders and replace them with others whose views are more compatible with those of the rebels. The result is not only new leadership but also new policies and new objectives. This image describes what is meant by *apostasía.* And sadly it also describes what happened to the Early Christian Church, according to the New Testament. Because of rebellion against the authority and doctrine of the apostles, the Early Church came to an end less than a century after its formation.[3]

As the process of *apostasía* developed, doctrines that inspired Church leaders had taught were corrupted and changed by others not of similar inspiration, the authority to act in God's name was taken from the earth, and the Christianity that existed thereafter, despite the honorable efforts of many individuals in it, did not enjoy divine endorsement as the Lord's own church. The Apostasy, then, refers to the circumstances that brought about the demise of the Early Church and to the period of time from its fall—about A.D. 100—until the time of the Restoration, beginning in 1820. But for most of the world, the Apostasy continues today.

Seducing Spirits

Perhaps the most remarkable witness of the apostasy of New Testament Christianity is the New Testament itself. Its writers prophesied that apostasy would take place and have a grave effect on their work. Those prophecies are the best place to start as we endeavor to understand what happened to the Early Church. They are important because they show us that Christ and the apostles anticipated the Apostasy and especially because they shed light on the nature of it and the process that brought it about. The following is an outline of some relevant verses.[4]

Matthew 24:5, 9–11. "Many" false Christs "shall deceive many" (24:5). "Then shall many be offended" (24:10). The word *offended* is used to translate the Greek *skandalízō,* which means to "trip." In a religious context such as this, it means to "give up one's faith": "many will turn away from the faith" (NIV), or "many will fall from their faith" (REB).[5] And "many false prophets shall rise, and shall deceive many" (24:11).

Acts 20:29–31. "Grievous wolves" will "enter in among" the

Church, and they will not spare the flock (20:29). "Of your own selves" men will arise, teaching "perverse things" so they can "draw away disciples after them" (20:30), or "in order to get the disciples to break away and follow them" (REB).

2 Thessalonians 2:1–12. The *apostasía* (Paul wrote *the,* not *a*) will take place (2:3): "the rebellion" (NIV, NRSV), "the Great Revolt" (JB). Satan—the "man of sin," "the son of perdition"—will come to the fore (2:3). He will sit in God's place as though he were God (2:4). This "mystery of iniquity" was being held back at the time Paul was writing until God withdrew the power that restrained it (2:6–8).

1 Timothy 4:1–3. In "the latter times," that is, the final days of the Early Church,[6] "some shall depart from the faith," following "seducing spirits, and doctrines of devils" (4:1). Examples of false teachings are a prohibition against marriage and the introduction of unauthorized dietary restrictions (4:3).

2 Timothy 4:3–4. There would be a rejection of "sound doctrine" (4:3). Having "itching ears" for religion, they will obtain teachers after their own liking (4:3). They will "turn away their ears from the truth" and turn to "fables" (4:4).

2 Peter 2:1–3. "There shall be false teachers among you" (2:1), who will "secretly introduce" (NIV) "damnable heresies" (2:1). "Many" will follow them (2:2), as a result of which "the way of truth" will be blasphemed (2:2). Thus they will "make merchandise of you" with false doctrine (2:3): "feigned words" (KJV), "stories they have made up" (NIV), "sheer fabrications" (REB).

1 John 2:18. "Ye" were warned that "antichrist" would come in "the last time," which, according to John, was the time in which he wrote.

Jude 1:4, 17–19. There had been warnings long ago about people infiltrating and perverting the faith: "certain men crept in unawares" (1:4). The apostles warned of "mockers" in the "last time" (1:17–18).

Revelation 13:1–9. Satan's beast will blaspheme "against God" and his work (13:6). He will "make war with the saints" and will "overcome them" (13:7). He will have power over "all that dwell upon the earth" (13:8).

These passages paint a disheartening picture of the future of the Early Church, because it is obvious that both Jesus and his apostles knew that apostate influences would have a powerful effect on it. The verses cited show clearly the pattern of how the Apostasy would work: the rejection of true doctrine, the appearance of self-appointed teachers, and the introduction of man-made religion. Subsequent history shows that the Church did not survive the process intact.[7]

Watching the Apostasy Happen

In addition to foretelling the spread of apostasy, the New Testament recorded much of it as it was taking place. The apostles' letters show them struggling with false teachings and practices that were making their way into the Church. In the earliest letters these problems were relatively minor and perhaps were remedied by sound apostolic teaching. But as time progressed, the false ideas against which the apostles contended became increasingly malignant and increasingly successful. As the Church grew, so also did the cancerous elements within it that finally led to its death. The New Testament recorded the process while it happened.[8]

Apostate practices are mentioned in a number of New Testament verses. Paul contended against those who formed factions by playing favorites with Church leaders (1 Cor. 1:10–16; 3:3–10; 11:18). The Corinthian Saints allowed a case of incest to go uncorrected (1 Cor. 5:1–13), and they engaged in inappropriate observance of the sacrament (1 Cor. 11:23–34). Uninspired notions concerning the gifts of the Spirit led them to distorted behavior (1 Cor. 14:1–14, 33). Evil speaking against the apostle Paul was evident (2 Cor. 11–12; Gal. 1). Some Church members were transforming their faith into a Judaized Christianity and were bringing into the Church Jewish holidays (Gal. 4:10) and Jewish ritual (Gal. 5:2–4).

False beliefs play an even more prominent role than do apostate practices in the documents of the New Testament. For example, some Thessalonian Saints had developed the idea that the second coming of Christ was "at hand" (2 Thes. 2:2–4). Some elsewhere had apparently developed mistaken notions about the relationship between faith and works (James 2:14–17, 26). Some Corinthian Church members were teaching that Jesus had not risen from the dead and that there is no resurrection (1 Cor. 15:1–58). Some Galatians were turning to what the apostle Paul called "another gospel," under the influence of those who would "pervert the gospel of Christ" (Gal. 1:6–7). They believed that the law of Moses was necessary for salvation (Gal. 3:1–5).

These examples all come from the period between A.D. 50 and 60. It may be argued that some of these problems would not be of major consequence, assuming that the corrective teaching in the apostles' letters and visits would be received and obeyed. But as is evident in the earliest Christian writings of the second century, by the end of the first century the apostles were gone,[9] and Christianity had lost its doctrinal anchor. These events suggest that the cumulative effect of false beliefs was more successful than the apostolic efforts to correct them.

Beginning in the 60s, doctrinal problems of a more serious nature grew in the Early Church. They clearly threatened the Church's existence and jeopardized the salvation of those who were affected by them.

It is in this period of history that we see the first evidences of what later became known as Gnosticism. Most of what we know of Gnosticism comes from sources a century or more after the days of the apostles, so we understand it best in its fully developed form of later years. But the New Testament gives unmistakable evidence that it was already developing and gaining ground while the Early Church was still alive. Gnosticism was an aberrant Christian doctrine that taught that physical matter and everything associated with it were evil. Because God could not consist of matter or even be the creator of matter, all material creation had to be looked upon as perverse. Some Gnostics believed in a chain of lower deities, each less holy than the one above. The lowest of these, the evil Jehovah of the Old Testament, created the material world.

In his epistle to the Colossians, Paul contended with a doctrinal heresy that he neither named nor described. But the words he used to warn the Colossian Saints against it suggest that it was Gnosticism in an early form. Paul's emphasis on Christ's supremacy in the universe (Col. 1:16–19; 2:9–10) and his warning against the worship of "angels" (Col. 1:15–2:23) seem to respond to Gnostic belief in lower deities. Paul gave a stern warning against accepting any doctrine that was different than the apostolic message that he had taught: "As ye have therefore received Christ Jesus the Lord, so walk ye in him: rooted and built up in him, and stablished in the faith, as ye have been taught, abounding therein with thanksgiving. Beware lest any man spoil you through philosophy and vain deceit, after the tradition of men, after the rudiments of the world, and not after Christ" (2:6–8). "Let no man beguile you" (2:18).

The Pastoral Epistles also show evidence of early Gnosticism. Paul's warnings against "genealogies" likely had reference to the descending chain of Gnostic deities. He wrote of "fables and endless genealogies" (1 Tim. 1:4), "vain babblings" (1 Tim. 6:20), "foolish questions, and genealogies" (Titus 3:9). He also warned against "what is falsely called *knowledge*" (1 Tim. 6:20, NIV, NRSV). "Knowledge" ("science" in the KJV) is the word used to translate the Greek *gnōsis,* from which the word *Gnosticism* comes. The Gnostics believed they had a special revealed *gnōsis,* or knowledge, by which they alone understood scripture, knew

God, and were saved. This knowledge, they believed, was not available to the uninitiated mainstream of Christianity.

John's letters, perhaps the latest writings in the New Testament, show additional evidence of Gnosticism creeping into the Early Church. The immediate apostate doctrine was *Docetism*—the belief that Jesus did not really come in the flesh (1 Jn. 4:2–3; 2 Jn. 1:7). Docetism was a product of the fundamental philosophy that all matter is evil. Because Jesus therefore could not have actually had a material body, he only seemed, or appeared, to come in the flesh.

It does not take much imagination to realize the consequences of this kind of belief. Like John, we can see that this doctrine denies the reality of Christ's mortal experiences, his suffering and death in the Atonement, his physical resurrection, and ours as well. John pointed out that the Saints had been warned that "antichrist" would come in the last days of the Church (1 Jn. 2:18). They are here, he wrote, and they came from among the Saints (1 Jn. 2:18–19). Many false prophets have arisen (1 Jn. 4:1). For John, the test of antichrist was whether one believed that Jesus actually came in the flesh (1 Jn. 4:2–3). As an eyewitness of the Savior he reminded his readers: "We have heard," "we have seen with our eyes," "we have looked upon, and our hands have handled, of the Word of life" (1 Jn. 1:1). He pleaded with the Saints to hold on to true doctrine: "Let that therefore abide in you, which ye have heard from the beginning. If that which ye have heard from the beginning shall remain in you, ye also shall continue in the Son, and in the Father. . . . These things have I written unto you concerning them that seduce you" (1 Jn. 2:24, 26).

Other varieties of apostasy developed in the Early Church and are evidenced in the New Testament. Paul spoke of "profane and vain babblings," which "will increase unto more ungodliness. And their word will eat as doth a canker" (2 Tim. 2:16–17). Two men guilty of spreading false doctrine had destroyed the faith of some by teaching that the final resurrection had already taken place

(2 Tim. 2:17–18). Paul and his teachings were being rejected: "This thou knowest, that all they which are in Asia be turned away from me" (2 Tim. 1:15). Paul had taught the gospel in the Roman province of Asia more than a decade earlier, and his message had been accepted by tremendous numbers (Acts 19:8–22). Now they were "all" turning from him and his message. Jude lamented the rejection of "the faith which was once delivered unto the saints" (Jude 1:3). He spoke of those who "reject authority, and defame dignitaries" (Jude 1:8).[10] He said that his readers had been warned long ago about people infiltrating and perverting the faith (Jude 1:4). They are here, he said (Jude 1:4). The apostles had warned of "mockers" in the last days of the Church (Jude 1:17–18). They are here, Jude wrote. They do not have the Spirit, and they are dividing the Saints (Jude 1:19).

John's Revelation provides additional evidence of the growth of apostasy. He spoke of the existence of false apostles (Rev. 2:2), of false prophecy (2:20–24), and extensively of apostate doctrine and behavior (Rev. 2:4–6, 14–16, 20–24; 3:2–4, 15–17). If John's words paint a fair picture of the overall status of Early Christianity near the end of the first century, we cannot avoid the conclusion that the prophecies of apostasy were then being fulfilled. Of the seven churches addressed in the book of Revelation, only two were not condemned. One of the five condemned churches was ready to die because of its sins; another was to be spit out of God's mouth. The rest were guilty of serious error, and each was told in strong terms that if it did not repent it would be rejected.

Finally, in what we assume is the last-written document of the New Testament, we have an example of direct rejection of the Lord's anointed leader. Diotrephes, a local Church leader who "loveth to have the preeminence" among the Saints (3 Jn. 1:9), rejected John, the senior and probably the only remaining apostle at the time. John had written to him, but Diotrephes would not receive him. In fact, Diotrephes excommunicated those who would (3 Jn. 1:10).

This was apostasy by any definition. John promised to deal with the offending leader when he could, but if Diotrephes did not recognize John's authority, no doubt he would not have responded to his discipline, either. Now in the third generation of Christian history, we see not only doctrinal apostasy taking place but also an act of open rebellion against priesthood authority. This was not without significant consequences: those who rejected John severed the final legitimate link of doctrine and priesthood between Christ and the church that bore his name.

With Tears

When Paul met with the elders of the Church in Asia at what would be the end of his ministry among them, he counseled them with deep feelings about what he foresaw in their future:

"Take heed therefore unto yourselves, and to all the flock, over the which the Holy Ghost hath made you overseers, to feed the church of God, which he hath purchased with his own blood. For I know this, that after my departing shall grievous wolves enter in among you, not sparing the flock. Also of your own selves shall men arise, speaking perverse things, to draw away disciples after them. Therefore watch, and remember, that by the space of three years I ceased not to warn every one night and day with tears" (Acts 20:28–31).

Significantly, Paul warned Church leaders not only to watch out for their flock but also to watch out for themselves. Among those "grievous wolves" who would enter and not spare the flock would be some of those same leaders, who, having been entrusted with the Lord's Church, would speak "perverse things, to draw disciples after them."

History has not left us a full record of the Apostasy, though we have New Testament prophecies foretelling it and New Testament examples of its taking place. But when our historical evidence begins again in the next centuries, we see a different church, teaching a different gospel. And we know that despite the warnings and the tears, something both dramatic and tragic has taken place.

Notes

1. See Justin Martyr (A.D. 110–65), *Hortatory Address to the Greeks,* 8; and Hegessipus, in Eusebius, *Church History,* 3.32.7–8. These can be found in A. Roberts and J. Donaldson, eds., *The Ante-Nicene Fathers,* 10 vols. (reprint, Grand Rapids, Mich.: Eerdmans, 1951); and P. Schaff and H. Wace, eds., *The Nicene and Post-Nicene Fathers,* 2d series, 14 vols. (reprint, Grand Rapids, Mich.: Eerdmans, 1983).

2. See especially Hegessipus and also Irenaeus, *Against Heresies;* Clement of Alexandria, *The Stromata, or Miscellanies;* Tertullian, *Against Marcion, Against Valentinius, Prescription against Heretics,* and *Scorpiace.* All of these are available in Roberts and Donaldson, *Ante-Nicene Fathers.*

3. See Chapter 3, 19–30.

4. For a much fuller discussion, see Kent P. Jackson, "Watch and Remember: The New Testament and the Great Apostasy," in *By Study and Also by Faith: Essays in Honor of Hugh W. Nibley on the Occasion of His Eightieth Birthday,* ed. John M. Lundquist and Stephen D. Ricks, 2 vols. (Salt Lake City: Deseret Book and the Foundation for Ancient Research and Mormon Studies), 1:81–95; and "Early Signs of the Apostasy," *Ensign,* Dec. 1984, 8–10.

5. Bible verses quoted are from the King James Version unless otherwise noted. Some passages are from the following English translations: JB, Jerusalem Bible; NIV, New International Version; NRSV, New Revised Standard Version; REB, Revised English Bible.

6. See Jackson, "Watch and Remember," 89–90.

7. See Chapter 3, 19–30.

8. See the fuller discussions in Jackson, "Watch and Remember," 95–117, and "Early Signs of the Apostasy," 10–16.

9. See n. 1. Clement of Rome (ca. A.D. 96) and Ignatius of Antioch (ca. 107), like Justin and Hegessipus, wrote as though the days of the apostles were past. See *1 Clement,* 42.1–5; 44.1–3; 47.1–6; and *Ignatius to the Magnesians,* 6.1 and 13.2 in Kirsopp Lake, trans., *The Apostolic Fathers,* 2 vols. (Cambridge, Mass.: Harvard University Press, 1949), vol. 1.

10. Bo Reicke, *The Epistles of James, Peter, and Jude,* Anchor Bible 37 (Garden City, N.Y.: Doubleday, 1964), 201.

Chapter 3

A New Generation of Christianity

In the early years after the resurrection of Jesus, the apostles added members to their number as vacancies required. It appears that the first item of apostolic business after Jesus' ascension was the selection of one to take the place of Judas (Acts 1:21–26). This action establishes the principle, which is confirmed by the practice today of The Church of Jesus Christ of Latter-day Saints, that apostolic succession was to be continued and that the ancient apostles intended to replace members of the Twelve each time one died. In addition to Matthias, three others we are aware of became apostles after Jesus' ascension: James (Acts 12:17; Gal. 1:19), Barnabas (Acts 14:14), and Paul (Acts 14:14). These three were called early in the Church's history—before A.D. 50. But neither scripture nor other historical evidence gives us any indication of the calling of others. It thus seems reasonable to suggest that near the middle of the first century, the calling of apostles came to an end and the apostleship died out. As far as we know, by the 90s only John remained. When he left his public ministry around A.D. 100, apostleship ceased, and the keys of the kingdom were taken.

The transformation of Christian doctrine was a process that must have happened with varying results in different places. But once the keys of the kingdom—which include the keys of revelation—were gone, the true Church of Jesus Christ was no longer in existence. Thus John's departure was the end of the Lord's

Church in the Old World. The withdrawal of apostolic power did not take place by accident. Had it been God's will, he would have chosen others to hold the keys and to continue the succession of the Twelve. But it appears that the rejection of true doctrine and authority was so widespread the Church could not continue.

The Great and Abominable Church

In the Book of Mormon, Nephi wrote about the time of the early apostles and prophesied of a "great and abominable church" whose founder would be the devil. This church would oppose the Saints and yoke them "with a yoke of iron" and thus bring them "down into captivity." In part, it would do that by removing things "which are plain and most precious" from the scriptures and from the gospel itself. The scriptural record we know as the Bible would not go forth to the nations until it had been corrupted "through the hands of the great and abominable church," leaving it less pure and reliable than it had been when it was first written (1 Ne. 13:4–6, 20–29).

Some Latter-day Saints, reading Nephi's descriptions in 1 Nephi 13, envision medieval monks tampering with the Bible to change it according to their own desires. And they see the church of Rome as the great and abominable church of which Nephi wrote. Neither of these interpretations is correct. According to Nephi, the corruption of the biblical text and the removal of "plain and most precious" things from the gospel would take place before the Bible would go to the world (1 Ne. 13:29). That the spread of the Bible was underway early in the second century A.D. is evident in the fact that New Testament passages are quoted often in the earliest Christian writings of that period.[1] The Catholic Church was no more responsible for the Apostasy than were the Baptists, the Presbyterians, or any other of today's churches; like all other Christians since the first century A.D., they were the inheritors of it. The Apostasy had been underway for more than two centuries before what we call the Catholic Church came into existence.[2] The monks and priests who carefully preserved and copied Bible manuscripts came even later. The keys of the kingdom had left the Church with John, and the process of doctrinal evolution had been underway since the Church began. Medieval Christianity was the *result* of the Apostasy, not the cause.[3]

Who, then, were the responsible parties, the ones whom history must see as accountable for the demise of the Early Christian Church? The answer is suggested in the New Testament.[4] Christ and the Twelve foretold and later witnessed the time when Church members would look beyond the simple doctrines of the gospel and bring new ideas into the Christian faith. Though pagans and persecutors often caused difficulties for early Christians, from the historical record there is no reason to believe that persecution had anything to do with the Apostasy, and the evidence does not point to Church members abandoning the faith to revert to their ancestral paganism. Nor do the sources suggest that the Apostasy was the result of Christians becoming less active in their faith or losing interest in it.

Instead, we see zealous Church members who were not content with "sound doctrine" but still had "itching ears" for religion (2 Tim. 4:3–4). And they did what their counterparts do in our own day. They sought out what a modern apostle has called "alternate voices,"[5] teachers whose words they found to be more "pleasing unto the carnal mind" (Alma 30:53)—more intellectually stimulating, more in style with contemporary ideas, or more spiritually titillating—than were the teachings of the Lord's authorized servants. In due time this process resulted in a spiritual transformation in the Church. The divinely revealed authority of apostles was replaced by the self-appointed authority of intellectuals.

The Early Church died from internal, self-inflicted wounds brought about by the introduction of alien ideas that gained widespread acceptance at the expense of the pure doctrine of Christ.

There must have come a time near the middle of the first century A.D. when the Lord, knowing the direction Church members were going, instructed his apostles to stop perpetuating the Twelve. False ideas were becoming more popular than revealed doctrine, self-appointed teachers were becoming more influential than true messengers, and slowly a revolution was taking place that in a matter of decades would overthrow the gospel, the priesthood, and the Church of Jesus Christ.

When the Savior established his Church, the apostles were sent forth to bear witness of him to the world, to gather and save all the souls who would accept their message, and to leave behind the record we call the New Testament. They did not fail in their appointed calling. But at the appropriate time, in light of the growing Apostasy and having accomplished the mission for which they had been sent, they were called home.

In the Book of Mormon, we learn that Christ established his Church in ancient America just as he had in Palestine, with authorized servants representing him and acting and teaching in his name. Sadly, what happened to the Lord's Church in the Mediterranean world happened to its counterpart in the Americas as well. Because of pride, those who once had been followers of Christ "did dwindle in unbelief and wickedness" (4 Ne. 1:34) until the Church of Christ was no longer in existence. In the Old World, Christianity continued, albeit in a different form. But in the New World, every vestige of it was soon removed or thoroughly perverted to the point that the gospel was completely obliterated from the memories of later generations. We are not aware of the Church of Jesus Christ existing anywhere on earth after the close of the Book of Mormon.

After the Apostles

Jesus' ministry took place in the early thirties of the first century A.D. The Gospels, which record his ministry, were probably written within a generation of that time.[6] The book of Acts continues Church history until about A.D. 63. James's letter was probably written in the mid fifties, and Peter's two letters were written before his death in about 67. Paul's letters span from the early fifties until about 67. The last of these, 2 Timothy, carries a somber tone with repeated warnings about the growing heresies. So also does Jude's letter, written perhaps a decade later.[7] John's writings, recorded near the end of the century, show unmistakable evidence of the spread of false doctrine and false leaders.

Paul had foretold that apostasy and aberrant behavior would be found in the "latter times" (*hústeroi kairoí;* 1 Tim. 4:1). Jude stated that he and his readers were living then in the "last time" (*éschatos chrónos*), when the warning prophecies were being fulfilled (Jude 1:17–19). John stated emphatically concerning his own day—and repeated the phrase for emphasis—"it is the last time" (*eschátē hōra;* 1 Jn. 2:18), which could be translated more literally, "it is the last hour." These phrases refer to the last days of the Church, not the last days of the world. And they provide significant evidence that inspired leaders knew the Church would come to an end. Those were the very days in which Jude and John wrote, both of whom knew that they were living in the Church's final hour, through revelation and because the prophecies concerning it were coming to pass.

We know very little about the history of the Church from the mid sixties until midway into the next century. But given the evidence within the New Testament, I suggest that John remained active in his public ministry long enough to be a witness that the prophecies were fulfilled, when there were too few in the Church who would "endure sound doctrine" (2 Tim. 4:3) to allow the Church to carry on.

After the days of the apostles, and thus after the New Testament ended, a new Christian literature began to develop. The earliest writers of the post–New Testament era are frequently called the Apostolic Fathers, because it was believed that they knew, or knew persons who knew, the apostles themselves.

Because of this connection with the generation of the apostles, the works and words of these early writers became authoritative among Christians of later generations.[8]

The earliest of these was a man named Clement, who was the bishop of Rome shortly before the end of the first century.[9] Clement wrote to the church in Corinth in about 96 to urge the Christians there to reject overt acts of rebellion that had occurred there recently. In what could be described as a coup d'etat, the Corinthians had removed from office their leaders who had been appointed by apostles, installing others in their places.

Clement emphasized, on doctrinal grounds, the importance of sustaining those who had been called by authority. "Christ received His commission from God, and the Apostles theirs from Christ." The apostles, in turn, set apart bishops and others to preside in the congregations.[10] "We cannot think it right for these men now to be ejected from their ministry, when, after being commissioned by the Apostles (or by other reputable persons at a later date) with the full consent of the Church, they have since been serving Christ's flock."[11]

Providing an impressive witness for the reality of the Apostasy, Clement pointed out the consequences of the Corinthians' rejection of their priesthood leaders: "All righteousness and peace among you is at an end. Everywhere men are renouncing the fear of God; the eye of faith has grown dim, and instead of following the commandments, and living as becomes a citizen of Christ, each one walks after the desires of his own wicked heart."[12]

Clement spoke of the apostles in the past tense and gave no indication that there were any still in the church. Another important document, the *Shepherd of Hermas,* written perhaps in part quite early in the second century, also acknowledges that the apostles were gone.[13]

Ignatius of Antioch[14] wrote around 107 and knew that he was in the postapostolic era.[15] In his preserved writings, which consist of seven short letters, additional evidence for the Apostasy is apparent. Ignatius saw that apostate influences were working hard in the church.[16] He was especially concerned about the spread of Docetism, the doctrine that denied the physical reality of Jesus and his work.[17] He pleaded with his readers to stand firmly behind those who had been chosen to lead them—the bishops and the elders. They had been called by the apostles or by others after the time of the apostles. He believed that this link of authority would tie the Christians as closely as they could be tied to the apostolic age and that it would be a safeguard against the false beliefs that were circulating in the church.[18]

Polycarp, the bishop of Smyrna early in the second century,[19] was believed in antiquity to have known John, the last of the Twelve.[20] In his only extant work, an epistle to the church in Philippi from about 107, he warned against Docetism and other evils,[21] urging the Philippians to "turn back to the word which was delivered to us in the beginning."[22] A treatise called *The Epistle of Barnabas,* probably written before 135,[23] identifies its time as the "last days" (*éschatai hēmérai*), "lawless times" in which "the insidious infiltration of the Dark One" was taking place.[24]

Although Christian writers of the early second century knew they were living in dark times for the church, their own words and teachings present a Christianity that seems increasingly alien to readers of the New Testament. Ignatius's warnings show evidence that he was well aware of changes taking place in the church, of threatening doctrines and self-appointed teachers, and of the need to hold fast to the last remaining links to the apostles. But without even knowing it, he himself was an example that the church had already passed into the new age. Ignatius saw himself as a defender of orthodoxy, but Latter-day Saints will recognize in his words some troubling signs that the orthodoxy that remained was no longer that of the pristine Church. The widespread celebrity status that Ignatius enjoyed, though he was only a local bishop, seems out of harmony with the scriptures. The way he confidently took it upon himself to write letters instructing other congregations also seems irregular and points to a day in which there was no longer a central authority in the church.[25] Most noteworthy, however, was his craving for martyrdom, a desire that has no precedent or justification in any scripture.[26]

The *Epistle of Barnabas* uses an extreme interpretive method that allegorizes passage after passage from the Old Testament, reducing history to metaphor.[27] This mode of interpretation became very popular in Christianity over the third and fourth centuries after Christ.

By the middle of the second century, Bishop Polycarp of Smyrna was an old man. A document called *The Martyrdom of Polycarp,* written shortly after his death in 155,[28] records that he was so revered by his disciples that he never had to unfasten his shoes. "He had never been accustomed to do this before, since the faithful used to vie with one another in their eagerness to touch his bare skin—such universal veneration had the saintliness of his life earned for him."[29] When he was executed for his Christianity, an eyewitness disciple recorded, "We did gather up his bones—more precious to us than jewels, and finer than pure gold—and we laid them to rest in a spot suitable for the purpose."[30]

A book called the *Didache, or Teaching of the Twelve Apostles,* is believed to have been written before 150, with much of its content coming perhaps even before the end of the first century.[31] Thus it could reflect some of the earliest Christian ideas of the postapostolic age. Latter-day Saints will find in the *Didache* a number of beliefs and practices that are manifestly out of harmony with revelation—notably so, given the early date of the book's composition.

The *Didache* gives us history's first reference to baptism by sprinkling. Though it identifies immersion in running water as the preferred method, it allows for sprinkling if immersion is not practical.[32] This unscriptural innovation destroys the purpose of baptism by removing the doctrinal symbolism of death, burial, and new life that is taught so well by Paul in the New Testament (Rom. 6:3–4; Col. 2:12; 3:1). Similarly, the *Didache*'s sacramental prayers[33] show nothing in common with Jesus' biblical words concerning the ordinance (Matt. 26:26–28; 1 Cor. 11:23–26) nor with the prayers that have been revealed from God in modern scripture (Moro. 4:3; 5:2; D&C 20:77, 79). The *Didache* versions lack entirely the ordinance's doctrinal foundation: there is no reference to witnessing or making a covenant, and there is no mention of the bread and wine being emblematic representations of Christ.

A final innovation of the *Didache* that is worth noting is a brief administrative instruction: "Appoint therefore for yourselves bishops and deacons."[34] While this, on the surface, may not seem like a major issue, it is in fact symptomatic of a fundamental redefinition of the Christian Church that had already taken place before the *Didache* was written. The New Testament pattern was not that the congregations would choose their own leaders but that divinely called apostles, or those specifically assigned by apostles, chose and appointed those who would preside, even in local congregations (e.g., Acts 14:23; Titus 1:5).

Without Apostles

Jesus gave the apostles instructions on how to continue with his work after his departure (e.g., Matt. 28:19–20; Acts 1:2–3). It is clear that the Church was to carry on and that the leadership of the Twelve would continue that of the Master in both their authority and their service in Christ's name. But nowhere in the New Testament are there instructions on how to administer the Church after the departure of the Twelve. For example, there are no plans for how to keep calling and setting apart new leaders without the apostles, or for organizing the Church in areas where the gospel would be introduced, or for receiving continuing revelation in behalf of the Church as the apostles had done to meet its ever-changing needs.

The New Testament simply does not foresee the Lord's Church in existence without apostles, nor does it make any preparation for that possibility. That was not because Jesus and the Twelve did not care, or because they anticipated that the apostleship would endure forever. The reason is clear, and it is as simple as it is ominous: Without apostles, there is no Church of Jesus Christ.

Notes

1. See the references in the marginal notes to Clement, Ignatius, Polycarp, and the *Didache;* in Kirsopp Lake, trans., *The Apostolic Fathers,* vol. 1 (Cambridge, Mass.: Harvard University Press, 1949).

2. There is no convenient point in history to locate the beginning of what we now call the Roman Catholic Church, which evolved over the centuries after the departure of the apostles. The reign of Constantine (A.D. 312–37) is perhaps the best period in which to start, because many of the church's distinguishing features were formalized during the fourth century after Christ. Though the term *Catholic* is attested earlier, the "Roman" and the "Catholic" character of the church developed over the course of later centuries.

3. See Stephen E. Robinson, "Early Christianity and 1 Nephi 13–14," in *First Nephi: The Doctrinal Foundation,* ed. Monte S. Nyman and Charles D. Tate Jr. (Provo, Utah: Religious Studies Center, Brigham Young University, 1988), 177–91.

4. See Chapter 2, 8–18.

5. Dallin H. Oaks, "Alternate Voices," *Ensign,* May 1989, 27–30.

6. See Kent P. Jackson and Robert L. Millet, eds., *The Gospels,* Studies in Scripture Series, vol. 5 (Salt Lake City: Deseret Book, 1986), 38–48, 61–67, 92–95, 109–11.

7. We do not know if Jude was an apostle. He calls himself "the servant of God, called of Jesus Christ" (Jude 1:1, JST), and he refers to the apostles in the third person and in the past tense (1:17–18).

8. See Lake, *Apostolic Fathers,* and Maxwell Staniforth, trans., *Early Christian Writings: The Apostolic Fathers* (New York: Dorset, 1968).

9. See Lake, *Apostolic Fathers,* 8–121; Staniforth, *Early Christian Writings,* 23–59.

10. *1 Clement,* 42.2–4; in Staniforth, *Early Christian Writings,* 45.

11. *1 Clement,* 44.3; in Staniforth, *Early Christian Writings,* 46.

12. *1 Clement,* 3.4; in Staniforth, *Early Christian Writings,* 24.

13. See *Shepherd of Hermas,* 13.1; 94.1; 102.2; in J. B. Lightfoot and J. R. Harmer, trans., Michael W. Holmes, ed. and rev., *The Apostolic Fathers,* 2d ed. (Grand Rapids, Mich.: Baker, 1989), 189–290.

14. See Lake, *Apostolic Fathers,* 166–277; Staniforth, *Early Christian Writings,* 61–131.

15. As implied in Ignatius, *To the Magnesians,* 13.2; *To the Trallians,* 2.2; *To the Smyrnaeans,* 8.1.

16. E.g., *To the Ephesians,* 9.1; *To the Trallians,* 6.1; *To the Smyrnaeans,* 4.1.

17. E.g., *To the Magnesians,* 11.1; *To the Trallians,* 9.1–10.1; *To the Smyrnaeans,* 1.1–4.2; 5.2.

18. See *To the Ephesians,* 3.2; 6.1; *To the Trallians,* 2.1–2.

19. See Lake, *Apostolic Fathers,* 279–301; Staniforth, *Early Christian Writings,* 133–50.

20. Ireneus, *Against Heresies,* 3.3.4; Tertullian, *Prescription against Heretics,* 32; in A. Roberts and J. Donaldson, eds., *The Ante-Nicene Fathers,* 10 vols. (reprint, Grand Rapids, Mich.: Eerdmans, 1951).

21. *To the Philippians,* 7.1.

22. *To the Philippians,* 7.2; in Lake, *Apostolic Fathers,* 293.

23. See Lake, *Apostolic Fathers,* 335–409; Staniforth, *Early Christian Writings,*187–222.

24. *Epistle of Barnabas,* 4.9; in Staniforth, *Early Christian Writings,* 197.

25. See *To the Philadelphians,* 7.1–2; 10.1–2; *To Polycarp,* 7.2.

26. "I [am] praying for a combat with the lions" (*To the Trallians,* 10.1; in Staniforth, *Early Christian Writings,* 97). "I am truly in earnest about dying for God. . . . Pray leave me to be a meal for the beasts, for it is they who can provide my way to God. I am His wheat, ground fine by the lions' teeth to be made purest bread for Christ. . . . How I look forward to the real lions that have been got ready for me! . . . This is the first stage of my discipleship; and no power, visible or invisible, must grudge me my coming to Jesus Christ. Fire, cross, beast-fighting, hacking and quartering, splintering of bone and mangling of limb, even the pulverizing of my entire body—let every horrid and diabolical torment come upon me. . . . I am yearning for death with all the passion of a lover" (*To the Romans,* 1.1; 5.2–3; 7.2; in Staniforth, *Early Christian Writings,* 104–6).

27. See, for example, the imaginative interpretations of Old Testament dietary laws in the *Epistle of Barnabas,* 10.1–9.

28. Staniforth, *Early Christian Writings,* 151–67; for the dating, see 138–41 and *Encyclopedia of the Early Church* (New York: Oxford University Press, 1992), s.v. "Polycarp."

29. *Martyrdom of Polycarp,* 13.2; in Staniforth, *Early Christian Writings,* 160.

30. *Martyrdom of Polycarp,* 18.2; in Staniforth, *Early Christian Writings,* 162.

31. Lake, *Apostolic Fathers,* 303–33; Staniforth, *Early Christian Writings,* 223–37.

32. *Didache,* 7.1–3.

33. Ibid., 9.1–4.

34. Ibid., 15.1; in Lake, *Apostolic Fathers,* 331.

Chapter 4

The Journey of Christianity

A discussion of the Apostasy rightly focuses on the Church in the first century A.D. The philosophers, councils, and creeds that led to medieval and modern Christianity are a separate matter, a part of the aftermath of the Apostasy many years later. But the development of traditional Christianity is a subject of interest to us, because it explains the origins of the Christian faith that existed at the time of the Restoration and that still exists today. Thus we will examine some of the major events and individuals of Christianity's formative years.[1] The following examples were chosen because they were key elements in Christianity's evolution and because they are representative of others.

In the centuries after the fall of the Early Church, many people continued to believe in Christ and acknowledge him as the source of their salvation. Christianity grew as converts flocked to its message, often in the face of severe persecution. But the Christian religion that became a political and social force in the Roman empire was not the same as that which had existed when the Lord's apostles were on the earth, endowed with the keys of the kingdom and the authority to speak and act in Christ's name. Inasmuch as the keys of the priesthood are also the keys of revelation,[2] it was inevitable that once the apostleship was taken from the Church, so also would be taken the divine guidance that it had enjoyed under the leadership of the Twelve. Believers were thus left to their own resources as Christianity journeyed into the future on an uncharted path, where its doctrine continued to develop with the passage of time. The result, however well-intentioned the people may have been, was a new Christian faith that included fundamental teachings that are largely at variance with the revelations of heaven.

Philo, Clement, and Origen

In its early years, Christianity found itself increasingly exposed to the cultural and philosophical influences of its surroundings. The entire New Testament took place within the sphere of Greek culture, which in previous centuries had become the culture of a huge area of the ancient world. After the conquests of Alexander the Great in the fourth century before Christ, Hellenism, the Greek culture of Alexander and his successors, spread dramatically throughout the Mediterranean area and into western Asia. It became the culture of the day, in due time supplanting many of the native cultures or changing them radically. Greek thought was very attractive to many because it placed man—particularly educated, intellectual man—at the center of the universe and gave him the keys to find what was perceived as truth. Native belief systems in many cases proved unable to retain their character in the face of the popularity of Greek culture. Over the centuries, indigenous religions underwent profound changes, as their beliefs were syncretized or substantially compromised by the imported ideas of the Greeks.

Judaism was not immune to the influences of Hellenism, particularly in the Hellenistic city of Alexandria, in Egypt, which had a very large population of Jews. The Jews there were thoroughly Greek in many ways, speaking Greek as their native tongue, accepting Hellenism as their native culture, and incorporating much of Greek thought into their religion. Jews in Palestine and Mesopotamia were more conservative, but even there Greek ideas made their way into their religion.

Philo of Alexandria (ca. 15 B.C. to A.D. 50) was a Jewish philosopher who was roughly contemporary with Jesus. He is important to our understanding of the development of Christian theology not only because of his influence on later Christian thinkers but also because his efforts to Hellenize Judaism illustrate the likely process of the Hellenization of Christianity.

Philo wrote scriptural commentaries and philosophical treatises that were defenses of the Jewish faith. In his writing he argued that the religion of Moses and the philosophy of the Greeks were compatible sources of truth, with the philosophy being derivative of the religion. To show their compatibility, he explained Judaism in terms that made it acceptable within the Hellenistic cultural context. And in doing so, he created what might be considered the first successful synthesis of Greek philosophy and revealed religion. Philo defended the Old Testament as God's revelation, yet he freely explained away as allegory much of its historical and doctrinal content, especially anything that stood out in contrast to prevailing cultural interpretations. That is particularly true of his concept of Deity. His primary philosophical influence was Plato, and like other students of Plato in the Hellenistic period, Philo adopted a belief in God that contrasted sharply with the God of the Old Testament.[3]

Philo rejected all anthropomorphic references to the God of Israel, accepting instead the view of Deity that was in style among the Greeks of his generation. Thus he believed that the passages that depict God with humanlike shape or other humanlike characteristics are to be explained as metaphor. Anticipating Christian theology of later generations, he taught that God's existence could be known but that it is impossible to know anything else about him.

Though his effect on Judaism was minimal (because Jewish thought developed along different lines), Philo's influence on the evolution of Christianity was enormous. Early Christian theologians, who like Philo merged philosophy and revelation, invoked him as a model. In their teaching, he and his writings became a forerunner to the development of classical Christian theology, as well as medieval philosophy in general. His influence was especially felt in the thought of Clement, Origen, and Ambrose.

Clement of Alexandria (150–215) was an important Christian apologist of the second and third centuries.[4] His contribution to church history was in his efforts to explain and promote Christianity in terms that would be acceptable to the intellectuals of his time. Like Philo, he created a synthesis of his own religion and Greek philosophy. In his view, philosophy was to the Greeks what the law of Moses was to the Jews—one of the paths whereby individuals could be brought to the higher revelation of Christianity.[5] Drawing from the Platonic tradition of Greek philosophy, Clement believed in a transcendent God who was beyond all comprehension. And even Christ, he taught, "was entirely impassible; inaccessible to any movement of feeling—either pleasure or pain."[6] Clement was succeeded at his school in Alexandria by his student Origen (185–254), who followed the precedent of his teacher and the earlier example of Philo in the process of accommodating his religion to Greek thought. Like Clement, Origen was well versed in Greek philosophy and, significantly, he received some of his training in it under Ammonius Saccas, the founder of the philosophy called Neoplatonism.

Origen was a Christian theologian and writer of profound importance.[7] A scholar of the Bible, he wrote extensive treatises on doctrinal and scriptural topics, large commentaries on biblical texts, and defenses of Christianity against pagans and heretics. Among his most important writings is a text called *On First Principles,* a large work of theology. Not all of his many works have survived, however, in part because some of his writings were so lengthy as to make copying them impractical. But some did not survive because later generations had mixed feelings about his doctrinal speculations.

Origen wrote in a generation of theological freedom, before

the time when the ecumenical councils of the fourth and later centuries codified the official doctrines of the church. In those councils and in the writings of contemporary theologians, some of Origen's beliefs were rejected as dangerous, and he himself was identified frequently as a heretic. Among the most heretical of his beliefs was his teaching of the premortal existence of human souls. He taught that those who are now mortals existed before birth, where, being agents with free will, they made choices. Except for Christ, all fell to some degree from their pure state. The most wicked and rebellious in that premortal setting fell to become devils. Origen's view of Christ's status was another factor that earned him the disapproval of later theologians. In a time when the doctrine of the Trinity was in the early stages of its evolution, Origen taught that the Son, though divine, was subordinate to the Father. In the councils of the next two centuries, when the trinitarian unity of Father, Son, and Holy Ghost was officially formulated, this subordinationist belief was viewed as false and was rejected.[8]

Although Latter-day Saint readers may see an element of truth in some of Origen's teachings, other aspects of his theology are less easily harmonized with revelation. His God, for example, had much more in common with the god of Platonic philosophy than with the God of the Old and New Testaments. Even in his own lifetime he was accused of corrupting Christianity with pagan philosophy. Like Philo, he used an extremely allegorical interpretive method when reading scripture and believed that the highest interpretation was a "spiritual exegesis" that we would say shows little resemblance to a passage's original context or intent. Physical resurrection, for example, was viewed as a metaphor for a deeper spiritual process. His asceticism was legendary, even to the point that he castrated himself to avoid physical temptation.[9] His life and writings became influential in establishing monasticism in the church.

The One

While early apologists were attempting to make Christianity appear respectable within the context of Greek thought, a new strain of philosophy was developing that eventually had a permanent effect on the Christian faith, particularly on its doctrine of God.[10] Along with some other philosophers of his time, Philo of Alexandria is classified as a Middle-Platonist, representing a school of thought that two centuries after his day would blossom into the powerful and lasting Neoplatonism, the philosophy that in late antiquity was fused forever with Christian theology.

Neoplatonism was largely the creation of two non-Christian Alexandrian philosophers: Ammonius Saccas (who had been a teacher of Origen) and his student Plotinus. Its view of existence was characterized by a belief in multiple spheres of reality, the lowest being our universe with its limitations of time and space. The highest existence is described as the realm of an entity called "the One," "the ultimate principle, which is absolutely free from determinations and limitations and utterly transcends any conceivable reality, so that it may be said to be 'beyond being.'" Because this ultimate, transcendent, undefinable entity "has no limitations, it has no division, attributes, or qualifications; it cannot really be named, or even properly described as being, but may be called 'the One' to designate its complete simplicity. . . . Since this supreme principle is absolutely simple and undetermined (or devoid of specific traits), man's knowledge of it must be radically different from any other kind of knowledge. It is not an object (a separate, determined, limited thing) and no predicates can be applied to it; hence it can be known only if it raises the mind to an immediate union with itself, which cannot be imagined or described."[11]

Plotinus (205–70), the earliest Neoplatonic thinker whose words have been preserved, advocated this view of the ultimate essence and passed his teachings on to others. It soon became a powerful philosophy with wide-ranging influence. From the third century on, Christianity developed under the umbrella of Neoplatonism and its belief in "the One." Over the years the Christian faith learned from it, drew much of its strength and inspiration from it, absorbed much of its world view, and was influenced by it immeasurably. As a pagan school of thought Neoplatonism eventually died out, but as a philosophical foundation of Christianity it continues, even today. Predictably, and very sadly, at an early date "the One"—the unknowable, indefinable, ultimate reality of the philosophers—was identified with the God of the church. And Christianity has never been the same since.

Councils and Creeds

Beginning in the fourth century, more than two hundred years after the last apostle guided the Church, a process was developed to establish and standardize Christian beliefs. In a series of "ecumenical councils," church leaders debated, decided, and officially proclaimed the doctrines of their faith. The resulting policies, creeds, and doctrinal decisions—established by the authority of the bishops and the imperial power of the Roman/Byzantine state—are the foundations of Christianity even to our day. Thus the councils serve a formative function in traditional Christianity that is similar to that of the First Vision and the coming of Moroni in our own religion.

Seven ecumenical councils in late antiquity and the early Middle Ages are accepted by Catholics and Orthodox as establishing the fundamental beliefs of their faith. Some Protestants accept all seven councils, but others—following the lead of Martin Luther—accept only the first four.[12] It must be stated from the outset that Latter-day Saints accept none of them, coming as they did many years after the Lord had withdrawn from the earth his Church with the authority to speak in his name. Christian doctrines had already undergone centuries of transformation before the earliest councils met to clarify and codify the religious

The site of Constantine's lakeside palace at Nicea (modern İznik, Turkey), where the first Council of Nicea took place and the doctrine of the Trinity was officially established for the Christian church

traditions that they had received. Still, these councils were among the most important events in history, because in them was developed what the world today knows as Christianity.

The First Council of Nicea (325) was brought about as a result of what is called the Arian controversy.[13] Arius was a theologian who taught that Christ is not truly divine but is a finite, created being who had a beginning. Only God the Father is self-existent; Jesus is not self-existent and thus could not be God. Arianism was an effort to reconcile a literal reading of the New Testament text to Neoplatonism, with its absolutely unique and transcendent Deity. Arians believed that Christ, though the most perfect creation in the material world, was entirely unlike God, who was eternal and uncreated. And Christ was subordinate to God's will.

Arius's doctrine was opposed primarily by Athanasius, another prominent theologian of the time. The controversy caused enough concern that Constantine, the Roman emperor, called a large meeting of bishops at his palace in Nicea (in northwest Turkey) to settle the matter. Constantine, who only later was baptized a Christian, presided at the meeting. At issue was the long-standing question whether Jesus was "of the same substance" (*homoousion*) as the Father, or whether he was "of like substance." In short, are Jesus and the Father the same being, or is Jesus something separate who is *like* the Father?

The question may seem unusual to some modern readers, but within the philosophical context of the fourth century it was an important issue. Platonic tradition maintained the absolute uniqueness of Deity. And "the One" of Neoplatonism was necessarily unknowable, indefinable, and utterly unlike anything else in existence. Jesus, in contrast, is described in the New Testament as a man who, though divine, had attributes common to other humans. How could he be both God and something radically other than God at the same time?

The council decided in favor of the views of Athanasius that the Son is of one substance with the Father and not a separate individual. That decision preserved the absolute singularity of God and avoided the problem of having someone other than him with status similar to his. But how the Father and the Son could be the same essence—two persons within the same being—was to be a mystery, something not intended to be understood. Like most everything else about God, it was unknowable.

The decision of the Council of Nicea established, with permanent force, the doctrine that the Father and the Son are one incomprehensible being.[14] Every other detail of the Christian faith, passed down through sixteen centuries and hundreds of millions of people, rests on that fundamental belief that was codified then as the official doctrine of the church. In due time the theology of Nicea would be refined to fully state the doctrine of the Trinity, the belief in the oneness of the Father, the Son, and the Holy Ghost. Later councils clarified the details, but the core of the

Nicene trinitarian doctrine has remained the very cornerstone of the Christian faith to the present time.

The second ecumenical council was held at Constantinople. The emperor Theodosius I convened it to deal with the continuing debate about the nature of the Trinity.[15] The previous year, before his baptism, he had issued an edict mandating belief in the consubstantiality of the Father, the Son, and the Holy Ghost as a condition for being a Christian. In the summer of 381 he called the council, inviting 150 Greek-speaking bishops to deal with the matter. The council reaffirmed the doctrine of Nicea, putting a virtual end to Arianism as a viable alternative theology. And it more fully defined the doctrine of the Trinity and the equality of the Holy Ghost with the Father and the Son: the Holy Ghost is of the same essence as the Father and the Son and is coexistent with them in the Trinity.

The official statement of this council is called popularly "the Nicene Creed," but more accurately it is "the Niceno-Constantinopolitan Creed." It reads in part: "We believe in one God the Father almighty, maker of heaven and earth, of all things visible and invisible; And in one Lord Jesus Christ, the only-begotten Son of God, begotten from the Father before all ages, [God of God,] light from light, true God from true God, begotten not made, of one substance with the Father. . . . And in the Holy Spirit, the Lord and life-giver, Who proceeds from the Father [and the Son], Who with the Father and the Son is together worshiped and together glorified."[16]

Notes

1. In this chapter and in Chapter 5, 42–51. For general information on some of the factors that contributed to the development of Christian theology, see *The New Encyclopaedia Britannica,* 32 vols. (Chicago/London: Encyclopaedia Britannica, 1993), 16:259–66, 272–87, 315–23; *Encyclopedia of Religion,* 16 vols., ed. Mircea Eliade (New York: Macmillan, 1987), 4:138–44; 6:17–22. See

also J. N. D. Kelly, *Early Christian Creeds,* 2d ed. (London: Longmans, 1960), 205–331; and W. H. C. Frend, *The Rise of Christianity* (Philadelphia: Fortress, 1984), 161–650.

2. Andrew F. Ehat and Lyndon W. Cook, eds., *The Words of Joseph Smith: The Contemporary Accounts of the Nauvoo Discourses of the Prophet Joseph* (Provo, Utah: Religious Studies Center, Brigham Young University, 1980), 38–39.

3. For Philo, see David Winston, "Philo Judaeus," *Encyclopedia of Religion,* 11:287–90, and references cited there.

4. See Frend, *Rise of Christianity,* 368–73. Clement's works are found in A. Roberts and J. Donaldson, eds., *The Ante-Nicene Fathers,* 10 vols. (reprint, Grand Rapids, Mich.: Eerdmans, 1951), 2:163–605. See also Elizabeth A. Clark, "Clement of Alexandria," *Encyclopedia of Religion,* 3:533–34, and references cited there.

5. See *Stromata (Miscellanies),* 1.5, 16.

6. *Stromata (Miscellanies),* 6.9; in Roberts and Donaldson, *Ante-Nicene Fathers,* 2:496.

7. See Frend, *Rise of Christianity,* 373–83. For Origen's collected works, see Roberts and Donaldson, *Ante-Nicene Fathers,* 4:221–669; 10:287–512.

8. For an introduction to Origen's thought, see Henri Crouzel, "Origen," *Encyclopedia of Religion,* 11:108–11.

9. Eusebius, *History of the Church,* 6.8; in Philip Schaff and Henry Wace, eds., *A Select Library of Nicene and Post-Nicene Fathers,* 2d series, 14 vols. (reprint, Grand Rapids, Mich.: Eerdmans, 1986), 1:254.

10. For a general overview of platonic thought and Christianity, see A. H. Armstrong and H. J. Blumenthal, "Platonism after Plato," *Encyclopaedia Britannica,* 25:899–906.

11. Ibid., 900–901.

12. Roman Catholics accept a total of twenty-one councils, spanning from the first at Nicea to the most recent, Vatican II, in the 1960s.

13. See Kelly, *Early Christian Doctrines,* rev. ed. (San Francisco: Harper and Row, 1978), 223–51; Frend, *Rise of Christianity,* 494–501.

14. For the creed that was produced at the council, see Henry Bettenson, ed., *Documents of the Christian Church,* 2d ed. (London: Oxford, 1967), 25.

15. See Frend, *Rise of Christianity,* 635–41.

16. Kelly, *Early Christian Creeds,* 297–98. Western additions are in brackets. This creed is the only one accepted by both the Roman Catholic and the Eastern Orthodox churches. It is also accepted by most Protestants.

Chapter 5

The God of the Philosophers

Historians of religion recognize well that the traditional Christian concept of God is to a large extent the product of Greek philosophy's influence on post–New Testament Christianity. What few understand, however, is how tragic the consequences of that are. Joseph Smith taught the true doctrine of God when he said: "God, who sits in yonder heavens, is a man like yourselves. That God that holds the worlds, if you were to see him today, you would see him like a man in form like yourselves. Adam was made in his image and talked with him and walked with him."[1] That, however, is not the doctrine of God that was developed in the early Christian centuries and that has survived into our day. We Latter-day Saints, who take for granted this idea of God, do not often realize how revolutionary it is within the broad context of today's Christian churches.[2]

Augustine

Augustine (A.D. 354–430), bishop of Hippo in North Africa, was Christianity's most significant figure in late antiquity.[3] No one individual has had a greater effect on the beliefs of the Christian faith. His writings helped create the culture of Western Europe in the Middle Ages, provided a doctrinal backdrop for certain aspects of the Protestant Reformation, and set much of the agenda for Christianity to the present day. He was a man of profound

Augustine (354–430), bishop of Hippo in North Africa, early Christian theologian. Fifteenth-century painting by Botticelli

importance to our understanding of the Christianity of the churches.

Augustine was born to a devout Christian mother and a non-Christian father.[4] Though his mother reared him to become a Christian, and though he was always quite knowledgeable about Christian beliefs, he did not convert until he was in his early thirties. As a young man he was well educated and was trained as a lawyer and rhetorician. During his studies, at about age twenty, he developed a passion for philosophy that never left him. Despite his mother's pleading that he accept Christianity, he found it shallow and uninteresting compared with the philosophical thought of the Greeks and Romans. And Christianity could not provide answers to the two questions that concerned him most: the question of God's nature, and the question of the origin of evil.

In his early twenties, Augustine converted to Manicheism, a religion with roots in Christianity, Zoroastrianism, and Gnosticism. Manicheism held that all of creation was the result of a cosmic battle between light and darkness. Human souls were elements of light trapped in the darkness of physical matter. Because matter was a manifestation of the darkness and souls were not intended to be trapped in flesh, celibacy and asceticism were encouraged as the superior mode of life. Augustine, however, had a mistress during the nine years of his Manichean experience and thus never attained to the highest order of his religion. In time he became disillusioned with Manicheism, primarily because as a philosophical system it was unable to answer his questions. Eventually he became embittered against it and attacked it in his later writings.

As Augustine continued his quest for truth, he accepted a professorship in Milan. There he heard the teaching of Ambrose (ca. 339–97), bishop of Milan and one of the foremost Christian intellectuals of the day.[5] In Ambrose, Augustine found a Christian thinker with deep philosophical roots, whose sermons introduced him to Neoplatonism and the writings of Plotinus, whom Ambrose quoted extensively.[6] In Plotinus and his philosophy, Augustine felt that he at last had found answers to life's questions. He embraced Neoplatonism, and it provided the philosophical perspective for the rest of his life.

But there remained the question of Christianity. Augustine's mother continued to urge her son to convert, and finally he did. He was baptized by Ambrose on Easter in 387. Foremost among his reasons was a spiritual experience in which he read a passage from Paul that encouraged the Saints to overcome their physical lusts (Rom. 13:14). That experience changed his life by motivating him to set aside the things of the flesh—foregoing marriage forever—and surrender himself to God. But other factors also had an appeal for him and aided in his conversion. In his earlier years he had found the Bible too unsophisticated for his interests, particularly its depiction of God in human form with humanlike characteristics.[7] But in Ambrose's teaching he found a Christian interpretation that was worthy of the best of philosophers. Ambrose rejected a literal reading of the text and developed allegorical interpretations in the tradition of Philo and Origen, both of whose works he knew well and had taken to heart. That method, as questionable as it may seem to Latter-day Saints, gave Augustine an interest in the Bible that he had never felt before.

But perhaps his greatest attraction to the Christian faith was the natural compatibility he perceived between it and his chosen philosophy of Neoplatonism. It was the joining of the two that characterized his theology from that time on. Indeed, Augustine's great contribution to the development of Christianity was the lasting marriage, solemnized under the authority of his pen, between the philosophical school of Plato and what had once been the religion of Christ. As one scholar has written, "his mind was the crucible in which the religion of the New Testament was most completely fused with the Platonic tradition of Greek philosophy."[8] And his writings were the medium through which that synthesis was conveyed through the centuries of Christianity.

Augustine's conversion to Christianity was, to a very large degree, an outgrowth of his conversion to Neoplatonism. Before he found Neoplatonism and learned to see Christianity through its eyes, the religion of Jesus held little appeal for him. Especially attractive to him was Plotinus's concept of Deity—"the One," the absolute, unique essence that has neither attributes nor descriptive qualities. In that transcendent entity, Augustine was able to formulate his understanding of the God of the Bible. According to the Neoplatonic view, an essence called "mind," or "spirit," emanated from "the One." For Augustine it was a logical step to equate that essence with Christ, the Word of God that comes from the Father.

Augustine went on to have a long and brilliant career in which he became known throughout the Roman empire. In his own lifetime he was recognized as the greatest thinker of Christianity, whose views frequently established church doctrine. He was a prolific writer from whom about four hundred sermons and two hundred letters have been preserved. His books include *The City of God,* a treatise on the conflict between good and evil, and *Confessions,* a spiritual autobiography. His book *On the Trinity,* written in response to the Arian controversy,[9] engaged the debate concerning the nature of God and Christ and dealt with issues that would be discussed at the Council of Chalcedon in 451. He wrote that the Trinity is "a divine unity of one and the same substance in an indivisible equality; and therefore that they are not three Gods, but one God."[10] Taking issue with the position of Origen on the subject of Jesus' subordination to the Father, he taught that there is a perfect unity of rank in the Trinity, with neither member being greater than any other.[11] Yet in the end, as Augustine conceded, the Trinity is a mystery and cannot be understood. One thing that can be understood, however, is that God is utterly unlike man and unlike anything man in his loftiest imagination can conceive of.[12]

Augustine continued to struggle with his question concerning the origin of evil. He concluded that it came about as the result of Adam's fall. As he examined the Fall in his sermons and writings, he developed doctrine that would stand the test of time and remain forever part of Christian tradition. Indeed, much of the inherited view of Adam and the Fall is a legacy of Augustine, including the general view of the depravity of human nature that set the moral tone for the Middle Ages.

The doctrine of grace, as understood in Christian tradition, is also largely Augustine's contribution.[13] He taught that though humans have agency, that agency is not sufficient to enable them to do good and overcome evil. The capacity to do good can only exist as a gift of grace from God. In that teaching he was opposed publicly by the British theologian Pelagius, who contended that humans, endowed with agency, are indeed capable of choosing good and doing it. Were it not so, Pelagius argued, God's judgments against them could not be just. Implicit in Pelagius' point of view was a rejection of the accepted doctrine of original sin, the inherited guilt of Adam's transgression.[14]

Augustine undertook a campaign of sermons and writings to refute the teaching of Pelagius. Its success was apparent in the fact that Pelagius and his doctrine were condemned at the First Council of Ephesus in 431 and also in the fact that Augustine's views prevailed to establish the accepted doctrine of grace. But as Augustine developed that doctrine, some of his ideas became solidified into a position that did not achieve universal acceptance. He taught that God alone determines salvation, independent of human effort, and that it is a mystery why some are chosen and others are not. God elects whom he will for salvation, and no act of ours can affect the choice.[15] In time he developed this teaching into an explicit doctrine of predestination—God's selection in advance of those who would be saved.

Many of Augustine's contemporaries and later Christians found his teachings on predestination to be excessive. Thus in the Catholic Church they never were viewed as official doctrine.[16] But centuries later they reemerged in the teachings of John Calvin, a great admirer of Augustine, who brought them into the mainstream of Protestant thought during the Reformation. Today, Augustine's views on grace and predestination are vital elements in the doctrine of significant portions of Christianity.

Some of Augustine's teachings on the Fall were also not fully accepted into the Christian mainstream but nonetheless had a lasting influence on traditional doctrine. Even before his conversion to Christianity, Augustine wrestled with feelings of guilt for physical instincts that showed the power of his flesh over his spirit. As a Christian, he developed a belief in original sin that had its focus on sexuality as the evidence for the fallen state of humankind. He believed that humans inherit the guilt of Adam's sin through birth, because conception is dependent on sexual passion. And sexual desire and the sexual act are the surrender of the spirit to carnal lusts. All humans are therefore fallen, he believed, because all were brought into life through the victory of the flesh over the spirit. In part as a result of Augustine's teaching, as well as the ascetic beliefs of such of his contemporaries as Jerome (347–420), Medieval Christianity inherited an ambivalent attitude toward sexuality and toward human nature in general.

True God and True Man

"When the Savior shall appear we shall see him as he is. We shall see that he is a man like ourselves. And that same sociality which exists among us here will exist among us there, only it will be coupled with eternal glory, which glory we do not now enjoy" (D&C 130:1–2).

The councils of the fifth, sixth, and seventh centuries dealt with the topic of the character of Jesus Christ, the foremost matter of debate among the theologians of the time. At issue was to what extent Jesus had a human nature in addition to his divine nature. Was he actually two separate persons (one human and one divine) acting in agreement within Christ, as the Nestorians maintained? Or did he possess a single, divine nature and no human nature at all, as claimed by the Monophysites?

The Council of Ephesus in 431 officially declared Christ's dual nature. That was also the council that condemned Pelagius and Pelagianism, thus affirming as church doctrine the idea of original sin and rejecting the concept that humans have sufficient agency to do good.

The Council of Chalcedon in 451 affirmed the two-nature doctrine of Ephesus, stating that Christ has both a complete divine nature and a complete human nature, both of which dwell in him

The remains of the Church of St. Mary at Ephesus (western Turkey), site of the Council of Ephesus in 431

"without confusion, without change, without division, without separation; . . . the characteristics of each nature being preserved and coming together to form one person and subsistence, not as parted or separated into two persons, but one and the same Son and Only-begotten God the Word."[17]

The Second Council of Constantinople in 553 articulated again the decision of Chalcedon with greater emphasis on Jesus' divinity.[18] The Third Council of Constantinople, 680–81, concluded that Christ has two separate wills corresponding with his two separate natures.

The last of the councils that are accepted by both Orthodox and Catholic Christians was the Second Council of Nicea in 787, which dealt with what is called the "Iconoclastic controversy." The veneration of icons—paintings of saints and scriptural persons—had been a long-standing practice, especially in the Eastern church. It had been forbidden in 726, after which users of icons had been persecuted. The council reaffirmed the legitimacy of venerating images and also the practice of calling upon the saints for intercession.

Without Body, Parts, or Passions

By the time of Joseph Smith, the doctrines of the early theologians and councils had been rooted deeply in Christian thought for many centuries. It seemed as though the great debates of the early generations of Christian history had settled the matter of the nature of God and Christ forever. Later Catholic theologians, as well as Protestant theologians in their time, debated questions of doctrine among themselves, but few ventured far afield of the decisions that had been made by the founders of the received Christian faith. As shown in this important Protestant confession, the God of the philosophers remained:

"There is but one only living and true God, who is infinite in being and perfection, a most pure spirit, invisible, without body, parts, or passions, immutable, immense, eternal, incomprehensible. . . . God hath all life, glory, goodness, blessedness, in and of himself; and is alone in and unto himself all-sufficient, not standing in need of any creatures which he hath made. . . . In the unity of the Godhead there be three persons, of one substance, power, and eternity: God the Father, God the Son, and God the Holy Ghost. The Father is of none, neither begotten nor proceeding; the Son is eternally begotten of the Father; the Holy Ghost eternally proceeding from the Father and the Son."[19]

Notes

1. Andrew F. Ehat and Lyndon W. Cook, eds., *The Words of Joseph Smith: The Contemporary Accounts of the Nauvoo Discourses of the Prophet Joseph* (Provo, Utah: Religious Studies Center, Brigham Young University, 1980), 344; spelling and punctuation modernized.

2. For background introductions, see *The New Encyclopaedia Britannica,* 32

vols. (Chicago/London: Encyclopaedia Britannica, 1993), 16:259–66, 272–87, 315–23; *Encyclopedia of Religion,* 16 vols., ed. Mircea Eliade (New York: Macmillan, 1987), 4:138–44; 6:17–22. See also J. N. D. Kelly, *Early Christian Creeds,* 2d ed. (London: Longmans, 1960), 205–331; and W. H. C. Frend, *The Rise of Christianity* (Philadelphia: Fortress, 1984), 651–906.

3. See John Burnaby, "Augustine," *New Encyclopaedia Britannica,* 14:397–401; Warren T. Smith, "Augustine of Hippo," *Encyclopedia of Religion,* 1:520–27.

4. The main primary source for the information on Augustine's life is his autobiographical work *Confessions.* See Augustine, *Confessions,* trans. R. S. Pine-Coffin (New York: Penguin, 1983); Philip Schaff, ed., *The Nicene and Post-Nicene Fathers,* 1st ser., 14 vols. (reprint, Grand Rapids, Mich.: Eerdmans, 1983), 1:27–207; see also Frend, *Rise of Christianity,* 659–83. Augustine's works are collected in vols. 1–8 of Schaff, *The Nicene and Post-Nicene Fathers.*

5. For an overview of Ambrose's career, see Frend, *Rise of Christianity,* 618–26.

6. See discussion of "the One" in Chapter 4, 36–37.

7. Augustine, *Confessions,* 3.5; 6.3–4.

8. Burnaby, "Augustine," 397.

9. See Chapter 4, 38–39.

10. *On the Trinity,* 1.4; in Schaff, *Nicene and Post-Nicene Fathers,* 3:20.

11. *On the Trinity,* 1.7–8.

12. Ibid., 8.2.

13. See the discussion in Frend, *Rise of Christianity,* 673–80.

14. Pelagius did not reject the idea of God's grace. For him, God's grace was evidenced in the fact that he gave us agency to choose good or evil, laws to govern our lives, and the example and redemptive work of Jesus Christ.

15. See *On the Predestination of the Saints,* 1–43.

16. See Burnaby, "Augustine," 399–400.

17. From the statement adopted by the Council of Chalcedon; Henry Bettenson, ed., *Documents of the Christian Church,* 2d ed. (London: Oxford, 1967), 51.

18. See Frend, *Rise of Christianity,* 848–53.

19. "The Westminster Confession of Faith, 1647," 2.1–3, in Schaff, *The Creeds of Christendom,* 3 vols., 4th ed. (New York: Harper, 1919), 3:606–8.

Chapter 6

The God of Revelation

We must remember that the individuals who contributed to the development of Christian theology, who participated in the debates, wrote the creeds, and defined the doctrines, were doing so many years after the apostasy of the Early Church, when Church members rebelled against the light that they had received from Jesus and the apostles. But it must also be stated frankly that those who created what the world knows today as Christianity did so without the authority to act in God's name in an age when the heavens were not open to the church. Given what they knew and did not know about the gospel, some might argue that they did the best they could in the absence of prophetic direction. Still, when we compare what resulted through the creeds and councils with what is taught in the revelations of God, we can see that at almost every turn they made decisions that took Christianity ever farther away from its revealed roots. The Church of Jesus and the apostles had become the church of the intellectuals. Because of that, it is unlikely that a Christian of the first century A.D., who had received the gospel from Jesus or his messengers, could have recognized much in the Christianity of three or four centuries later.

Are Latter-day Saints Christians?

If the definition of a Christian is one who worships God and Christ as depicted in the doctrines and creeds of historical

Christianity, then Latter-day Saints are not Christians. Our views on the nature of the Father and the Son diverge irreconcilably from the inherited beliefs of other churches, because our beliefs come from a different source.

If the definition of a Christian is one whose religion has resulted from the historical processes that created modern Christianity, then Latter-day Saints are not Christians. Our roots do not go back through the centuries of Christian history: we are not part of that family tree. Our beliefs do not descend through the councils or the philosophical developments that contributed to making Christianity what it is today. Nor does the institution of our Church. Though we cherish our association with good people of all faiths, particularly those who share with us a belief in the life and mission of Jesus Christ, we confess that their doctrines are foreign to us. In many ways, we do not even share the same understanding of the Bible, since we read it in the light of modern revelation and therefore very differently from the way other churches do. And though some external forms in LDS culture are part of the broader Christian tradition—such as our church architecture, our observance of Christmas, and many of our hymns—our religion is something fundamentally different from the traditional Christian faith.[1]

But if the definition of a Christian is one who loves and believes in Jesus Christ, recognizes his atoning sacrifice as the only means of salvation, and tries to follow his teachings, then Latter-day Saints are Christians. "We believe in God, the Eternal Father, and in His Son, Jesus Christ, and in the Holy Ghost" (Article of Faith 1). "We believe that through the Atonement of Christ, all mankind may be saved, by obedience to the laws and ordinances of the Gospel" (Article of Faith 3). "We talk of Christ, we rejoice in Christ, we preach of Christ, we prophesy of Christ, and we write according to our prophecies, that our children may know to what source they may look for a remission of their sins"

(2 Ne. 25:26). Because of these beliefs, we view ourselves without reservation or hesitation as Christians.[2]

It is not surprising that Latter-day Saints find it difficult to understand the doctrine of the Trinity and the value of the debates, councils, and philosophical developments that led to the formation of classical Christian theology. But in attempting to comprehend the idea of the Trinity, we miss its point and try to do something that is not meant to be done. The trinitarian unity of the Father, the Son, and the Holy Ghost—three persons in one being—is considered in Christian theology to be a mystery, a principle that is beyond human ability and out of the realm of mortal understanding. Christians in the early centuries determined that God, by his very nature, must be something entirely other than anything earthly. If humans could describe, define, understand, or even imagine him, he would be finite and thus not divine. He cannot, therefore, be contained in a body, a shape, a place, or a time, nor can he have anything like human characteristics or emotions. The beauty of this doctrine, the churches believe, is that it exalts and glorifies God by seeing him as beyond anything within the grasp of human experience or human reasoning. Were it otherwise, he would not be God.

We may wonder if anyone could read the New Testament and come to the same conclusions about God that were reached in the early councils, unless one had already learned the doctrine through the official teachings of one's church. The idea of the Trinity has no biblical foundation. The idea of an indefinable, unknowable God is simply not found in the New Testament, in which Jesus speaks of the Father in the third person—as a *person*—repeatedly and consistently, leaving no room for misunderstanding. The Bible describes the God of the Old and New Testaments as clearly within the reach of human comprehension. He is not depicted as mysterious or distant but as one who—though perfect, all-powerful, and divine—is near, approachable, and fully endowed with the wide range of feelings and emotions that humans experience.[3] Moreover, the Bible gives every indication that God has a body like that of humans (Gen. 1:26–27; Ex. 33:11; Deut. 4:28; Acts 7:56). Were one to read the Old and New Testaments without the teachings of the churches, one would conclude that God is a divine man.

By the time of Jesus, Jews were already beginning to explain away biblical descriptions of God's attributes.[4] Christians followed suit, dismissing the biblical God—with his body, emotions, and other "humanlike" characteristics—as metaphor and thereby transforming the God of whom Jesus spoke in the New Testament into the very different God of the Greek intellectuals. The councils, in their turn, accelerated and confirmed both the process and the outcome through codification and creeds. Modern-day theologians have done the same. Today, the Latter-day Saint doctrines that Christian clerics and academics find most disagreeable are those that deal with the nature of God: that he is an exalted man, that he has a body, that Christ is his literal Son, and that we are his children.

Many Christians believe, both intuitively and through their Bible reading, in the God of revelation, despite the doctrines of some of their churches. When we explain the Godhead to our friends, we are frequently told, "I have always believed that." The official theologies of the churches remain to a great extent the domain of only the learned among them. But among the humble members of their flocks are many who have come to understand the God of the scriptures—a God whom they can really know. And they sense, as though instinctively, that they have a real kinship with him.

Notes

1. As described in the Presbyterian Church's 1995 policy statement on their relationship with the LDS faith, Latter-day Saints are not part of "the historic apostolic tradition of the Christian Church." "Relations with The Church of Jesus

Christ of Latter-day Saints and Its People: Position Paper, the Presbyterian Church (U.S.A.), adopted January 21, 1995." The quotation comes from page 1 of the resolution made to the 207th General Assembly (1995), attached to the Position Paper.

2. Concerning the role of Jesus Christ in the Latter-day Saint faith, see Topical Guide in the LDS edition of the King James Version of the Bible, 240–58. See also Daniel H. Ludlow, ed., *Jesus Christ and His Gospel* (Salt Lake City: Deseret Book, 1994), a compilation of articles from Daniel H. Ludlow, ed., *The Encyclopedia of Mormonism,* 5 vols. (New York: Macmillan, 1992).

3. See the examples in R. Scott Burton, "The Nature of God in the Psalms," in Kent P. Jackson, ed., *1 Kings to Malachi,* Studies in Scripture Series, vol. 4 (Salt Lake City: Deseret Book, 1993), 426–36, 441–47.

4. See M. Catherine Thomas, "From Malachi to John the Baptist: The Dynamics of Apostasy," in Jackson, *1 Kings to Malachi,* 476–80.

Chapter 7

Preparing the World for the Restoration

By 1820, the effects of the apostasy of Christianity had already been felt for more than seventeen hundred years in the Old World and for about fourteen hundred years in the New World. It is important to understand that the Apostasy was found not only in the places where the Lord's Church had once existed in ancient times but worldwide. For much of humankind, the Apostasy had been underway since the beginning of history. What Isaiah had foretold concerning the last days was now true universally: "The darkness shall cover the earth, and gross darkness the people" (Isa. 60:2).

As we consider the Apostasy, we should not restrict our thinking to religious matters. The world's apostasy covered all areas of human endeavor as completely as it covered all geographical regions of the earth. Every aspect of society was, and for the most part still is, affected by it. Philosophy, science, economics, government, and culture all developed to a large extent in the absence of gospel light and thus reflect the things of the world more than the things of God. When society entered the modern period, it brought with it the baggage of thousands of years of human misdirection, all of which needed to be redefined, restructured, or reinvented by the Restoration.

But there were bright lights even in the midst of the general darkness. Though the Lord had taken his Church from the earth, he had not altogether withdrawn his Spirit, and many were touched by it. In the years after the fall of the ancient Church, millions of persons, in every corner of the world, continued to come and go through the normal processes of birth and death. Many of those—perhaps most—were honorable women and men. Where the gospel has not been available, there have always been individuals who have faithfully lived up to all the light and knowledge they possessed, for which the redemptive work for the dead will provide them with every gospel opportunity. The Lord's Spirit was not idle, for many significant contributions to human happiness and well-being came during those days through the good efforts of honorable persons and the inspiration of God. But the fulness of the gospel was not available. In a profound way, the sun had set, and the world had entered an era of darkness. Yet that darkness was not to last forever; when the world was ready, the dawning of the Restoration would come.

As the new day approached, the Lord was active in human affairs and influenced some significant developments. Those developments are important not only because they blessed the lives of individuals but because they helped prepare the way for the restoration of the gospel. As such, we can view them as part of God's plan and see that they were essential ingredients in making the world ready for the Lord's work of the latter days.

The Protestant Reformation

The Protestant Reformation was, in its simplest form, a rebellion against the power of the Church of Rome. We frequently think of it as beginning with the work of such reformers as Martin Luther and John Calvin in the sixteenth century, but its roots include the humanism of the Renaissance and the work of earlier reformers and dissidents. In an effort to reform the church, Luther and others published grievances they had with various church practices and policies. Most of the Reformation leaders taught that true authority in Christianity rested in the Bible rather than in the church. Thus they opposed nonbiblical practices—such as celibacy, the veneration of saints, and the selling of indulgences—and sought to make the Bible available to lay Christians. In doing these things, the Protestants brought about a liberation of the Bible and made it, and not the church, the focus of their religion. Soon the movement took on a political aspect also, as several European rulers joined the reformers in seeking political as well as religious independence from Rome. By the end of the sixteenth century, the landscape of Western Europe was changed forever in politics, culture, and religion. And that new landscape was transplanted to North America when colonists began emigrating in large numbers to the New World. Among them were the forebears of Joseph Smith and others of his generation.[1]

From a Latter-day Saint point of view, the Reformation perpetuated many of the theological problems that it had inherited from late antiquity: the God of the Greek intellectuals remained the God of the Protestant churches, and the theological framework of medieval Christianity remained mostly intact. The Reformation also introduced its own share of doctrinal misinformation, including a belief in predestination among Calvinists and a rejection of the idea of priesthood authority among Protestants in general. Even so, the Reformation must be viewed as a positive development in the preparation of the world for the Restoration. It helped set the stage for the great latter-day work in two important ways.

First, the Reformation made it possible for religious diversity to exist on a large scale in the world of Western Christianity. Without it, Joseph Smith would have had to contend with the opposition of a single, powerful Christian religion rather than establishing the restored Church in an era of relative diversity. Creating a new church was not a unique idea in the Prophet's day, and the existence of a variety of churches was taken for granted.

Second, the Reformation encouraged independent study of the

John Calvin (1509–64), theologian and a leader of the Reformation

Bible and independent religious thinking. Before the Reformation, few Bibles existed in Western Europe in languages other than Latin, which had long ago ceased to be a common spoken tongue. Because knowledge of Latin was a monopoly held by the church and some few others educated by the church, the clergy controlled access to the word of God. By Joseph Smith's time, however, literacy had increased dramatically, and most literate Christians had access to the Bible in their own language. That allowed them to read the Bible independent of clergy and even independent of church affiliation. Many Christians in the early nineteenth century were thus amateur Bible scholars in their own right and had drawn their own conclusions about religious matters. Not surprisingly, many through their own study and contemplation of the Bible had come to believe in a God who was radically different from the God of Ambrose, Augustine, and the creeds.

The Political and Social Climate of America

With the founding of the United States of America only decades before Joseph Smith's birth in one of its New England states, constitutional law was established that helped prepare the political environment in which the gospel could be restored. The United States Constitution reflects early North America's appreciation for such individual liberties as freedom of conscience and freedom of expression. These were part of the culture of Joseph Smith's day, and when the United States came into existence, they became part of its most fundamental law.

The First Amendment to the Constitution stipulates the freedoms that were to play an important role in facilitating the Restoration. It reads, in part: "Congress shall make no law respecting an establishment of religion, or prohibiting the free exercise thereof; or abridging the freedom of speech, or of the press; or the right of the people peaceably to assemble." While these stipulations were understood at the time to apply only to the federal government, most state constitutions contained similar guarantees. These restrictions, imposed on government by a sovereign people, did away with the possibility of a government-sponsored religion, affirmed the right of citizens to worship according to their own choice, and protected their freedom to assemble and to express their convictions openly.

That these developments were undertaken by the will of the Lord is stated in revelation (D&C 101:80). Their importance to the restoration of the gospel is clear. The Church was established in a land in which government could neither promote nor hinder any religious movement, thereby allowing the gospel to be restored and Church members to practice it without governmental opposition.[2]

It is important that we recognize the Lord's hand at work in lands throughout the world, preparing them to receive his restored Church. The same culture that created a fertile environment for the Restoration in America provided many faithful converts in

Canada. Great Britain was certainly prepared by God to provide an unsurpassed harvest of converts in the nineteenth century. In their time, continental Europe, Australia, South and Central America, Asia, and Africa have all been moved upon by the Spirit of the Lord in preparation for the gospel message. Political and social circumstances continue to change, and laws have been established in nations across the world that enable the gospel to be taught and the Saints to practice it freely.

The Preparation of a Prophet

Joseph Smith wrote, "I was born . . . of goodly parents who spared no pains to instructing me in the Christian religion."[3] He was raised in the home of honorable, believing Christians who taught him of Christ and instilled in him a love for the truth. That was one important aspect of his environment that prepared him for his life's work. Although his parents were religious, religiosity in that day did not necessarily include membership in a church. In the early nineteenth century, Americans may have been more religious than they are now, but a much smaller proportion belonged to churches.[4] Many Americans, like the Smiths, practiced their religion at home, including prayer and Bible study, but were not affiliated with any particular church organization, even if they frequently attended one of the churches in their area.[5] Not until shortly before the First Vision did some members of the Smith family formally join a church (JS–H 1:7).

In the Prophet's later writings, he told of events that took place in his youth that helped prepare him for the First Vision. Soon after his family moved to the area of Palmyra and Manchester in western New York, there developed "an unusual excitement on the subject of religion" (JS–H 1:5).[6] It was an intense spread of religious fervor, and the deep effect it had on him is reflected in the words he used to describe it: "[an] extraordinary scene of religious feeling . . . a scene of great confusion and bad feeling . . . a strife of words and a contest about opinions" (JS–H 1:6). This excitement, he

Palmyra, New York, Main Street, looking northwest.
Photo by George Edward Anderson, 1907

recorded, was brought about by competition between local churches for converts among the unaffiliated people of the area. For a serious boy in his early teens such as Joseph Smith was, this religious excitement became the source of much reflection and much confusion. "My mind at times was greatly excited," he wrote. And "in the midst of this war of words and tumult of opinions, I often said to myself: What is to be done? Who of all these parties are right; or, are they all wrong together" (JS–H 1:9–10). This was important for him to know, he said, for "I knew not who was right or who was wrong, and I considered it of the first importance that I should be right in matters that involve eternal consequences."[7]

With the question clearly in mind, Joseph Smith set out to find the answer. He had learned through experience that visiting the churches and listening to their messages only brought him more confusion. And he had learned also that an appeal to the Bible would not answer his question, "for the teachers of religion of the different sects understood the same passages of scripture so differently as to destroy all confidence in settling the question by an appeal to the Bible" (JS–H 1:12). Yet though the Bible could not tell him which church to join, it was the Bible that led him to the source that would answer his question. That source was prayer.

As the Prophet later recounted his First Vision, he looked back on his reading of James 1:5 as a pivotal event in his search for truth. Its effect on him was profound, and it led him to the unavoidable conclusion that he "must either remain in darkness and confusion, or else must do as James directs, that is, ask of God" (JS–H 1:13).

From our vantage point later in history, we can see God at work in these circumstances, just as in other things that helped set the stage for the Restoration. The Lord was challenging Joseph Smith to seek truth in every way he knew how. But it seems that before the First Vision could take place, the young man needed to ask the right question, a question that gradually worked its way into his heart as he was exposed to different religious denominations, each claiming to have the right way to know and to please God.

How carefully and how thoroughly the Lord had set everything in place to lead Joseph Smith into what we now reverently call the Sacred Grove. In addition to preparing a culture and a country in which the Restoration could succeed, the Lord also prepared the heart of a young man who had been chosen from the councils in heaven to do a great work. When the time was right, the Holy Ghost bore witness to him of a biblical promise concerning the answering of prayer, and he learned that he could obtain his desired knowledge by that means. Accordingly, he went into the woods to ask of God.

Notes

1. Standard encyclopedias may be consulted for basic information on the Protestant Reformation. See also De Lamar Jensen, "Protestant Reformation," in Daniel H. Ludlow, ed., *The Church and Society* (Salt Lake City: Deseret Book,

1992), 413–15, and bibliography cited there; or in Daniel H. Ludlow, ed., *The Encyclopedia of Mormonism,* 5 vols. (New York: Macmillan, 1992), 1171–72.

2. See Rex E. Lee, "Constitutional Law," and Ralph C. Hancock, "Constitution of the United States of America," in Ludlow, *Church and Society,* 114–18 and 118–22; or in Ludlow, *Encyclopedia of Mormonism,* 315–17 and 317–19.

3. Dean C. Jessee, ed., *The Papers of Joseph Smith,* 3 vols. (Salt Lake City: Deseret Book, 1989–97), 1:3; spelling and punctuation modernized.

4. See Milton V. Backman Jr., *Joseph Smith's First Vision: The First Vision in Its Historical Context* (Salt Lake City: Bookcraft, 1971), 53–56.

5. See Richard L. Bushman, *Joseph Smith and the Beginnings of Mormonism* (Urbana and Chicago: University of Illinois Press, 1984), 36–39.

6. For a discussion of this period, see Backman, *Joseph Smith's First Vision,* 53–111.

7. Journal, 9 November 1835; Jessee, *Papers of Joseph Smith,* 2:69; spelling and punctuation modernized.

Chapter 8

The First Vision

In the earliest days of the history of the Church, Joseph Smith apparently spoke less frequently about the First Vision than he did about other sacred experiences. In public addresses and publications, greater emphasis seems to have been placed on the coming of John the Baptist, which signified the restoration of authority, and on the coming of Moroni, which represented the revelation of new doctrine. Near the end of his ministry, however, the Prophet spoke of the First Vision more frequently. Undoubtedly the great care with which he treated it was out of reverence for it. And there is good reason to treat it reverently. As glorious as the later visitations of heavenly messengers were, nothing on earth could surpass the appearance of the Father and the Son. It was the crowning event of the restoration of the gospel and one of the crowning events of all human history. In fact, in all of scripture it is the only recorded instance of the Father and the Son appearing together on earth. President Ezra Taft Benson called it "the greatest event that has occurred in this world since the resurrection of the Master." [1]

By the end of the Prophet's lifetime, he may have told the story of the First Vision on many occasions. Yet his own written accounts of it have been preserved in only five places. We will examine them all, thereby allowing Joseph Smith himself, the only mortal witness of the event, to explain it as it happened. In these accounts, the Prophet tells his story in his own words.

Because the accounts were written under different circumstances and perhaps with different readers in mind, the emphasis in them varies from one to the next. And because of what they describe and the fact that the Prophet himself wrote or dictated them, each one is a precious record.[2]

The five accounts are presented here in the order in which they were written. The Prophet's words have been preserved in each of them exactly as they were recorded, but for ease of reading, the spelling and punctuation have been modernized. Because doing that may overlay a modern shading onto the original documents, references to the unedited texts are provided in the notes. The paragraphs in the accounts are also numbered for ease of discussion.[3]

The 1832 Draft History

The first known effort of Joseph Smith to record his sacred experiences was a document written in 1832. This history covers events from the Prophet's birth through the arrival of Oliver Cowdery to assist in the translation of the Book of Mormon. The following excerpt, which is the earliest written report of the First Vision in existence, is entirely in Joseph Smith's own hand, making it an even more remarkable document because he usually dictated his words to scribes. We could assume that his original intention was to prepare the manuscript for publication, but that is not certain. It was never completed, and it remained in rough-draft condition throughout his lifetime.[4]

1 At about the age of twelve years, my mind became seriously impressed with regard to the all-important concerns for the welfare of my immortal soul, which led me to searching the scriptures, believing, as I was taught, that they contained the word of God.

2 Thus, applying myself to them, and my intimate acquaintance with those of different denominations, led me to marvel exceedingly, for I discovered that they did not adorn their profession by a holy walk and

godly conversation[5] agreeable to what I found contained in that sacred depository. This was a grief to my soul.

3 Thus from the age of twelve years to fifteen, I pondered many things in my heart concerning the situation of the world of mankind—the contentions and divisions, the wickedness and abominations, and the darkness which pervaded the minds of mankind.

4 My mind became exceedingly distressed, for I became convicted[6] of my sins.

5 And by searching the scriptures I found that mankind did not come unto the Lord, but that they had apostatized from the true and living faith, and there was no society or denomination that built upon the gospel of Jesus Christ as recorded in the New Testament.

6 And I felt to mourn for my own sins and for the sins of the world, for I learned in the scriptures that God was the same yesterday, today, and forever, that he was no respecter to persons, for he was God.

7 For I looked upon the sun, the glorious luminary of the earth, and also the moon, rolling in their majesty through the heavens, and also the stars shining in their courses, and the earth also upon which I stood, and the beast of the field and the fowls of heaven and the fish of the waters, and also man walking forth upon the face of the earth in majesty and in the strength of beauty, whose power and intelligence in governing the things which are so exceeding great and marvelous [are] even in the likeness of him who created them.

8 And when I considered upon these things my heart exclaimed, "Well hath the wise man said, 'It is a fool that saith in his heart there is no God'" [Ps. 14:1].

9 My heart exclaimed, "All these bear testimony and bespeak an omnipotent and omnipresent power, a being who maketh laws and decreeth and bindeth all things in their bounds, who filleth eternity, who was and is and will be from all eternity to eternity."

10 And when I considered all these things and that that Being seeketh such to worship him as worship him in spirit and in truth, therefore I cried unto the Lord for mercy, for there was none else to whom I could go and obtain mercy.

11 And the Lord heard my cry in the wilderness. And while in the attitude of calling upon the Lord in the sixteenth[7] year of my age, a pillar of light above the brightness of the sun at noon day came down from above and rested upon me, and I was filled with the Spirit of God.

12 And the Lord opened the heavens upon me, and I saw the Lord

Path leading to the Sacred Grove, Manchester Township, New York.
Photo by George Edward Anderson, 1907

and he spake unto me, saying, "Joseph, my son, thy sins are forgiven thee. Go thy way, walk in my statutes, and keep my commandments. Behold, I am the Lord of glory. I was crucified for the world, that all those who believe on my name may have eternal life."

13 "Behold, the world lieth in sin at this time, and none doeth good, no not one. They have turned aside from the gospel and keep not my commandments. They draw near to me with their lips, while their hearts are far from me."

14 "And mine anger is kindling against the inhabitants of the earth to visit them according to their ungodliness, and to bring to pass that which hath been spoken by the mouth of the prophets and apostles. Behold and lo, I come quickly, as it [is] written of me, in the cloud clothed in the glory of my Father."

15 And my soul was filled with love, and for many days I could rejoice with great joy, and the Lord was with me. But [I] could find none that would believe the heavenly vision. Nevertheless, I pondered these things in my heart.

The 1835 Journal Account

In November 1835, Joseph Smith was visited in Kirtland, Ohio, by a well-known religious eccentric who went by the name "Joshua the Jewish Minister."[8] During their conversations, the Prophet related to him some of his early experiences, including the First Vision. The following is the Prophet's journal entry documenting that conversation, as recorded by his scribe. This account, too, was never published in Joseph Smith's day and thus has also been preserved in rough-draft form.[9]

1 Being wrought up in my mind respecting the subject of religion and looking at the different systems taught the children of men, I knew not who was right or who was wrong. And I considered it of the first importance that I should be right in matters that involve eternal consequences.

2 Being thus perplexed in mind, I retired to the silent grove and bowed down before the Lord, under a realizing sense that he had said, if the Bible be true, "Ask, and you shall receive; knock and it shall be opened; seek and you shall find" [Matt. 7:7]; and again, "If any man lack wisdom, let him ask of God, who giveth to all men liberally, and upbraideth not" [James 1:5].

3 Information was what I most desired at this time, and with a fixed determination to obtain it, I called upon the Lord for the first time, in the place above stated, or in other words I made a fruitless attempt to pray.

4 My tongue seemed to be swollen in my mouth, so that I could not utter. I heard a noise behind me like some person walking towards me. I strove again to pray but could not. The noise of walking seemed to draw nearer. I sprang up on my feet and looked around but saw no person or thing that was calculated to produce the noise of walking.

5 I kneeled again. My mouth was opened and my tongue liberated, and I called on the Lord in mighty prayer.

6 A pillar of fire appeared above my head. It presently rested down upon me and filled me with joy unspeakable. A personage appeared in the midst of this pillar of flame, which was spread all around and yet nothing consumed.

7 Another personage soon appeared like unto the first. He said unto me, "Thy sins are forgiven thee." He testified unto me that Jesus Christ is the Son of God.

8 And I saw many angels in this vision.

9 I was about fourteen years old when I received this first communication.

The 1838 "History of Joseph Smith" (JS–H)

The longest and best-known of the Prophet's accounts of his First Vision was dictated to a scribe in 1838 as part of his official history, which eventually became the *History of the Church.*[10] It shows every indication of having been written with great care. It is the most deliberate, the most detailed, and the most formal of the accounts. It was first published in Nauvoo, Illinois, in 1842 and is now included in the Pearl of Great Price.[11] Thus it is the only account that has been canonized as scripture. Today we know it as "Joseph Smith–History" ("JS–H"). The verse numbers are from the Pearl of Great Price.

9 My mind at times was greatly excited, the cry and tumult were so great and incessant. The Presbyterians were most decided against the Baptists and Methodists, and used all the powers of both reason and sophistry to prove their errors, or, at least, to make the people think they were in error. On the other hand, the Baptists and Methodists in their turn were equally zealous in endeavoring to establish their own tenets and disprove all others.

10 In the midst of this war of words and tumult of opinions, I often said to myself: What is to be done? Who of all these parties are right; or, are they all wrong together? If any one of them be right, which is it, and how shall I know it?

11 While I was laboring under the extreme difficulties caused by the contests of these parties of religionists, I was one day reading the Epistle of James, first chapter and fifth verse, which reads: *If any of you lack wisdom, let him ask of God, that giveth to all men liberally, and upbraideth not; and it shall be given him.*

12 Never did any passage of scripture come with more power to the heart of man than this did at this time to mine. It seemed to enter with great force into every feeling of my heart. I reflected on it again and again, knowing that if any person needed wisdom from God, I did; for how to act I did not know, and unless I could get more wisdom than I then had, I would never know; for the teachers of religion of the different

sects understood the same passages of scripture so differently as to destroy all confidence in settling the question by an appeal to the Bible.

13 At length I came to the conclusion that I must either remain in darkness and confusion, or else I must do as James directs, that is, ask of God. I at length came to the determination to "ask of God," concluding that if he gave wisdom to them that lacked wisdom, and would give liberally, and not upbraid, I might venture.

14 So, in accordance with this, my determination to ask of God, I retired to the woods to make the attempt. It was on the morning of a beautiful, clear day, early in the spring of eighteen hundred and twenty. It was the first time in my life that I had made such an attempt, for amidst all my anxieties I had never as yet made the attempt to pray vocally.

15 After I had retired to the place where I had previously designed to go, having looked around me, and finding myself alone, I kneeled down and began to offer up the desires of my heart to God. I had scarcely done so, when immediately I was seized upon by some power which entirely overcame me, and had such an astonishing influence over me as to bind my tongue so that I could not speak. Thick darkness gathered around me, and it seemed to me for a time as if I were doomed to sudden destruction.

16 But, exerting all my powers to call upon God to deliver me out of the power of this enemy which had seized upon me, and at the very moment when I was ready to sink into despair and abandon myself to destruction—not to an imaginary ruin, but to the power of some actual being from the unseen world, who had such marvelous power as I had never before felt in any being—just at this moment of great alarm, I saw a pillar of light exactly over my head, above the brightness of the sun, which descended gradually until it fell upon me.

17 It no sooner appeared than I found myself delivered from the enemy which held me bound. When the light rested upon me I saw two Personages, whose brightness and glory defy all description, standing above me in the air. One of them spake unto me, calling me by name and said, pointing to the other—*This is My Beloved Son. Hear Him!*

18 My object in going to inquire of the Lord was to know which of all the sects was right, that I might know which to join. No sooner, therefore, did I get possession of myself, so as to be able to speak, than I asked the Personages who stood above me in the light, which of all the sects was right (for at this time it had never entered into my heart that all were wrong)—and which I should join.

The Sacred Grove, Manchester Township, New York

19 I was answered that I must join none of them, for they were all wrong; and the Personage who addressed me said that all their creeds were an abomination in his sight; that those professors were all corrupt; that: "they draw near to me with their lips, but their hearts are far from me, they teach for doctrines the commandments of men, having a form of godliness, but they deny the power thereof."

20 He again forbade me to join with any of them; and many other things did he say unto me, which I cannot write at this time. When I came to myself again, I found myself lying on my back, looking up into heaven. When the light had departed, I had no strength; but soon recovering in some degree, I went home. And as I leaned up to the fireplace, mother inquired what the matter was. I replied, "Never mind, all is well—I am well enough off." I then said to my mother, "I have learned for myself that Presbyterianism is not true."

The 1842 "Church History"

John Wentworth, publisher of the *Chicago Democrat,* requested that Joseph Smith write for him an article about the Church, which he planned to send to a friend who was writing a book. Accordingly, what has come to be known as the "Wentworth Letter" was written. The article apparently never was published in Wentworth's newspaper or in the book, but the Prophet published it himself in the *Times and Seasons* in Nauvoo.[12] It was the first of the Prophet's accounts to appear in print.[13] The article discusses the First Vision, the coming forth of the Book of Mormon, and the history of the Church. It ends with a brief sketch of some beliefs of the Church which we now call the Articles of Faith. Unlike the 1832 and 1835 accounts, this document was prepared for publication, presumably for readers who were not Latter-day Saints.

In 1843 the Prophet was asked to prepare a chapter on the Latter-day Saints for a book on various religious beliefs. It was published shortly before his death the next year. The account of the First Vision in it is almost identical to that in the 1842 "Church History."[14]

1 When about fourteen years of age, I began to reflect upon the importance of being prepared for a future state. And upon enquiring the plan of salvation, I found that there was a great clash in religious sentiment. If I went to one society they referred me to one place, and another to another, each one pointing to his own particular creed as the *summum bonum* of perfection.

2 Considering that all could not be right, and that God could not be the author of so much confusion, I determined to investigate the subject more fully, believing that if God had a church it would not be split up into factions, and that if he taught one society to worship one way, and administer in one set of ordinances, he would not teach another principles which were diametrically opposed.

3 Believing the word of God, I had confidence in the declaration of James: "If any man lack wisdom, let him ask of God, who giveth to all men liberally, and upbraideth not; and it shall be given him" [James 1:5].

4 I retired to a secret place in a grove and began to call upon the Lord.

5 While fervently engaged in supplication, my mind was taken away from the objects with which I was surrounded. And I was enwrapped in a heavenly vision and saw two glorious personages who

exactly resembled each other in features and likeness, surrounded with a brilliant light which eclipsed the sun at noonday.

6 They told me that all religious denominations were believing in incorrect doctrines, and that none of them was acknowledged of God as his church and kingdom.

7 And I was expressly commanded to "go not after them," at the same time receiving a promise that the fullness of the gospel should at some future time be made known unto me.

The 1843 *Pittsburgh Gazette* Interview

In 1843 Joseph Smith was interviewed by a reporter from the *Pittsburgh Weekly Gazette.* The following is his brief account of the First Vision as it was reported in that newspaper.[15]

1 The Lord does reveal himself to me. I know it. He revealed himself first to me when I was about fourteen years old, a mere boy. I will tell you about it.

2 There was a reformation among the different religious denominations in the neighborhood where I lived, and I became serious and was desirous to know what church to join.

3 While thinking of this matter, I opened the Testament promiscuously[16] on these words in James: "Ask of the Lord, who giveth to all men liberally, and upbraideth not" [James 1:5]. I just determined I'd ask him.

4 I immediately went out into the woods where my father had a clearing and went to the stump where I had stuck my axe when I had quit work. And I kneeled down and prayed, saying, "O Lord, what church shall I join?"

5 Directly I saw a light, and then a glorious personage in the light, and then another personage. And the first personage said to the second, "Behold my beloved Son, hear him."

6 I then addressed this second person, saying, "O Lord, what church shall I join?" He replied, "Don't join any of them; they are all corrupt."

7 The vision then vanished, and when I came to myself, I was sprawling on my back, and it was some time before my strength returned.

The Heavenly Vision

When we consider the importance of the restoration of the gospel, which was initiated by the First Vision, and the millions of lives that have been and will continue to be blessed by it—both on the earth and in the spirit world—we can only begin in some small way to grasp the significance of this event. It was certainly one of the greatest occurrences of all time.

The Prophet seems to have been selective regarding what he made known of the sacred event in his five known accounts of the vision. We have no idea, for example, how long it lasted, and he wrote that the Lord told him "many other things" that he was not at liberty to share with others. In answer to his mother's concerned question about what had happened to him, he responded only with the amazing understatement that he had learned for himself "that Presbyterianism is not true" (JS–H 1:20). We respect the confidentiality of what the Lord has chosen not to make public and acknowledge that we are greatly blessed to learn all that he allowed his prophet to tell us. (In the following summary and in later chapters, the citations refer to the accounts by date, followed by the paragraph or verse number).[17]

Joseph Smith emphasized that he knew, even at a young age, that all was not right with the world and that he as well as others needed to learn how to live worthy of divine favor (1832:1–6, 10). For him, the pressing issue was to find a church whose teachings were in harmony with God's will (1835:1–2; JS–H 1:10; 1842:1–2; 1843:2). It was this question that led him eventually to a biblical verse that promises wisdom to those who earnestly seek it at the hand of God, James 1:5 (1835:2–3; JS–H 1:11–13; 1842:3; 1843:3). One account also mentions another verse with the same message, Matthew 7:7 (1835:2). In accordance with the scriptural promise, Joseph Smith went to the Lord and prayed in faith (1832:11; 1835:2–3; JS–H 1:14–15; 1842:4–5; 1843:4), whereupon Satan attacked him, trying to abort his prayer (1835:4–5; JS–H 1:15–16). Indescribable glory appeared with and surrounded the heavenly Personages—"a pillar of light above the brightness of the sun" (1832:11; JS–H 1:16), "a pillar of fire" (1835:6), "a brilliant light which eclipsed the sun at noonday"

(1842:5), "a light" (1843:5). God the Father appeared to Joseph Smith (1835:6; JS–H 1:17; 1842:5; 1843:5), as did his Son Jesus Christ (1832:12; 1835:7; JS–H 1:17; 1842:5). They "exactly resembled each other in features and likeness" (1842:5). The Father bore testimony of the Son (JS–H 1:17; 1843:5), and the Son delivered the message to Joseph Smith (1832:12–14; JS–H 1:17–20; 1843:5–6).

The Prophet was informed that his own sins were forgiven (1832:12; 1835:7). He was then told, in some detail, that the world lay in sin and the fullness of truth was not to be found on earth (1832:13–14; JS–H 1:19; 1842:6; 1843:6). Thus he was expressly forbidden to join any church (JS–H 1:19–20; 1842:7; 1843:6), but he was promised that "at some future time" "the fullness of the gospel" would be made known to him (1842:7).

Only one of the accounts reveals that he "saw many angels in this vision" (1835:8), which should confirm our caution that there is much about the First Vision we do not know at the present time.

The glorious experience was accompanied by a feeling of "great joy" (1832:15), or "joy unspeakable" (1835:6), which lasted "for many days" (1832:15). And the Prophet's soul "was filled with love" (1832:15).[18]

Notes

1. *Ensign,* June 1971, 34.

2. Important contemporary accounts of the First Vision written by others include Orson Pratt, *Interesting Account of Several Remarkable Visions, and of the Late Discovery of Ancient American Records* (Edinburgh: Ballantyne and Hughes, 1840); Orson Hyde, *Ein Ruf aus der Wüste* (Frankfurt, 1842); and a diary entry of Alexander Neibauer, 24 May 1844. These are found in Dean C. Jessee, ed., *The Papers of Joseph Smith,* 3 vols. (Salt Lake City: Deseret Book, 1989–97), 1:387–91, 402–9, and 459–61, respectively.

3. For additional discussion and composite texts that include information from Joseph Smith and other early sources, see Milton V. Backman Jr.,

Eyewitness Accounts of the Restoration (Orem, Utah: Grandin Book, 1983), 1–32.

4. The unedited original is found in Jessee, *Papers of Joseph Smith,* 1:1–10.

5. *Conversation* here, as in the King James Version of the Bible, means "behavior." See Noah Webster, *An American Dictionary of the English Language* (New York: S. Converse, 1828; facsimile reproduction, San Francisco: Foundation for American Christian Education, 1980), s.v. "conversation."

6. Meaning "convinced." Webster, *Dictionary,* second definition of *convict* (verb). See also KJV, John 8:9.

7. That the Prophet listed his age here as fifteen is of little consequence. This account was a draft and was never checked and edited for publication. All the other accounts list his age at fourteen (1835:9; JS–H 1:14; 1842:1; and 1843:1). Presumably he later consulted with older family members to be reminded of the correct year.

8. Joshua's real name was Robert Matthews. He claimed to be a literal descendant and also the reincarnation of the ancient apostle Matthias.

9. The scribe was Warren Parrish. The unedited original is in Jessee, *Papers of Joseph Smith,* 2:68–69.

10. See Joseph Smith, *History of the Church of Jesus Christ of Latter-day Saints,* ed. B. H. Roberts, 2d ed. rev., 7 vols. (Salt Lake City: Deseret Book, 1957).

11. See *Times and Seasons* 3, no. 10 (15 March 1842): 726–28; and 3, no. 11 (1 April 1842): 748–49. The heading was "History of Joseph Smith." When the *Pearl of Great Price* was created in 1851, it was included under the heading "Extracts from the History of Joseph Smith."

12. *Times and Seasons* 3, no. 9 (1 March 1842): 706–10. The heading was "Church History." The First Vision is discussed at 706–7.

13. The earliest of all published accounts of the First Vision was written by Elder Orson Pratt while he was serving a mission in Scotland. It is contained in his pamphlet *Interesting Account of Several Remarkable Visions.*

14. Joseph Smith, "Latter Day Saints," in I. Daniel Rupp, *An Original History of the Religious Denominations at Present Existing in the United States* (Philadelphia, 1844), 404–10. The text is preserved in Jessee, *Papers of Joseph Smith,* 1:445–58. The First Vision is discussed at 1:448–49 of Jessee, *Papers of Joseph Smith.*

15. "The Prairies, Nauvoo, Joe Smith, the Temple, the Mormons, etc.," *Pittsburgh Weekly Gazette* 58 (15 September 1843): 3. See Jessee, *Papers of Joseph Smith,* 1:438–44. Reprinted in the 23 September 1843 *New York Spectator.*

16. That is, "without order," "indiscriminately." Webster, *Dictionary,* s.v. "promiscuously." According to Alexander Neibaur, the Prophet said that when

he opened his Bible, "the first passage that struck him" was James 1:5. See Jessee, *Papers of Joseph Smith,* 1:461.

17. For a comprehensive harmony of each recorded element of the First Vision, see Backman, *Eyewitness Accounts,* 201–3.

18. See Rodney Turner, "The Visions of Moses," in Robert L. Millet and Kent P. Jackson, eds., *The Pearl of Great Price,* Studies in Scripture Series, vol. 2 (Salt Lake City: Randall Book, 1985), 50–51.

Chapter 9

Lessons from the Sacred Grove

The First Vision is one of history's greatest revelations of sacred doctrine. It is the beginning of the process by which the Church was restored, but in addition it is in its own right a magnificent restoration of truths that could be found nowhere else on earth.

It is not difficult to imagine that this revelation was an overpowering experience for a fourteen-year-old boy, even one with the maturity and sensitivity that characterized young Joseph Smith. Likely the experience was so unexpected and so overpowering that he did not understand all he saw and heard in it until he had matured and learned more of the gospel through subsequent revelations. Aside from the five accounts discussed previously, we have no record in his words of his ever discussing in detail what he learned from the First Vision. Still, we can gain much through a careful study of what he recorded of the sacred event, including several important doctrines. In this discussion, the accounts are cited by date and paragraph or verse numbers.

The Reality and Nature of Satan

Even before Joseph Smith learned anything else in his First Vision, he was made aware in a dramatic way of the existence and power of Satan, who seized him and nearly overcame him. He recognized that an unseen force wanted to destroy him, and it was only through the approach of the pillar of light that he was delivered from that fate (1835:4–5; JS–H 1:15–16). From Satan's attack on the Prophet, we see that the adversary has some power to manipulate the elements to do his will, a fact that is borne out in a later revelation to Joseph Smith (D&C 61:4–5, 15–19).[1] We do not know what the limitations on that power are, but it is clear from the Prophet's record that Satan's power is real and frighteningly potent. In fact, Joseph Smith thought that he was going to die (JS–H 1:15–16).

As a believer in the Bible, the Prophet presumably believed in the devil before he had the First Vision. But the First Vision proves Satan's existence, which is more important today than it was then because much of Christianity has now abandoned belief in the reality of the adversary. The First Vision also establishes that Satan knew Joseph Smith. Through a later revelation we learn that Satan was present with "the noble and great ones" in the premortal councils (Abr. 3:22–28), where Joseph Smith certainly was also present, where his calling was probably known, and where he was foreordained to do his great earthly work.[2] After the First Vision the Prophet marveled that someone such as himself would attract the attention of so many "of the great ones of the most popular sects of the day, and in a manner to create in them a spirit of the most bitter persecution and reviling" (JS–H 1:23). Those individuals were merely attempting, like many others since them, to complete the deed that Satan had failed to accomplish in the Sacred Grove. Joseph Smith was not, contrary to his own assessment at the time, "an obscure boy" (JS–H 1:22). As he learned in due time, he was one of the great ones of the Father's children, whose mission would affect the lives of millions of others.

Satan knew that. By the spring of 1820 he had enjoyed enormous power over human hearts for many centuries. Now, with the calling of Joseph Smith and the restoration of true religion to the earth, the doom of the devil's kingdom was assured.

Apostasy and Restoration

The First Vision teaches the reality of the Apostasy and the need for the Restoration. In response to Joseph Smith's question about which church he should join, the Lord told him that he should "join none of them, for they were all wrong." The Lord elaborated that "all their creeds were an abomination in his sight; that those professors were all corrupt; that: 'they draw near to me with their lips, but their hearts are far from me, they teach for doctrines the commandments of men, having a form of godliness, but they deny the power thereof'" (JS–H 1:19).

Because these clear and straightforward statements come from a prophet reporting the words of Jesus Christ, we need to take them seriously, believe them, and understand them. We must recognize that the Lord's chastisement was directed not at honorable individuals who had been led into confusion by the wrong ideas of others but rather at false doctrine and at those who perpetrated it.

As a result of apostate forces that had existed in ancient times and had been at work continuously into Joseph Smith's day, true religion was nowhere to be found, neither in the Palmyra-Manchester area nor anywhere on earth. All religions were therefore "corrupt" (1843:6), despite the best efforts of many who were in them. The doctrines of Christianity, having been removed for many centuries from their original revealed source, were "commandments of men" and not of God. Even though some beliefs had "a form of godliness," they denied God's power (JS–H 1:19) because they were not revealed by him, acknowledged by him, nor administered under the hands of his authorized servants. As a result, even the most honorable of believers were living their lives contrary to the Lord's plan: "The world lieth in sin at this time, and none doeth good, no not one. They have turned aside from the gospel and keep not my commandments" (1832:13). The Prophet summarized the Lord's message: "They told me that all religious denominations were believing in incorrect doctrines, and that none of them was acknowledged of God as his church and kingdom. And I was expressly commanded to 'go not after them'" (1842:6–7).

But what of those whom the Lord characterized as drawing near to him with their lips but whose hearts were far from him? (JS–H 1:19; 1832:13). Those were individuals who professed religion but were hypocrites because their hearts were not consistent with their words. To profess is "to make open declaration of; to avow or acknowledge."[3] Those who did so dishonestly added the sin of hypocrisy to their false doctrine. Unfortunately, Joseph Smith soon had experiences with many such individuals.

These conditions demonstrate that there was a need for a restoration of gospel truth to the earth. The Prophet never told us whether he was informed at that time of his own role in the process. Perhaps his calling was explained to him then, or perhaps that message was reserved to be explained at a later date by Moroni (see JS–H 1:33, 54).[4] His only comment was that he received "a promise that the fullness of the gospel should at some future time be made known" to him (1842:7).

The Reality and Nature of God

Certainly the greatest doctrinal contribution of the First Vision is what it teaches us about God. Its revelations concerning Deity are especially important because they follow on the heels of many centuries of confusion and misinformation on this topic since the Apostasy began. When false influences alter or supplant true religion, the first target is the nature of God, as can be seen in the teachings of the periods that followed the Old and New Testaments.[5] The world witnessed the consequences of that in the early centuries of Christian history. The first task of the Restoration was to reestablish the true doctrine of God so individuals could know him, understand what is revealed concerning

The First Vision, stained-glass window, Salt Lake City, Utah

him, and worship him in righteousness. The First Vision began that process in a profound way.

First, we learn from the First Vision that God exists. Perhaps in Joseph Smith's day the revelation of this knowledge was not as significant as it is in our own era of disbelief. But even then, the assurance that there is a God in heaven, confirming the Bible's testimony of this truth, was a revelation of profound importance. That someone in modern times has spoken with God bears testimony to his reality and stands as a witness of it to all the world.

Second, from the First Vision we have evidence that God knows us and hears and answers our prayers. That may have been a new insight to the young Prophet, who had never before made an attempt to pray such as he did on that occasion (JS–H 1:14). Those who have had experience with prayer take for granted that God knows us and cares for us. But that knowledge is perhaps the single most important thing lacking in the lives of millions of people worldwide. It is sad to know that even many in the world who pray have been taught that God is so far removed from us that one cannot actually converse with him or that prayer consists of reciting set phrases rather than offering the sincere personal expressions of an honest individual's heart.

That God knew Joseph Smith is evident in that He came to him and addressed him by name (1832:12; JS–H 1:17). From the Prophet's experience we can rightly infer that God knows each of us as well.

Third, the First Vision teaches that humans are, just as the Bible says, created in the literal image of God. This truth was rejected by early Christian theologians because it clashed so fundamentally with the prevailing philosophies of the time, which had long since rejected the possibility of a bodily God. From the First Vision we learn that God is neither shapeless, indefinable, nor unknowable. Although we do not know whether Joseph Smith learned in the First Vision that God has flesh and bones, it can be stated that he learned then that God and humans are in the same form, something that many Christians had already assumed from their reading of the Bible. Later revelations taught him more (D&C 130:22), including the truth that God is our Father and the ultimate destiny of his faithful children is to become as he is.[6]

Fourth, from the First Vision we know that God the Father and his Son Jesus Christ are two separate individuals with distinct personal identities. The New Testament clearly teaches this truth, but the ancient Christian councils rejected it. Under the influence of Greek thought, they devised in its place the nonscriptural trinitarian mystery that the Father, the Son, and the Holy Ghost are one being who consists of three different persons. That has been the fundamental theology—the most basic core belief—of the Christian world since the fourth century after Christ, and it continues to be at the very foundation of Orthodox, Catholic, and Protestant Christianity today. The First Vision proves it mistaken and shows instead the separate identities of the Father and the Son.

Fifth, the Prophet also learned in the First Vision that the Father and the Son "exactly resembled each other in features and likeness" (1842:5).

Sixth, the First Vision teaches us that God is a being of awesome glory. A "pillar of light" (JS–H 1:16)—"a brilliant light which eclipsed the sun at noonday" (1842:5)—rested on Joseph Smith, driving away the power of Satan and creating an environment in which the Prophet could stand in the presence of Deity. He learned from subsequent revelations and experiences that to endure God's presence, one needs to be immersed in God's glory (Moses 1:2, 11; D&C 76:19–20). The Prophet described this glory as "above the brightness of the sun" (JS–H 1:16). From his earthbound perspective he had nothing else to which he could compare it, so his analogy drew from the brightest thing he had ever seen. The glory that accompanied the Father and the Son was far brighter than that.

Seventh, the First Vision teaches us something of the priesthood order of heaven: Christ, though divine, is subordinate to God the Father. The Father appeared first, followed by the Son (1835:6–7; 1843:5). The Father introduced and bore testimony of the Son (JS–H 1:17; 1843:5), who then delivered the message to Joseph Smith (1832:12–14; 1843:6). These matters are only briefly mentioned in the Prophet's accounts and are not discussed in any detail, but they teach us some important things. President Joseph Fielding Smith stated: "All revelation since the fall has come through Jesus Christ. . . . The Father has never dealt with man directly and personally since the fall, and he has never

The First Vision, stained-glass window, Brigham City, Utah

appeared except to introduce and bear record of the Son."[7] That truth is consistent with the evidence from the First Vision.

Eighth, from the First Vision we gain an additional witness of the divine, redemptive mission of Jesus Christ. The Father's introduction, "This is My Beloved Son" (JS–H 1:17; cf. 1843:5), is sufficient endorsement of the Savior's work and worthiness. "He testified unto me that Jesus Christ is the Son of God" (1835:7). "I am the Lord of glory," Jesus told the Prophet, "I was crucified for the world, that all those who believe on my name may have eternal life" (1832:12). And Jesus will come again: "I come quickly, as it [is] written of me, in the cloud clothed in the glory of my Father" (1832:14).

It is not difficult to see that the First Vision responds in fundamental ways to the creeds and councils that created traditional Christian theology. By means of this supernal revelatory event, centuries of doctrinal misdirection were wiped away and replaced with eternal but long-lost truth. The Restoration is thus not a reformation of Christianity nor a refinement of its beliefs and practices. Like the First Vision itself, it is a radical departure from traditional Christianity that sets in its place a whole new system of beliefs entirely independent of past tradition. The First Vision opened a new day in the history of God's dealings with humankind.

The Reality of the First Vision

As a doctrinal revelation, the First Vision is certainly on a par with the greatest of the revelations in the Doctrine and Covenants. Indeed, it seems safe to say that we learn more about God from it than we do from any other revelation. One cannot imagine a more profound and enlightening event to begin the return of lost truth, starting with the most fundamental principles of theology. But the First Vision did even more than reveal new light on doctrinal topics, as important as that is. It also began the historical process we call the Restoration, and as such it holds a unique and supremely significant position as an event of sacred history.

Did the First Vision actually take place? Though some may be uncomfortable with the idea of God appearing to a frontier farm boy, for Latter-day Saints the historical reality of the event is foundational and not subject to negotiation. To say that the First Vision was not an actual event—a real occurrence that took place as Joseph Smith described it—is to deny everything about it. How can one disbelieve the First Vision and believe anything else of the gospel that the Lord restored through Joseph Smith? If one rejects or modifies any part of his testimony concerning it, one is rendering it meaningless by rejecting the man who witnessed it and taught us about it. The definition of a Latter-day Saint is, among other things, one who accepts at face value the literal, historical reality of the First Vision. President Ezra Taft Benson taught: "This message constitutes the heart and the foundation of the Church. If Joseph Smith's testimony of seeing God the Father and His Son, Jesus Christ, is not true, then Mormonism represents a false system of belief. But if this vision was reality—and there are thousands who attest that it is by the verifying witness of God's Holy Spirit—then the Church of Jesus Christ was and is restored on earth again."[8]

Through the power of the Holy Ghost, all who humbly seek enlightenment from God can receive an assurance that the First Vision took place. As they come to accept the Prophet's testimony of it, they can witness that it is true, that it really happened, and that their lives have been blessed immeasurably because of it.

Notes

1. See Joseph Fielding Smith, *Church History and Modern Revelation,* 4 vols. (Salt Lake City: Deseret News Press, 1946–47), 1:207.

2. Andrew F. Ehat and Lyndon W. Cook, eds., *The Words of Joseph Smith: The Contemporary Accounts of the Nauvoo Discourses of the Prophet Joseph* (Provo, Utah: Religious Studies Center, Brigham Young University, 1980), 367.

3. Noah Webster, *An American Dictionary of the English Language* (New York: S. Converse, 1828; facsimile reproduction, San Francisco: Foundation for American Christian Education, 1980), s.v. "profess." A professor is one who "makes open declaration of his sentiments or opinions; particularly, one who makes a public avowal of his belief in the Scriptures and his faith in Christ," ibid., s.v. "professor."

4. In his 1842 account of what Moroni told him, the Prophet said: "I was informed that I was chosen to be an instrument in the hands of God to bring about some of his purposes in this glorious dispensation" (1842:11).

5. See M. Catherine Thomas, "From Malachi to John the Baptist: The Dynamics of Apostasy," in Kent P. Jackson, ed., *1 Kings to Malachi,* Studies in Scripture Series, vol. 4 (Salt Lake City: Deseret Book, 1993), 476–80.

6. See Chapter 23, 242–50.

7. Joseph Fielding Smith, *Doctrines of Salvation,* 3 vols., comp. Bruce R. McConkie (Salt Lake City: Bookcraft, 1954–56), 1:27.

8. Ezra Taft Benson, *Come unto Christ* (Salt Lake City: Deseret Book, 1983), 74.

Chapter 10

The Coming of Moroni

The process of restoring the gospel was not resumed until more than three years after the First Vision. Then, with the appearance of Moroni on the night of 21–22 September 1823, the Restoration was underway with a dramatic burst of interaction between heaven and earth. Even though Joseph Smith was only seventeen years old at the time, he was assuming his foreordained role as the Prophet of the Restoration. It was a role from which he would never be released, the responsibility of which he would carry with him every day of his life.

The Prophet was prepared for his life's mission under the guidance of Moroni, an ancient American prophet who was the caretaker of the Book of Mormon and who became in the latter days the mentor and tutor of young Joseph Smith.[1] Moroni's appearance to the Prophet is described in succinct terms in Doctrine and Covenants 20:5–8:

> 5 After it was truly manifested unto this first elder that he had received a remission of his sins, he was entangled again in the vanities of the world;
>
> 6 But after repenting, and humbling himself sincerely, through faith, God ministered unto him by an holy angel, whose countenance was as lightning, and whose garments were pure and white above all other whiteness;
>
> 7 And gave unto him commandments which inspired him;

8 And gave him power from on high, by the means which were before prepared, to translate the Book of Mormon.

We also know of the coming of Moroni through the testimony of Joseph Smith, who experienced it, spoke of it publicly, and proclaimed its reality in conjunction with the coming forth of the Book of Mormon. Based on what they learned from him, both Oliver Cowdery and Orson Pratt published accounts of Moroni's appearance before the Prophet did.[2] But we are greatly blessed that on four known occasions, Joseph Smith himself recorded on paper his eyewitness experience. Like the narratives of the First Vision, these four accounts bear testimony of the event and of the Prophet who experienced it. Following are all four accounts of Moroni's first visits in the order in which they were written. As with the Prophet's narratives of the First Vision, of which these are the continuation, his words are preserved exactly as they were recorded but with punctuation and spelling modernized. The paragraphs are numbered as well. References to the original documents are in the notes.[3]

The 1832 Draft History

Joseph Smith's 1832 narrative of the coming of Moroni was dictated to a scribe, unlike the account of the First Vision that immediately precedes it, which was written in the Prophet's own hand.[4] This history was not completed or edited for publication in the Prophet's lifetime.[5]

16 But after many days, I fell into transgressions and sinned in many things, which brought a wound upon my soul. And there were many things which transpired that cannot be written, and my father's family have suffered many persecutions and afflictions.

17 And it came to pass, when I was seventeen years of age, I called again upon the Lord, and he showed unto me a heavenly vision. For behold, an angel of the Lord came and stood before me, and it was by night. And he called me by name, and he said the Lord had forgiven me my sins.

18 And he revealed unto me that in the town of Manchester, Ontario County, New York, there were plates of gold upon which there were engravings which were engraven by Moroni and his fathers, the servants of the living God in ancient days, and deposited by the commandments of God and kept by the power thereof, and that I should go and get them.

19 And he revealed unto me many things concerning the inhabitants of the earth which since have been revealed in commandments and revelations. And it was on the twenty-second day of September A.D. 1823.[6] And thus he appeared unto me three times in one night and once on the next day.

The 1835 Journal Account

Dating from November 1835 is a diary entry that narrates the continuation of the Prophet's words to "Joshua the Jewish Minister," an eccentric religionist of the time. It too was not published while Joseph Smith was alive.[7]

10 When I was about seventeen years old, I saw another vision of angels. In the night season after I had retired to bed, I had not been asleep but was meditating upon my past life and experience. I was very conscious that I had not kept the commandments, and I repented heartily for all my sins and transgression and humbled myself before him whose eyes are over all things.

11 All at once the room was illuminated above the brightness of the sun. An angel appeared before me. His hands and feet were naked, pure and white, and he stood between the floors of the room, clothed with purity inexpressible. He said unto me, "I am a messenger sent from God. Be faithful and keep his commandments in all things."

12 He told me of a sacred record which was written on plates of gold. I saw in the vision the place where they were deposited. He said the Indians were the literal descendants of Abraham.

13 He explained many of the prophesies to me. One I will mention, which is in Malachi, fourth chapter: "Behold the day of the Lord cometh," etc. [Mal. 4:1];

14 Also that the Urim and Thummim was hid up with the record, and that God would give me power to translate it with the assistance of this instrument. He then gradually vanished out of my sight, or the vision closed.

15 While meditating on what I had seen, the angel appeared to me again and related the same things and much more, also the third time, bearing the same tidings, and departed. During the time I was in this vision, I did not realize anything around me except what was shown me in this communication.

16 After the vision had all passed, I found that it was nearly daylight. . . .

The 1838 "History of Joseph Smith" (JS–H)

The following narrative is an excerpt from the Prophet's most formal history, which we now have as the seven-volume *History of the Church.*[8] This part was first published under the Prophet's direction in the Church's newspaper in Nauvoo, Illinois, in 1842.[9] It is now contained in the Pearl of Great Price as part of the "Joseph Smith–History," and thus it carries the added importance of being scripture. It is by far the longest and most detailed of the Prophet's accounts of Moroni's coming. The verse numbers are those of the Pearl of Great Price.

28 During the space of time which intervened between the time I had the vision and the year eighteen hundred and twenty-three—having been forbidden to join any of the religious sects of the day, and being of very tender years, and persecuted by those who ought to have been my friends and to have treated me kindly, and if they supposed me to be deluded to have endeavored in a proper and affectionate manner to have reclaimed me—I was left to all kinds of temptations; and, mingling with all kinds of society, I frequently fell into many foolish errors, and displayed the weakness of youth, and the foibles of human nature; which, I am sorry to say, led me into divers temptations, offensive in the sight of God. In making this confession, no one need suppose me guilty of any great or malignant sins. A disposition to commit such was never in my nature. But I was guilty of levity, and sometimes associated with jovial company, etc., not consistent with that character which ought to be maintained by one who was called of God as I had been. But this will not seem very strange to any one who recollects my youth, and is acquainted with my native cheery temperament.

29 In consequence of these things, I often felt condemned for my

Log home of Joseph Smith Sr. family, Palmyra Township, New York, where the Prophet was living at the time of the First Vision (1820) and where Moroni appeared (1823). Painting by Al Rounds

weakness and imperfections; when, on the evening of the above-mentioned twenty-first of September, after I had retired to my bed for the night, I betook myself to prayer and supplication to Almighty God for forgiveness of all my sins and follies, and also for a manifestation to me, that I might know of my state and standing before him; for I had full confidence in obtaining a divine manifestation, as I previously had one.

30 While I was thus in the act of calling upon God, I discovered a light appearing in my room, which continued to increase until the room was lighter than at noonday, when immediately a personage appeared at my bedside, standing in the air, for his feet did not touch the floor.

31 He had on a loose robe of most exquisite whiteness. It was a whiteness beyond anything earthly I had ever seen; nor do I believe that any earthly thing could be made to appear so exceedingly white and brilliant. His hands were naked, and his arms also, a little above the wrist; so, also, were his feet naked, as were his legs, a little above the ankles. His head and neck were also bare. I could discover that he had no other clothing on but this robe, as it was open, so that I could see into his bosom.

32 Not only was his robe exceedingly white, but his whole person was glorious beyond description, and his countenance truly like lightning. The room was exceedingly light, but not so very bright as immediately around his person. When I first looked upon him, I was afraid; but the fear soon left me.

33 He called me by name, and said unto me that he was a messenger sent from the presence of God to me, and that his name was Moroni; that God had a work for me to do; and that my name should be had for good and evil among all nations, kindreds, and tongues, or that it should be both good and evil spoken of among all people.

34 He said there was a book deposited, written upon gold plates, giving an account of the former inhabitants of this continent, and the source from whence they sprang. He also said that the fulness of the everlasting Gospel was contained in it, as delivered by the Savior to the ancient inhabitants;

35 Also, that there were two stones in silver bows—and these stones, fastened to a breastplate, constituted what is called the Urim and Thummim—deposited with the plates; and the possession and use of these stones were what constituted "seers" in ancient or former times; and that God had prepared them for the purpose of translating the book.

36 After telling me these things, he commenced quoting the prophecies of the Old Testament. He first quoted part of the third chapter of Malachi; and he quoted also the fourth or last chapter of the same prophecy, though with a little variation from the way it reads in our Bibles. Instead of quoting the first verse as it reads in our books, he quoted it thus:

37 *For behold, the day cometh that shall burn as an oven, and all the proud, yea, and all that do wickedly shall burn as stubble; for they that come shall burn them, saith the Lord of Hosts, that it shall leave them neither root nor branch.*

38 And again, he quoted the fifth verse thus: *Behold, I will reveal unto you the Priesthood, by the hand of Elijah the prophet, before the coming of the great and dreadful day of the Lord.*

39 He also quoted the next verse differently: *And he shall plant in the hearts of the children the promises made to the fathers, and the hearts of the children shall turn to their fathers. If it were not so, the whole earth would be utterly wasted at his coming.*

40 In addition to these, he quoted the eleventh chapter of Isaiah, saying that it was about to be fulfilled. He quoted also the third chapter of

Acts, twenty-second and twenty-third verses, precisely as they stand in our New Testament. He said that that prophet was Christ; but the day had not yet come when "they who would not hear his voice should be cut off from among the people," but soon would come.

41 He also quoted the second chapter of Joel, from the twenty-eighth verse to the last. He also said that this was not yet fulfilled, but was soon to be. And he further stated that the fulness of the Gentiles was soon to come in. He quoted many other passages of scripture, and offered many explanations which cannot be mentioned here.

42 Again, he told me, that when I got those plates of which he had spoken—for the time that they should be obtained was not yet fulfilled—I should not show them to any person; neither the breastplate with the Urim and Thummim; only to those to whom I should be commanded to show them; if I did I should be destroyed. While he was conversing with me about the plates, the vision was opened to my mind that I could see the place where the plates were deposited, and that so clearly and distinctly that I knew the place again when I visited it.

43 After this communication, I saw the light in the room begin to gather immediately around the person of him who had been speaking to me, and it continued to do so until the room was again left dark, except just around him; when, instantly I saw, as it were, a conduit open right up into heaven, and he ascended till he entirely disappeared, and the room was left as it had been before this heavenly light had made its appearance.

44 I lay musing on the singularity of the scene, and marveling greatly at what had been told to me by this extraordinary messenger; when, in the midst of my meditation, I suddenly discovered that my room was again beginning to get lighted, and in an instant, as it were, the same heavenly messenger was again by my bedside.

45 He commenced, and again related the very same things which he had done at his first visit, without the least variation; which having done, he informed me of great judgments which were coming upon the earth, with great desolations by famine, sword, and pestilence; and that these grievous judgments would come on the earth in this generation. Having related these things, he again ascended as he had done before.

46 By this time, so deep were the impressions made on my mind, that sleep had fled from my eyes, and I lay overwhelmed in astonishment at what I had both seen and heard. But what was my surprise when again I beheld the same messenger at my bedside, and heard him rehearse or

repeat over again to me the same things as before; and added a caution to me, telling me that Satan would try to tempt me (in consequence of the indigent circumstances of my father's family), to get the plates for the purpose of getting rich. This he forbade me, saying that I must have no other object in view in getting the plates but to glorify God, and must not be influenced by any other motive than that of building his kingdom; otherwise I could not get them.

47 After this third visit, he again ascended into heaven as before, and I was again left to ponder on the strangeness of what I had just experienced; when almost immediately after the heavenly messenger had ascended from me for the third time, the cock crowed, and I found that day was approaching, so that our interviews must have occupied the whole of that night.

The 1842 "Church History"

The following account continues Joseph Smith's history from what is sometimes called the "Wentworth Letter." It was first published in Nauvoo in 1842 and was the first of these narratives to appear in print.[10] The Prophet published it again two years later, with only minor changes, in a book on American religions.[11]

8 On the evening of the twenty-first of September, A.D. 1823, while I was praying unto God and endeavoring to exercise faith in the precious promises of scripture, on a sudden a light like that of day, only of a far purer and more glorious appearance and brightness, burst into the room.

9 Indeed, the first sight was as though the house was filled with consuming fire. The appearance produced a shock that affected the whole body. In a moment a personage stood before me, surrounded with a glory yet greater than that with which I was already surrounded.

10 This messenger proclaimed himself to be an angel of God sent to bring the joyful tidings that the covenant which God made with ancient Israel was at hand to be fulfilled, that the preparatory work for the Second Coming of the Messiah was speedily to commence, that the time was at hand for the gospel, in all its fulness, to be preached in power unto all nations, that a people might be prepared for the millennial reign.

11 I was informed that I was chosen to be an instrument in the hands of God to bring about some of his purposes in this glorious dispensation.

12 I was also informed concerning the aboriginal inhabitants of this

country and shown who they were and from whence they came. A brief sketch of their origin, progress, civilization, laws, governments, of their righteousness and iniquity, and the blessings of God being finally withdrawn from them as a people was made known unto me.

13 I was also told where there were deposited some plates on which was engraven an abridgement of the records of the ancient prophets that had existed on this continent.

14 The angel appeared to me three times the same night and unfolded the same things.

A Messenger Sent from God

In an 1838 newspaper article, Joseph Smith wrote about the angel's coming: "Moroni, the person who deposited the plates, . . . being dead, and raised again therefrom, appeared unto me, and told me where they were; and gave me directions how to obtain them."[12] From 1820 to 1823, it appears that the work of restoration awaited only the continued maturing of the young Prophet Joseph Smith. When the time was right, the process of bringing lost truth back to earth was recommenced with the coming of Moroni, "a messenger sent from God" (1835:11).

By the time Joseph Smith was seventeen years old (1832:17; 1835:10), more than three years had passed since the First Vision. During that time, as he later related, he was subject to "the foibles of human nature" (JS–H 1:28) and felt himself unworthy, "which brought a wound upon [his] soul" (1832:16). His transgression, he stated, was that he "was guilty of levity, and sometimes associated with jovial company," which he felt was "offensive in the sight of God." The Prophet himself set these comments in proper perspective by noting that he never possessed a disposition to do evil. Indeed, the issue was not that his levity and associations were bad but that they were not in harmony with how one should act who had been called of God as he had (JS–H 1:28). Still, he "repented heartily" of these things (1835:10).

As he prayed for forgiveness on the night of 21 September 1823 (JS–H 1:28–29; 1842:8), a light came into his room that was "of a far purer and more glorious appearance and brightness" than the light of the sun at noonday (1842:8; JS–H 1:30). In that light, an angel of God appeared, standing in the air (1835:11; JS–H 1:30). The Prophet described the angel's manner of dress and said that even his clothing was "white and brilliant," with "a whiteness beyond anything earthly" that he had ever seen (JS–H 1:31). At first he felt fear, but that soon left him (JS–H 1:32). The angel called Joseph Smith by name (1832:17) and announced that he was a messenger from God whose name was Moroni (JS–H 1:33). He told the Prophet that his sins were forgiven (1832:17) and that God had a work for him to do (JS–H 1:33; 1842:11). He instructed him to keep himself worthy (1835:11) and informed him that his name would "be both good and evil spoken of among all people" (JS–H 1:33).

Moroni spoke about the natives of the Americas and told Joseph Smith that they were "the literal descendants of Abraham" (1835:12). He showed him "who they were and from whence they came." He learned of their ancestors in ancient times, "of their origin, progress, civilization, laws, governments," and of their "righteousness and iniquity" (1842:12). Moroni told the Prophet of a book that was the account of these ancient people, written by their prophets on gold plates. It had been concealed anciently and preserved to come forth in modern times (1832:18; 1835:12; 1842:13). It contained "the fulness of the everlasting Gospel" (JS–H 1:34). Joseph Smith was to translate it by means of an instrument called the Urim and Thummim, which was hidden with the record (1835:14; JS–H 1:35).

The angel taught Joseph Smith about his mission by quoting and explaining passages of scripture (1835:13; JS–H 1:36). In the Prophet's accounts of the experience, he cited specifically only a few passages (1835:13; JS–H 1:36–41), but he stated that Moroni quoted "many" others as well (JS–H 1:41). The angel revealed to him many things that were reaffirmed in subsequent revelations (1832:19).

Joseph Smith was instructed that once he received them, he was to show neither the plates nor the Urim and Thummim to anyone except those whom the Lord would designate. If he did otherwise, he would be destroyed (JS–H 1:42). He was allowed to see in vision the place where they were buried (1835:12), which was so vivid that he had no trouble finding the spot when he went there the next day (JS–H 1:42). After that, Moroni departed, and the room was dark again (1835:14; JS–H 1:43).

Moroni's mission was not complete with this one visit. Altogether he appeared three times that night, each time repeating the same message and then adding other information (1832:19; 1842:14). The next day he appeared twice more.

During the final visit of the night, he warned Joseph Smith that he should have only God's glory in mind when he dealt with the gold plates. Because of the poverty of his family, he would be tempted by Satan to consider their financial value. Moroni cautioned him that he "must not be influenced by any other motive" than that of building God's kingdom (JS–H 1:46). The consequences of disobedience to that injunction would become very real to him the following day.

During the angelic interviews, which opened and closed in succession, the Prophet was oblivious to everything but what he was shown in the visions (1835:15). That seems to have included the passage of time, for when the third appearance ended, he discovered that the night had run its course and it was morning. The visions had lasted the entire night (1835:16; JS–H 1:47).

Notes

1. See H. Donl Peterson, *Moroni: Ancient Prophet, Modern Messenger* (Bountiful, Utah: Horizon, 1983).

2. Oliver Cowdery, "Letter IV. To W. W. Phelps, Esq.," *Latter Day Saints' Messenger and Advocate* 1, no. 5 (February 1835): 77–80; "Letter VI. To W. W. Phelps, Esq.," *Messenger and Advocate* 1, no. 7 (April 1835): 108–12; "Letter

VII. To W. W. Phelps, Esq.," *Messenger and Advocate* 1, no. 10 (July 1835): 156–59; Orson Pratt, *Interesting Account of Several Remarkable Visions, and of the Late Discovery of Ancient American Records* (Edinburgh: Ballantyne and Hughes, 1840), 5–11. Part of Orson Pratt's account consists of material quoted from Oliver Cowdery's accounts.

3. A composite text from the words of Joseph Smith and others is found in Milton V. Backman Jr., *Eyewitness Accounts of the Restoration* (Orem, Utah: Grandin Book, 1983), 38–56.

4. Only the first four words, "But after many days," are in Joseph Smith's handwriting.

5. The scribe was Frederick G. Williams. The unedited original is found in Dean C. Jessee, ed., *The Papers of Joseph Smith,* 3 vols. (Salt Lake City: Deseret Book, 1989–97), 1:7–8.

6. The scribe recorded 1822 in the original draft. The correct year was 1823; see 1838:28; 1842:1.

7. It was dictated to Warren Parrish. The unedited original is in Jessee, *Papers of Joseph Smith,* 2:69–70.

8. Joseph Smith, *History of The Church of Jesus Christ of Latter-day Saints,* ed. B. H. Roberts, 2d ed. rev., 7 vols. (Salt Lake City: Deseret Book, 1957).

9. See "History of Joseph Smith," *Times and Seasons* 3, no. 11 (1 April 1842): 749; 3, no. 12 (15 April 1842): 753–54. In the original 1851 *Pearl of Great Price,* it was called "Extracts from the History of Joseph Smith."

10. "Church History," *Times and Seasons* 3, no. 9 (1 March 1842): 706–10. This account is found on page 707.

11. Joseph Smith, "Latter Day Saints," in I. Daniel Rupp, *An Original History of the Religious Denominations at Present Existing in the United States* (Philadelphia, 1844), 404–10. See Jessee, *Papers of Joseph Smith,* 1:449–50.

12. *Elders' Journal* 1, no. 3 (July 1838), 42–43.

Chapter 11

God's Work in the Last Days

One significant aspect of Moroni's appearance to Joseph Smith was the instruction he gave the young Prophet about his life's calling. Although it often does not receive as much attention as the message about the Book of Mormon, this part of the angel's visit is profoundly important in our history. Moroni introduced Joseph Smith to his mission and began to train him to assume his foreordained role to preside over the Lord's work of the last days.

The Prophet gave us only brief glimpses into what Moroni taught him. In the 1832 account he reported simply that he learned "many things concerning the inhabitants of the earth" (1832:19). In 1835 he said that Moroni "explained many of the prophecies" (1835:13). In his 1842 recitation he stated that Moroni taught him "that the covenant which God made with ancient Israel was at hand to be fulfilled, that the preparatory work for the Second Coming of the Messiah was speedily to commence, that the time was at hand for the gospel, in all its fulness, to be preached in power unto all nations, that a people might be prepared for the millennial reign." He added, "I was informed that I was chosen to be an instrument in the hands of God to bring about some of his purposes in this glorious dispensation" (1842:10–11).

Teaching from the Scriptures

Moroni taught Joseph Smith by quoting and discussing scripture. Through this process, the angel conveyed to him the messages and testimonies of ancient prophets who had seen and rejoiced in our day. In the 1835 account, the Prophet said that Moroni explained "many" prophecies to him, but he mentioned only one: Malachi 4. In the Joseph Smith–History (1:36–41), he mentioned five specific passages and recorded some of Moroni's comments concerning them: Malachi 3 ("part," perhaps vv. 1–4); Malachi 4:1–6; Isaiah 11:1–16; Acts 3:22–23; Joel 2:28–32.[1] The Prophet then added: "He quoted many other passages of scripture, and offered many explanations which cannot be mentioned here" (JS–H 1:41).

In 1835 Oliver Cowdery wrote a series of articles in the Church's newspaper, the *Messenger and Advocate,* regarding Moroni's appearance to Joseph Smith.[2] Written in Elder Cowdery's rich literary style, these articles contain lengthy discourses that represent the message conveyed by the angel Moroni. Elder Cowdery called his accounts "an outline of the conversation of the angel."[3] As in the Prophet's accounts, Oliver Cowdery's recitation shows Moroni teaching by quoting and explaining scripture.[4] These articles contribute a wealth of information about this sacred event and its importance. Obviously, Elder Cowdery was not with the Prophet when it happened, so the account is secondary. Yet we assume that Joseph Smith had rehearsed the event to his colleague on numerous occasions. Elder Cowdery had been the Prophet's scribe, and when he wrote the articles about Moroni he was assistant president of the Church. His intimate association with the Prophet, especially in the early part of his ministry, may have enabled him to know more about these events than anyone else except Joseph Smith.[5]

At the beginning of one of the accounts, Elder Cowdery wrote: "I have thought best to give a farther detail of the heavenly message, and if I do not give it in the precise words, shall strictly confine myself to the facts in substance."[6] At the end of his discussion of Moroni, "whose words I have been rehearsing," he wrote: "I have now given you a rehearsal of what was communicated to our brother. . . . I may have missed in arrangement in some instances, but the principle is preserved." He commented further: "You are aware of the fact, that to give a minute rehearsal of a lengthy interview with a heavenly messenger, is very difficult, unless one is assisted immediately with the gift of inspiration."[7]

How well he succeeded only God, Moroni, and Joseph Smith know for sure. Keeping in mind that it was an event at which only Moroni and Joseph Smith were participants, I am inclined, in general, to trust Elder Cowdery's record because he was working closely with the Prophet when he wrote it. Moreover, almost all of the passages of scripture quoted by Moroni in his accounts deal with the same topics as the passages mentioned by Joseph Smith.

When we combine the information provided by Oliver Cowdery with that recorded by the Prophet Joseph Smith, the following scriptures emerge in Moroni's message (those mentioned by the Prophet are in italics):

Deuteronomy 32:23–24
Deuteronomy 32:43
Psalm 100:1–2
Psalm 107:1–7
Psalm 144:11–12
Psalm 144:13
Psalm 146:10
Isaiah 1:7
Isaiah 1:23–24
Isaiah 1:25–26
Isaiah 2:1–4
Isaiah 4:5–6
Isaiah 11:1–16
Isaiah 29:11
Isaiah 29:13
Isaiah 29:14
Isaiah 43:6
Jeremiah 16:16
Jeremiah 30:18–21
Jeremiah 31:1
Jeremiah 31:6
Jeremiah 31:8
Jeremiah 31:9
Jeremiah 31:27–28
Jeremiah 31:31–33
Jeremiah 50:4–5
Joel 2:28–32
Malachi 3:1–4 (?)
Malachi 4:1–6
Acts 3:22–23
1 Corinthians 1:27–29

A View of the Last Days

Joseph Smith's prayer as he went to bed that autumn night was for a "manifestation" to know of his "state and standing" before the Lord (JS–H 1:29). What he received, in addition to that and in addition to the announcement of the Book of Mormon, was a powerful lesson about the mission of God's people from his day through the Millennium. The angel's message outlined not only the work of Joseph Smith but also the continuing destiny of the Church and kingdom of God. The passages of scripture he used to convey the message were not randomly chosen. They were carefully selected to provide clear and systematic instruction of profound importance.

What do we learn from the scriptures that the angel Moroni quoted concerning God's work in the latter days? As the following summary of his message shows, it was an amazingly rich revelation that built the foundation for all the revelations that have come to the Church since then.

Scattering and apostasy. As a result of apostasy that began in Old Testament times, the Lord destroyed and scattered the house of Israel. Because they were rebellious, corrupt, and uncaring, his once-covenant people became his "adversaries" and his "enemies" (Isa. 1:23–24). Thus he heaped "mischiefs upon them" and spent his arrows on them, burning them with hunger and devouring them with heat (Deut. 32:23–24), leaving their country desolate and their cities ruined (Isa. 1:7). Even in the latter days, the world would lie in sin. "This people draw near me with their mouth, and with their lips do honour me," the Lord said. But they "have removed their heart far from me, and their fear toward me is taught by the precept of men" (Isa. 29:13). These conditions set the stage for the Restoration.

The calling of the Prophet Joseph Smith. In the latter days, "God hath chosen the foolish things of the world to confound the wise, . . . the weak things of the world to confound the things

The statue of the angel Moroni on top of the Salt Lake Temple. Moroni's statue on Latter-day Saint temples symbolizes the announcement to the world that God's work of the last days has begun

which are mighty." Moroni used these words of Paul to describe the Prophet Joseph Smith, one who was despised by the world but chosen of God and worthy to stand in his divine presence (1 Cor. 1:27–29). He was the "rod out of the stem of Jesse" of whom Isaiah prophesied (Isa. 11:1), "a servant in the hands of Christ, . . . on whom there is laid much power" (D&C 113:4). He was also the "root of Jesse" whose work would stand as a rallying banner for all the world (Isa. 11:10), "unto whom rightly belongs the priesthood, and the keys of the kingdom, for an ensign, and for the gathering of my people in the last days" (D&C 113:6).[8] Bearing the keys of his calling, he would serve, perhaps more than any other, as the Lord's latter-day messenger, sent to prepare the way for the Savior's glorious coming (Mal. 3:1; cf. D&C 45:9).[9]

The opening of the heavens and the gift of the Holy Ghost. With the latter-day outpouring of light and knowledge to his Saints, the Lord would perform "a marvellous work" among them, causing the "wisdom" of the world to perish and the "understanding of their prudent men" to be hid (Isa. 29:14). Moroni reminded us that God would pour out his spirit on all flesh, empowering sons and daughters, servants and handmaids, old and young to prophesy, dream dreams, and otherwise enjoy the blessings of the gift of the Holy Ghost (Joel 2:28–29). With the Restoration would come a steady flow of new revelation to the Lord's Saints, contained now in latter-day scriptures and also in the inspired teachings and practices of the Church. Spiritual gifts would be restored as well, whereby all the Saints would be edified (D&C 46:9). Foremost among these would be the gift of testimony, a divine witness available to all, that Jesus is the Christ and that his Church has been restored.

The coming forth of the Book of Mormon. Much of Moroni's visit had to do with teaching Joseph Smith about the Book of Mormon. The Prophet was told that it contained "the fulness of the everlasting Gospel" (JS–H 1:34). How miraculous it was that the Lord had prepared, many centuries in advance, a book of inspired scripture ready to come forth at the beginning of his latter-day Restoration. It is "the keystone of our religion."[10] Sealed up to the world, it was opened to the humble young Prophet Joseph Smith and to all the humble who receive it today. It is indeed "a marvellous work" of God for our time, "a marvellous work and a wonder" (Isa. 29:11, 14).

The restoration of priesthood and keys. Part of the outpouring foretold by Joel (2:28–29) would be the restoration of the power of the priesthood. John the Baptist would appear to Joseph Smith and restore the Priesthood of Aaron. Peter, James, and John would come and bring the Melchizedek Priesthood. This restoration was vital not only because the priesthood is the power to act in God's name but also because it is the power to receive God's word by revelation and speak it on his behalf.[11]

Moroni foretold the restoration of true temple worship when he quoted Isaiah's words that in the last days, "the mountain of the Lord's house" would be established (Isa. 2:1–3). Although the ultimate fulfillment of this revelation will be millennial (see v. 4), it is also fulfilled to a degree each time a sacred house is constructed and dedicated to the Lord.

The angel quoted the last two verses of the Old Testament, Malachi 4:5–6, with significant modifications to the text (cf. JS–H 1:38–39). This passage, foretelling the coming of Elijah, is important enough that it appears not only in the Pearl of Great Price but also separately as section 2 of the Doctrine and Covenants (see also D&C 128:17). It is one of the most important scriptures of the Restoration because it announces the creation of the links of priesthood power that bind and seal both ordinances and generations on earth and in heaven. The prophecy was fulfilled on 3 April 1836, when Elijah, the ancient prophet who held the keys of the sealing power, appeared to Joseph Smith in the Kirtland Temple to restore those keys to earth (D&C 110:13–16).[12]

The gathering and restoration of Israel. Moroni quoted: "O give thanks unto the Lord, for he is good: for his mercy endureth for ever. Let the redeemed of the Lord say so, whom he hath redeemed from the hand of the enemy" (Ps. 107:1–2). The cause of this rejoicing would be the restoration of the house of Israel and their gathering back to the covenant fold, expressed in the language of promised lands (Ps. 107:3–7; Jer. 31:8–9). From their dispersed and scattered condition, they would respond to the voice of their Good Shepherd and the call of his earthly servants, "the watchmen upon the mount Ephraim," who would say, "Arise ye, and let us go up to Zion, unto the holy Mount of the Lord our God" (Jer. 31:6).[13] Joseph Smith would be the "root of Jesse," the Lord's Ephraimite servant who would announce Israel's return (Isa. 11:10; D&C 113:6).[14] By means of the keys that he would hold (D&C 110:11), the Lord would send out "fishers" and "hunters" (Jer. 16:16) to find them in the places of their scattering throughout the nations of the world. They would be gathered "from Assyria, and from Egypt, and from Pathros, and from Cush, and from Elam, and from Shinar, and from Hamath, and from the islands of the sea" (Isa. 11:11), or in other words, "from the east, and from the west, from the north, and from the south" (Ps. 107:3; Isa. 43:6; Jer. 31:8). From their bondage in sin and ignorance there would be a divinely prepared means of return—a "highway"—just as there had been when their ancestors returned from their bondage in Egypt (Isa. 11:16).

Moroni taught that this gathering would also be the restoration of the house of Israel, for the remnants of the two divided kingdoms—the "outcasts of Israel" and the "dispersed of Judah"—would set aside their enmity and become one (Isa. 11:12–13; Jer. 50:4). As we read elsewhere, in gathering to the covenants they would no longer be two kingdoms but one, under the kingship of Jehovah himself (Ezek. 37:15–22).

But with the gathering of only Israel and Judah, the Lord's work would not yet be complete. Moroni quoted scriptures that show that the gathering must also include the Gentiles, those who are not of the house of Israel by lineage but become so by covenant. The latter-day "ensign"—the restored gospel of Jesus Christ—would be the rallying standard to them as well as to the descendants of God's ancient people (Isa. 11:10). Gentiles, Israel, and Judah would come together "from the four corners of the earth" (Isa. 11:12). They would follow the path that leads to Zion and would say, "Let us join ourselves to the Lord in a perpetual covenant that shall not be forgotten" (Jer. 50:5).

Destruction and purification of the earth. Moroni quoted Malachi's prophecy: "For behold, the day cometh that shall burn as an oven, and all the proud, yea, and all that do wickedly shall burn as stubble," leaving them "neither root nor branch" (JS–H 1:37; Mal. 4:1). When the Lord prepares the world for his millennial reign, all that is unholy and impure in it must be removed. This process will be God's great act of universal judgment, in which the wicked will at long last receive the harvest of their evil and the righteous will enjoy the fruits of their worthiness. It will be the "great and dreadful day of the Lord" (Mal. 4:5), in which nations and individuals alike will be recompensed according to their behavior. Moroni quoted Malachi's words that Christ's appearance will be "like a refiner's fire, and like fullers' soap." Among those who will be purified at that time will be the sons of Levi, ancient Israel's Aaronic priesthood, whose purification will symbolize the restoration of Levi and Judah to the covenant fold of Israel, making them ready to present again "an offering in righteousness" to the Lord (Mal. 3:2–4). Truly, he will purge away all the impurities of those who wish to worship him, making them worthy to stand when he appears (Isa. 1:25; Mal. 3:2).

God's latter-day cleansing will be the event for which all earlier acts of judgment were types (e.g., Deut. 32:23–24). As we learn in modern revelation, it will begin at the Lord's own house (D&C 112:24–25), but it will soon involve all the nations of the world (e.g., Isa. 11:14–15). In some way that we do not understand, the Lord's Saints will be participants in this work (Isa. 11:14; Mal. 4:3), as will the angels, who will be sent to harvest the world (Mal. 4:1; D&C 86:4–7). Joseph Smith learned from Moroni that it will be accompanied by "wonders in the heavens and in the earth, blood, and fire, and pillars of smoke. The sun shall be turned into darkness, and the moon into blood" (Joel 2:30–31). And all who reject Jesus Christ will be found unworthy to remain when he comes (Acts 3:22–23; Deut. 18:15, 18–19).

The deliverance of the faithful. Scripture, both ancient and modern, assures us that the Lord will protect and deliver his covenant people from the calamities of the last days. Though not all will be spared from sickness, sorrow, and death—because our physical bodies are subject to these things—there will be a real and powerful force that will provide countless acts of divine deliverance for the Saints.[15] "Whosoever shall call on the name of the Lord shall be delivered," Moroni quoted, "for in mount Zion and in Jerusalem shall be deliverance, as the Lord hath said, and in the remnant whom the Lord shall call" (Joel 2:32).

The Second Coming. Joseph Smith learned that Christ will come again, as the scriptures have foretold. Moroni affirmed this truth by quoting Malachi's words that the Lord, whom we seek, will "suddenly come to his temple, even the messenger of the covenant, whom ye delight in: behold, he shall come" (Mal. 3:1). The coming of Christ to his temple may represent an appearance in one of the sacred buildings set apart to his name. But in that day, all the world will be his temple, for the entire planet and everything in it will be dedicated and consecrated. It will all be "holiness unto the Lord of hosts" (Zech. 14:20–21).

The blessings of the Saints. Several of the prophecies quoted by Moroni foretell the blessings that will come to the Lord's Saints as a result of God's latter-day work and especially as a result of Jesus' second coming. These things will be a cause of great happiness: "Make a joyful noise unto the Lord, all ye lands. Serve the Lord with gladness: come before his presence with singing" (Ps. 100:1–2; cf. Deut. 32:43; Jer. 30:19). Moroni quoted the psalmist: "The Lord shall reign for ever, even thy God, O Zion, unto all generations. Praise ye the Lord" (Ps. 146:10).

Christ's reign will be a source of unimaginable blessing to all the world. Moroni quoted Isaiah's prophecy that the Saints in that day will be taught by him and walk in his ways. When Jesus is the judge of the nations, his law and his word will go forth from Zion and Jerusalem (Isa. 2:3–4). "And the spirit of the Lord shall rest upon him, the spirit of wisdom and understanding, the spirit of counsel and might, the spirit of knowledge and of the fear of the Lord. . . . And he shall not judge after the sight of his eyes, neither reprove after the hearing of his ears: but with righteousness shall he judge the poor, and reprove with equity for the meek of the earth. . . . And righteousness shall be the girdle of his loins, and faithfulness the girdle of his reins" (Isa. 11:2–5; cf. D&C 113:1–2).

Quoting Isaiah, Moroni taught that Christ's righteous rule will establish peace in the hearts of all who dwell on earth. The Prophet learned that people will "beat their swords into plowshares, and their spears into pruninghooks: nation shall not lift up sword against nation, neither shall they learn war any more" (Isa. 2:4). This peace will extend to all flesh, both animal and human. "The wolf also shall dwell with the lamb, and the leopard shall lie down with the kid; and the calf and the young lion and the fatling together; and a little child shall lead them" (Isa. 11:6, 7–8; D&C 101:26). Indeed, the very nature of life will be changed such that predators and prey will live together in harmony. "They shall not hurt nor destroy in all my holy mountain" (Isa. 11:9).

Christ's coming will reestablish Israel's covenant with Jehovah and bring about the restoration of all that they have ever been promised (e.g., Isa. 1:26). That will include the continued gathering of Israel (Isa. 11:11–13), a process which began in the days of Joseph Smith but which will not be complete until "the earth shall be full of the knowledge of the Lord, as the waters cover the sea" (Isa. 11:9). Purified from sin, Israel's worship will again be acceptable to God (Mal. 3:4). Just as he had earlier broken and scattered them, he will now watch over them, build them, and plant them (Jer. 31:27–28; 30:18). And they will join with him in a "new covenant," "not according to the covenant that I made with their fathers in the day that I took them by the hand to bring them out of the land of Egypt; which my covenant they brake. . . . But this shall be the covenant that I will make with the house of Israel; after those days, saith the Lord, I will put my law in their inward parts, and write it in their hearts; and will be their God, and they shall be my people" (Jer. 31:31–33; cf. 31:1).

Moroni cited passages that show the outpouring of spiritual blessings in that day. With the "mountain of the Lord's house" established, people will flow from all nations to learn of God and his ways (Isa. 2:1–3). With his Spirit poured out on them in abundance, they will prophesy, dream dreams, and see visions (Joel 2:28–29).

Moroni showed that material blessings will also be their inheritance. They will grow like well-fed cattle (Mal. 4:2). Their sons will be like healthy plants, their daughters like polished stones. Their storehouses will be full of produce, and their flocks will increase beyond measure (Ps. 144:12–13). The Lord's power will overshadow them as it did ancient Israel—with a pillar of smoke by day and a pillar of fire by night. From heat, from storm, and from rain, the Lord will protect his people (Isa. 4:5–6), who will sing hymns of thanksgiving to him to celebrate the restoration of their nation, their prosperity, and their peace. "I will multiply them," he said, "and they shall not be few; I will also glorify them, and they shall not be small" (Jer. 30:18–21; cf. 31:27–28). In short, for all who will reverence Jehovah's name in that day, "the Sun of Righteousness" will rise, "with healing in his wings" (Mal. 4:2).

An Instrument in God's Hands

From Moroni, Joseph Smith received a breathtaking revelation of what the Lord had prepared for the last days, including his own work and that of the Church that would be established through his ministry. The message was meant to be learned and understood, not just heard. That became apparent when Moroni repeated it and reinforced it again and again. This was to be the mission of The Church of Jesus Christ of Latter-day Saints, and the Prophet needed to know it well.

When Joseph Smith was informed that he was called "to be an instrument in the hands of God to bring about some of his purposes" (1842:11), he could scarcely have imagined what the Lord had in store for him. But as he came to understand, over the next twenty-one years, who he was and where his work fit into the

Lord's whole plan, he learned that his calling was something extraordinary. "You don't know me; you never will," he said in the last year of his life. "I don't blame you for not believing my history. Had I not experienced it, I could not believe it myself."[16]

But in September 1823, his ministry to the world was yet to commence, and he still had much to learn. On the night of the angel's first appearance, he was presented with an overview, as we have seen in the summary of the scriptures that Moroni quoted. Details would follow later in dozens of revelations. But for now, the young Prophet was in a "missionary training center" for the next few years, until the time was right for his work to begin.

Notes

1. For a detailed analysis of these scriptures, see Kent P. Jackson, "The Appearance of Moroni to Joseph Smith," in Robert L. Millet and Kent P. Jackson, eds., *The Pearl of Great Price,* Studies in Scripture Series, vol. 2 (Salt Lake City: Randall Book, 1985), 348–59.

2. The articles are in the form of letters addressed to W. W. Phelps; "Letter IV. To W. W. Phelps, Esq.," *Latter Day Saints' Messenger and Advocate* 1, no. 5 (Feb. 1835): 77–80; "Letter VI. To W. W. Phelps, Esq.," *Messenger and Advocate* 1, no. 7 (April 1835): 108–12; "Letter VII. To W. W. Phelps, Esq.," *Messenger and Advocate* 1, no. 10 (July 1835): 156–59.

3. *Messenger and Advocate* 1, no. 10 (July 1835): 156.

4. In all, the angel used thirty passages according to Elder Cowdery's accounts. This list presents them in the order in which they appear in the narratives: 1 Cor. 1:27–29; Isa. 29:14; 29:13; 29:11; Ps. 100:1–2; 107:1–7; 144:11–12; Joel 2:28; Ps. 144:13; 146:10; Isa. 1:7; 1:23–24; Deut. 32:23–24; Isa. 1:25–26; Ps. 107:7; Isa. 2:1–4; 4:5–6; Jer. 31:27–28; 31:31–33; 30:18–21; 31:1; 31:8; Isa. 43:6; Jer. 50:4–5; 31:9; 31:6; Isa. 2:3; 11:15–16; Jer. 16:16; Deut. 32:43. The first four passages are from the February article (77–80), and the rest are from the April article (108–12).

5. In one of the two articles that contain these scriptures, Elder Cowdery used quotation marks to make it clear to the reader which were Moroni's words and which were his own. But in the other, in which most of the scriptures are cited, there are no quotation marks, and thus it is not clear which words are Elder Cowdery's and which are Moroni's. Perhaps Elder Cowdery did not feel that quotation marks were necessary; editorial customs were rather unstructured in

those days. Or perhaps he wanted to alert the reader to the fact that the message was (at least in part) reconstructed and not necessarily a verbatim transcript of the event.

6. *Messenger and Advocate* 1, no. 7 (April 1835): 109.

7. Ibid., 112.

8. See Keith A. Meservy, "God Is with Us," in Kent P. Jackson, ed., *1 Kings to Malachi,* Studies in Scripture Series, vol. 4 (Salt Lake City: Deseret Book, 1993), 102–3.

9. See Jackson, "Appearance of Moroni to Joseph Smith," 348–49.

10. Joseph Smith, *History of The Church of Jesus Christ of Latter-day Saints,* ed. B. H. Roberts, 2d ed. rev., 7 vols. (Salt Lake City: Deseret Book, 1957), 4:461.

11. See Andrew F. Ehat and Lyndon W. Cook, eds., *The Words of Joseph Smith: The Contemporary Accounts of the Nauvoo Discourses of the Prophet Joseph* (Provo, Utah: Religious Studies Center, Brigham Young University, 1980), 38–39.

12. See Joseph Smith's discussions of this passage in *Joseph Smith's Commentary on the Bible,* comp. and ed. Kent P. Jackson (Salt Lake City: Deseret Book, 1994), 69–74.

13. As worded in Oliver Cowdery's account. The KJV omits "the holy Mount of." *Messenger and Advocate* 1, no. 7 (April 1835): 111.

14. See Meservy, "God Is with Us," 102–3.

15. See references in Kent P. Jackson, "Prophecies of the Last Days in the Doctrine and Covenants and the Pearl of Great Price," in *The Heavens Are Open: The 1992 Sperry Symposium on the Doctrine and Covenants and Church History* (Salt Lake City: Deseret Book, 1993), 171–72.

16. Ehat and Cook, *Words of Joseph Smith,* 343; punctuation modernized.

Chapter 12

Obtaining the Ancient Record

Seventeen-year-old Joseph Smith had spent the night of 21–22 September 1823 in the company of a heavenly messenger, the angel Moroni, who taught him of God's purposes in the last days and introduced him to the Book of Mormon. The Prophet recounted that experience at four different times of which we have his written record. The following passages from those four accounts continue the narrative from the early morning of 22 September to the time at which he received the plates. As with the accounts given earlier, his words are preserved exactly as they were recorded but with punctuation and spelling modernized. The paragraphs are numbered as well, and references to the original documents are in the notes.

The 1832 Draft History

19 . . . And thus he appeared unto me three times in one night and once on the next day.

20 And then I immediately went to the place and found where the plates were deposited, as the angel of the Lord had commanded me, and straightway made three attempts to get them. And then, being exceedingly frightened, I supposed it had been a dream or vision, but when I considered, I knew that it was not. Therefore I cried unto the Lord in the agony of my soul, "Why can I not obtain them?"

21 Behold, the angel appeared unto me again and said unto me, "You have not kept the commandments of the Lord which I gave unto

you. Therefore you cannot now obtain them, for the time is not yet fulfilled. Therefore thou wast left unto temptation, that thou mightest be made acquainted with the power of the adversary. Therefore repent and call on the Lord. Thou shalt be forgiven, and in his own due time thou shalt obtain them."

22 For now I had been tempted of the adversary and sought the plates to obtain riches, and kept not the commandment that I should have an eye single to the glory of God.

23 Therefore I was chastened and sought diligently to obtain the plates, and obtained them not until I was twenty-one years of age.[1]

The 1835 Journal Account

16 After the vision had all passed, I found that it was nearly daylight. The family soon arose; I got up also. On that day while in the field at work with my father, he asked me if I was sick. I replied, I had but little strength. He told me to go to the house. I started and went part way and was finally deprived of my strength and fell, but how long I remained I do not know.

17 The angel came to me again and commanded me to go and tell my father what I had seen and heard. I did so. He wept and told me that it was a vision from God [and] to attend to it.

18 I went and found the place where the plates were, according to the direction of the angel. [I] also saw them, and the angel as before.

19 The powers of darkness strove hard against me. I called on God. The angel told me that the reason why I could not obtain the plates at this time was because I was under transgression, but to come again in one year from that time. I did so but did not obtain them, also the third and the fourth year, at which time I obtained them and translated them into the English language by the gift and power of God.[2]

The 1838 "History of Joseph Smith" (JS–H)

47 . . . Almost immediately after the heavenly messenger had ascended from me for the third time, the cock crowed, and I found that day was approaching, so that our interviews must have occupied the whole of that night.

48 I shortly after arose from my bed, and, as usual, went to the necessary labors of the day; but, in attempting to work as at other times, I found my strength so exhausted as to render me entirely unable. My

father, who was laboring along with me, discovered something to be wrong with me, and told me to go home. I started with the intention of going to the house; but, in attempting to cross the fence out of the field where we were, my strength entirely failed me, and I fell helpless on the ground, and for a time was quite unconscious of anything.

49 The first thing that I can recollect was a voice speaking unto me, calling me by name. I looked up, and beheld the same messenger standing over my head, surrounded by light as before. He then again related unto me all that he had related to me the previous night, and commanded me to go to my father and tell him of the vision and commandments which I had received.

50 I obeyed; I returned to my father in the field, and rehearsed the whole matter to him. He replied to me that it was of God, and told me to go and do as commanded by the messenger. I left the field, and went to the place where the messenger had told me the plates were deposited; and owing to the distinctness of the vision which I had had concerning it, I knew the place the instant that I arrived there.

51 Convenient to the village of Manchester, Ontario county, New York, stands a hill of considerable size, and the most elevated of any in the neighborhood. On the west side of this hill, not far from the top, under a stone of considerable size, lay the plates, deposited in a stone box. This stone was thick and rounding in the middle on the upper side, and thinner towards the edges, so that the middle part of it was visible above the ground, but the edge all around was covered with earth.

52 Having removed the earth, I obtained a lever, which I got fixed under the edge of the stone, and with a little exertion raised it up. I looked in, and there indeed did I behold the plates, the Urim and Thummim, and the breastplate, as stated by the messenger. The box in which they lay was formed by laying stones together in some kind of cement. In the bottom of the box were laid two stones crossways of the box, and on these stones lay the plates and the other things with them.

53 I made an attempt to take them out, but was forbidden by the messenger, and was again informed that the time for bringing them forth had not yet arrived, neither would it, until four years from that time; but he told me that I should come to that place precisely in one year from that time, and that he would there meet with me, and that I should continue to do so until the time should come for obtaining the plates.

54 Accordingly, as I had been commanded, I went at the end of each year, and at each time I found the same messenger there, and received

West side of the Hill Cumorah, Manchester Township, New York

instruction and intelligence from him at each of our interviews, respecting what the Lord was going to do, and how and in what manner his kingdom was to be conducted in the last days. . . .

59 At length the time arrived for obtaining the plates, the Urim and Thummim, and the breastplate. On the twenty-second day of September, one thousand eight hundred and twenty-seven, having gone as usual at the end of another year to the place where they were deposited, the same heavenly messenger delivered them up to me with this charge: that I should be responsible for them; that if I should let them go carelessly, or through any neglect of mine, I should be cut off; but that if I would use all my endeavors to preserve them, until he, the messenger, should call for them, they should be protected.

60 I soon found out the reason why I had received such strict charges to keep them safe, and why it was that the messenger had said that when I had done what was required at my hand, he would call for them. For no sooner was it known that I had them, than the most strenuous exertions were used to get them from me. Every stratagem that could be invented was resorted to for that purpose. The persecution became more bitter and severe than before, and multitudes were on the alert continually to get them from me if possible. But by the wisdom of God, they

remained safe in my hands, until I had accomplished by them what was required at my hand. When, according to arrangements, the messenger called for them, I delivered them up to him; and he has them in his charge until this day, being the second day of May, one thousand eight hundred and thirty-eight.[3]

The 1842 "Church History"

15 After having received many visits from the angels of God unfolding the majesty and glory of the events that should transpire in the last days, on the morning of the twenty-second of September A.D. 1827, the angel of the Lord delivered the records into my hands.[4]

At the Hill Cumorah

When the morning of 22 September 1823 dawned, Joseph Smith set out to perform his daily labors, despite his having been awake all night in the company of a heavenly messenger. But he soon found he had no strength to work. His father, seeing the young man's weakness, sent him back to the house. He fell unconscious on the way (1835:16; JS–H 1:48), remaining unaware of anything until he heard the angel's voice speaking to him again (1832:19; 1835:17; JS–H 1:49). Moroni related to Joseph Smith the same message that he had conveyed the night before, thereafter instructing him to go to his father and tell him of the vision and the commandments that he had been given (1835:17; JS–H 1:49). Father Smith's response was typical of how the Prophet's parents always received the revelatory experiences of their son. He told his young namesake that the vision was of God and that he should act in accordance with the angel's instructions (1835:17; JS–H 1:50).

The hill known as Cumorah is situated only three miles away from the Smith family farm, in the northern part of Manchester Township, New York. It is of course likely that the young Prophet had seen the hill many times, but from now on it would have a new significance in his life. He went to the hill, knowing it was the repository of the sacred record of which Moroni had spoken

(1832:20; 1835:18; JS–H 1:50). He recognized instantly the spot where the book was buried, so vivid had the vision been of its location (1835:12; JS–H 1:42, 50). The gold plates were in a stone box on the west side of the hill, near the top (JS–H 1:51–52).

But obtaining the plates was not as easy as the young man may have thought. He stated that when he saw them, "the powers of darkness strove hard" against him (1835:19). He tried three times to lift the plates out of the box but was unsuccessful (1832:20). Calling upon God, he asked why he could not obtain them (1832:20; 1835:19). In response, the Lord taught him some important principles.

When Moroni had appeared to Joseph Smith the night before, he warned him solemnly that Satan would seek to tempt him with the plates. The Prophet's family was of very modest means. Their every exertion was required to put food on the table through working their farm and hiring out as laborers for others. Because of these realities, the Prophet was warned that he must "have no other object in view in getting the plates but to glorify God, and must not be influenced by any other motive than that of building his kingdom" (JS–H 1:46). Needless to say, that would be a challenge for anyone, perhaps especially a seventeen-year-old boy. Oliver Cowdery reported that when the Prophet approached the hill he struggled within himself, as "a thought would start across the mind"[5] concerning the needs of his family and what such a treasure as the gold plates could do to alleviate their want (1832:21–22). "To use his own words it seemed as though two invisible powers were influencing, or striving to influence his mind," Elder Cowdery wrote.[6] Thus when the Prophet arrived at the hill and tried to lift the plates, Moroni appeared (1832:21; 1835:18) and forbade him to remove them (JS–H 1:53), telling him that he needed to repent. He would be forgiven in due time and would receive the record (1832:21), but for now the time was not right. Elder Cowdery added: "At that instant he looked to the Lord in prayer, and as he prayed darkness began to disperse from his mind and his soul was lit up as it was the evening before, and he was filled with the Holy Spirit; and again did the Lord manifest his condescension and mercy: the heavens were opened and the glory of the Lord shone round about and rested upon him."[7]

This event was an important experience in the training of Joseph Smith, and we too can learn much from it. First, the Lord's servants work according to the Lord's timetable, not their own. "The time is not yet fulfilled," Moroni said (1832:21; cf. JS–H 1:53), nor would it be until the Lord decreed that the Prophet was ready to obtain and translate the plates. Second, the Prophet was reminded of the power of Satan and of his continuing opposition to God's latter-day work. Moroni told him, "Therefore thou wast left unto temptation, that thou mightest be made acquainted with the power of the Adversary" (1832:21). He had felt the devil's power before, and he would continue to be reminded that satanic opposition would be an unrelenting reality through all of his ministry. According to Oliver Cowdery, the angel emphasized this point by showing the Prophet a vision of "the prince of darkness, surrounded by his innumerable train of associates."[8] Moroni said, "All this is shown, the good and the evil, the holy and impure, the glory of God and the power of darkness, that you may know hereafter the two powers and never be influenced or overcome by that wicked one."[9] Finally, the Prophet learned a lesson that all who serve God should learn. When we are on the Lord's errand, we must have no object in mind but to glorify him, and we must not be influenced by any motive but to build his kingdom (JS–H 1:46). Not even the most fleeting thought of personal profit or praise is acceptable for those who are in the Lord's service.

The Preparatory Years

Moroni told Joseph Smith that he would not receive the plates for another four years but that he was to return to the hill the following year on the same date and each year thereafter until the appointed time (1835:19; JS–H 1:53). Accordingly, on 22 September of each of the following four years, the Prophet went to the Hill Cumorah, where each time he was instructed by Moroni in preparation for his life's calling (1835:19; JS–H 1:54).

Oliver Cowdery wrote that Moroni gave the Prophet a "sign"—an irrefutable proof by which he would know that this was the Lord's work and that he would fulfill his promises. The sign was both sad and prophetic: "When it is known that the Lord has shown you these things, the workers of iniquity will seek your overthrow: they will circulate falsehoods to destroy your reputation, and also will seek to take your life."[10] The falsehoods intended to destroy Joseph Smith's reputation began almost immediately, continued throughout his life, and still circulate today. Some, no doubt, have made their way into the historical sources and are taken for granted to be true.[11] Given Moroni's statement that this would be a sign of the divinity of the Prophet's calling, it seems that we should view with caution and suspicion any and all information that seeks to disparage Joseph Smith's good name. "But remember this," Moroni continued, "if you are faithful, and shall hereafter continue to keep the commandments of the Lord, you shall be preserved to bring these things forth."[12]

During the years from 1823 to 1827, from Moroni's first appearance until the reception of the plates, the Prophet grew to manhood under angelic guidance. Each year the two met at the appointed time and place, and Moroni, his prophetic predecessor and tutor, trained him for his life's work. The Prophet recorded that through this process he "received instruction and intelligence . . . respecting what the Lord was going to do, and how and in what manner his kingdom was to be conducted in the last days" (JS–H 1:54). Thus were unfolded to him "the majesty and glory of the events that should transpire in the last days" (1842:15). And we, enjoying the light and knowledge made known through the Restoration, are the beneficiaries of what he learned.[13]

Emma Hale Smith (1804–79), wife of the Prophet Joseph Smith

The Prophet's education also included the schooling he received from life's experiences. In 1825 he hired on as a laborer with a Mr. Josiah Stoal of Chenango County, New York—an experience that was important, among other reasons, because it led to the kind of character assassination of which Moroni had warned him (JS–H 1:55–56).[14] During the time of his employment he boarded at the home of the Hale family in Harmony, Pennsylvania. There he met and fell in love with their daughter, Emma. The two were married in January 1827 and moved thereafter into the home of the Smith family in Manchester, New York (JS–H 1:57–58). It was there that they were living when the time came for the Prophet to obtain the plates.

Early in the morning of 22 September 1827, twenty-one-year-old Joseph Smith went to the Hill Cumorah for his annual visit. But this visit was unlike any other, because the time had come for

Frame home of Joseph Smith Sr. family, Manchester Township, New York, where the Smith family lived from 1825 to 1829. Joseph and Emma Smith lived in this home during 1827, and Oliver Cowdery lived in it while he taught school, 1828–29. Photo by George Edward Anderson, 1907

the Prophet to receive the ancient record. When Moroni met with him on this, the last of their annual meetings at that place, the angel warned him that he would be "cut off" if he did not safeguard the plates, "but that if [he] would use all [his] endeavors to preserve them, . . . they should be protected" (JS–H 1:59). Predictably, "every stratagem that could be invented" was used to wrest the plates from his care, necessitating his constant vigilance and exertion. "But by the wisdom of God" they were preserved (JS–H 1:60), and the Prophet was able to keep them secure until he finished the translation.[15]

Notes

1. The scribe was Frederick G. Williams. The unedited original is found in Dean C. Jessee, ed., *The Papers of Joseph Smith,* 3 vols. (Salt Lake City: Deseret Book, 1989–97), 1:8–9.

2. Dictated to Warren Parrish. The unedited original is in Jessee, *Papers of Joseph Smith,* 2:70–71.

3. See "History of Joseph Smith," *Times and Seasons* 3, no. 12 (15 April 1842): 754; 3, no. 13 (2 May 1842): 771–72.

4. A long, detailed description of the plates follows. See "Church History," *Times and Seasons* 3, no. 9 (1 March 1842): 707. Also published in Joseph Smith, "Latter Day Saints," in I. Daniel Rupp, *An Original History of the Religious Denominations at Present Existing in the United States* (Philadelphia, 1844), 404. See Jessee, *Papers of Joseph Smith,* 1:450.

5. *Latter Day Saints' Messenger and Advocate* 1, no. 10 (July 1835): 157.

6. Ibid.

7. *Messenger and Advocate* 2, no. 1 (October 1835): 198.

8. Ibid.

9. Ibid.

10. Ibid., 199.

11. Note the opening lines of Joseph Smith–History: "Owing to the many reports which have been put in circulation by evil-disposed and designing persons . . . , all of which have been designed by the authors thereof to militate against its character as a Church and its progress in the world—I have been induced to write this history, to disabuse the public mind, and put all inquirers after truth in possession of the facts" (JS–H 1:1).

12. *Messenger and Advocate* 2, no. 1 (October 1835): 199.

13. For Moroni's contributions to the Restoration, see H. Donl Peterson, *Moroni: Ancient Prophet, Modern Messenger* (Salt Lake City: Horizon, 1983).

14. See *Messenger and Advocate* 2, no. 1 (October 1835): 200–202.

15. Early reminiscences of the obtaining of the plates are found in Lucy Mack Smith, *Biographical Sketches of Joseph Smith the Prophet and His Progenitors for Many Generations* (Liverpool: S. W. Richards, 1853), 99–106; and Dean C. Jessee, ed., "Joseph Knight's Recollections of Early Mormon History," *BYU Studies* 17, no. 1 (autumn 1976): 32–34.

Chapter 13

Bringing Forth the Book of Mormon

The Book of Mormon is one of the most profound miracles of all time. As the "keystone of our religion,"[1] it plays a role in our lives that is not surpassed by any other book. The story of how it came to be is one of small things with great implications. Together those small things combined to become one of the great events in all of God's dealings with his children. The historicity of that event is in itself one of the cornerstones of our faith.

Translation

When it was learned that Joseph Smith had the gold plates, the persecutions and accusations of which Moroni had warned him began. In December 1827, just three months after he obtained the plates, those persecutions made it necessary for him to move from his family's home in Manchester, New York, to Harmony, Pennsylvania, where Emma's parents lived. They were able to make the journey through the generosity of a prosperous farmer of Palmyra, Martin Harris, who gave them fifty dollars.[2] Martin had been one of the earliest believers in Joseph Smith's calling, and this act of generosity characterized his commitment to the Lord's work. The young couple soon took up residence in a small

Martin Harris (1783–1875), generous benefactor of the Restoration and one of the Three Witnesses of the Book of Mormon

frame home, twenty-six by eighteen feet in size, on the Hale family property.

It soon became apparent that a full-time scribe would be necessary to facilitate the translation of the plates. In February 1828 Martin Harris went to Harmony and took a transcript of characters from the plates to the East, as recounted in the Prophet's history (JS–H 1:63–65). He then worked as the Prophet's scribe from April until mid-June. Together they made good progress that resulted in 116 pages of translation—the book of Lehi.[3]

We can understand the frustrations Martin's wife felt about her husband's being away from home for months, working on a strange religious project in which she did not share his belief. To satisfy her interests, as well as his own, Martin persuaded the Prophet to seek, and finally to obtain, permission from the Lord for him to take the manuscript back to Palmyra and show it to his wife and a few other specified individuals. It was during June or

July that the manuscript was lost, to the terrible grief and suffering of Joseph Smith and the divine condemnation of Martin Harris, whom the Lord in revelation called a "wicked man" (D&C 3:12; 10:1). Moroni took the plates and the Urim and Thummim from the Prophet, telling him that he too needed to repent (D&C 3:1–11). In September they were returned, but Martin was no longer requested to serve as scribe.

It is not difficult to imagine the Prophet's anguish over his lack of progress in translating the Book of Mormon. By the time the plates were returned to him, it had been a year since he first received them, and he had nothing to show for his time. During the remainder of that year and into the spring of the next, very little was accomplished, though Emma and the Prophet's brother Samuel assisted him somewhat as scribes.[4] But it was a full year and a half after the plates were received before real progress would be made on the translation. The Lord still had some miracles to perform.

During the fall of 1828 and the winter of 1829, a young schoolteacher named Oliver Cowdery taught in the Manchester-Palmyra area. Among his pupils were children of the Smith family. As part of his pay, Oliver boarded with the Smiths, who in time came to trust him and confided in him about the work in which their son Joseph was engaged. Oliver received a divine manifestation that the work was of God and that he was to be part of it.[5] Accordingly, at the end of the school year he went to Harmony, where on 5 April 1829 he introduced himself to the Prophet and told him that he had come to assist in the work. The translation began two days later and continued with miraculous vigor until the work was accomplished.

"These were days never to be forgotten," Elder Cowdery later wrote, "to sit under the sound of a voice dictated by the *inspiration* of heaven, awakened the utmost gratitude of this bosom! Day after day I continued, uninterrupted, to write from his mouth, as he translated, with the *Urim* and *Thummim,* or, as the Nephites would have said, 'Interpreters,' the history, or record, called 'The

Oliver Cowdery (1806–50), principal scribe for the Book of Mormon as well as parts of the Joseph Smith Translation and other revelations, one of the Three Witnesses of the Book of Mormon, and second elder of the Church

Book of Mormon.'"[6] The two labored together in Harmony through April and May of 1829, during which time most of the translation was completed. They were supported in their work by the generosity of Joseph Knight Sr., a farmer from nearby Colesville, New York. Brother Knight had come to believe in the divinity of the work some time earlier and provided food so the Prophet and Oliver would not be obliged to leave their calling to secure the necessities of life.[7] The Knights remained some of the Prophet's most faithful friends.

During those "days never to be forgotten," something extraordinary was taking place. "A marvelous work and a wonder" was being performed (Isa. 29:14), the importance of which we cannot overstate. The translation of the Book of Mormon was being revealed, an event that would influence eternally the lives of millions of persons by helping them return to the presence of God. Also, revelations were being received that would become the early

The home of Joseph and Emma Smith, Harmony, Pennsylvania, site of the translation of most of the Book of Mormon and the reception of several early revelations. The two-story section on the right was added after Joseph Smith's time.
Nineteenth-century photograph

sections of the Doctrine and Covenants. In a tiny village in a most remote and obscure corner of the earth, God was bringing to pass a miracle of unparalleled greatness. The little home in which the work was being done was the meeting place between heaven and earth, the most important building in the world.

Near the first day of June the Prophet and his scribe found it necessary to move to Fayette, New York. Persecution in the Harmony area had made it difficult to complete the translation there, so they asked the Whitmer family to allow them to continue the work at their Fayette home. The Whitmers were friends of Oliver Cowdery who had learned to trust his testimony of the Prophet's calling. They helped in the work by making available their house, where the translation was completed at the end of

June 1829. Members of the Whitmer family also assisted as scribes.

The Witnesses

At about the time the translation was finished, the Three Witnesses and the Eight Witnesses were shown the gold plates, as proclaimed in their testimonies published in every copy of the Book of Mormon.[8] When it was learned from the translation that there would be witnesses called to see the plates, Oliver Cowdery, David Whitmer, and Martin Harris went to the Prophet to ask that he ascertain through revelation whether they might be the witnesses. The Prophet inquired of the Lord, and a revelation to the three was received which told them they would indeed fill that role (D&C 17:1–9). Not long after the revelation came, they went with the Prophet into a wooded area near the Whitmer home in Fayette, where they knelt and prayed in succession. Martin Harris, believing that his presence was the reason no response was received, withdrew from the group.[9]

David Whitmer recalled: "All at once a light came down from above us and encircled us for quite a little distance around; and the angel stood before us. . . . A table was set before us and on it the records were placed. The Records of the Nephites, from which the Book of Mormon was translated, the brass plates, the Ball of Directors, the sword of Laban and other plates. While we were viewing them the voice of God spoke out of heaven saying that the Book was true and the translation correct."[10]

The Prophet recorded that the angel "turned over the leaves one by one, so that we could see them, and discern the engravings thereon distinctly." A voice from above said, "I command you to bear record of what you now see and hear."[11] Joseph Smith then withdrew from the others and found Martin Harris some distance away. As they prayed together, the manifestation was repeated to them.

Lucy Mack Smith, Joseph Smith's mother, remembered the

David Whitmer (1805–88), one of the Three Witnesses of the Book of Mormon

reaction of the Prophet and the witnesses when they returned to the house: "On coming in, Joseph threw himself down beside me, and exclaimed, 'Father, mother, you do not know how happy I am; the Lord has now caused the plates to be shown to three more besides myself. . . . I feel as if I was relieved of a burden which was almost too heavy for me to bear, and it rejoices my soul, that I am not any longer to be entirely alone in the world.' Upon this, Martin Harris came in: he seemed almost overcome with joy, and testified boldly to what he had both seen and heard. And so did David and Oliver, adding, that no tongue could express the joy of their hearts, and the greatness of the things which they had both seen and heard."[12]

Not long after the experience of the Three Witnesses, the Eight Witnesses saw and handled the plates.

With the exception of Oliver Cowdery and Martin Harris, the witnesses were all members of the Smith and Whitmer families,[13] individuals who already believed in Joseph Smith's work and were called to receive a manifestation and testify thereof to the world. Their testimonies are an important part of the coming forth of the Book of Mormon, because now there were others who could state with Joseph Smith: "We . . . have seen the plates. . . . And we also know that they have been translated by the gift and power of God, for his voice hath declared it unto us. . . . And we declare with words of soberness, that an angel of God came down from heaven, and he brought and laid before our eyes, that we beheld and saw the plates."[14]

In the revelation in which the Lord designated the Three Witnesses, he told them that they would see, in addition to the plates, "the sword of Laban, the Urim and Thummim, which were given to the brother of Jared upon the mount, when he talked with the Lord face to face, and the miraculous directors which were given to Lehi while in the wilderness, on the borders of the Red Sea" (D&C 17:1). The significance of these items is that they are all objects mentioned in the account in the Book of Mormon text itself—artifacts from the history in the book. This means that the Three Witnesses saw evidence not only that there was a divinely revealed book but also that the events described in it actually took place.

Since the beginning of the Restoration, the testimonies of the witnesses have been a problem for those who reject Joseph Smith. The lives of those men are well documented. They were respected in their communities and considered by their contemporaries to be not only of sound character but also of sound mind. Sadly, in the late 1830s each of the Three Witnesses left the Church, becoming disillusioned with Joseph Smith personally over matters of policy and beliefs. Two later were rebaptized, yet all three continued to maintain, even in their days of disassociation from the Church, that their published testimony was a true account of an actual supernatural event in which they had been participants.[15] Ironically, the disaffection of the witnesses adds to the credibility of their testimonies. Had the experience been fraudulent, the witnesses no doubt would have seized the opportunity to expose the Prophet as an impostor. But they remained true to their statements, even when they felt personal animosity toward Joseph Smith.

Today there are some who say that the Book of Mormon is true in the sense that its message is meaningful but propose that neither it nor the account of its origin is historical. The testimonies of the witnesses expose this point of view as nonsense by providing evidence that cannot be explained away. Reasonable men claimed throughout their lives that they saw an angel, handled the plates, and heard the voice of God. It is no wonder that the witnesses were foreknown by revelation and prepared by the Lord to perform their important calling to bear testimony of his work (D&C 17:1–9; Ether 5:1–4). The Book of Mormon still contains their "words of soberness," which are as valid today as they were in 1830 when the book first came off the press.

Publication

By the end of June 1829, Joseph Smith had completed the translation of the Book of Mormon into the English language. He had secured the copyright and now set out to hire a printer.[16] But he soon learned how intense the local sentiment was against the book. Religious leaders had warned their congregations against it and conspired to discourage them from buying it. As a result, printers in the area were reluctant to take on the project, for fear of sustaining financial loss. The Prophet was finally able to persuade a Palmyra printer and bookseller, Egbert B. Grandin, to publish the book. But Grandin agreed to do so only on the condition that he receive a guarantee for the money and not be dependent on sales. By doing that he would secure himself against losing a substantial investment. The agreement was made to print five thousand copies at a cost of three thousand dollars.

That was an enormous sum of money—far beyond the

Grandin Building, Palmyra, New York, the printshop and bookstore of E. B. Grandin, where the Book of Mormon was published in 1830

resources of the Smith family and of most other families of the day. But even for this, the Lord had made preparation. Martin Harris had inherited about half his farm from his father, who had settled in Palmyra more than thirty years earlier. The rest he had acquired through his labors. By 1829 the farm had enjoyed years of success to the point that Martin was, by contemporary standards, a prosperous man. Again he used his resources to help the cause of the coming forth of the Book of Mormon. He took out an eighteen-month mortgage with Grandin to guarantee the costs of printing the book. Money from its sales would be used to pay Grandin his three thousand dollars within the specified time. If the book did not raise enough money, part of the Harris farm would be sold to pay the debt.

Joseph Smith now had the translation, a printer, and the financial resources to publish the book. But he also had the memory of what had happened the last time he let the translation out of his

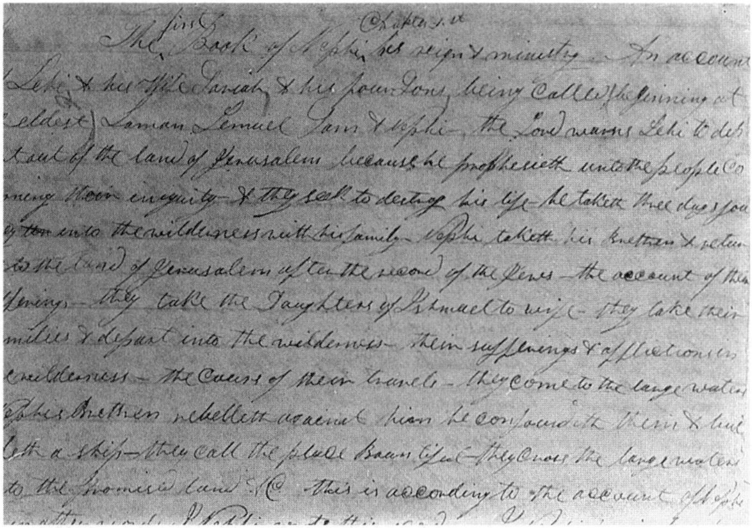

Chapter 1st
The first Book of Nephi his reign & ministry — An accoun
Lehi & his wife Sariah & his four Sons, being Called (the beginning at
eldest) Laman Lemuel Sam & Nephi — the Lord warns Lehi to dep
t out of the land of Jerusalem because he prophesieth unto the people Co
ning their iniquity & they seek to destroy his life — he taketh three days jou
y into the wilderness with his family — Nephi taketh his brethren & retur
to the land of Jerusalem after the record of the Jews — the account of thei
[illegible] — they take the Daughters of Ishmael to wife — they take their
milies & depart into the wilderness — their sufferings & afflictions in
wilderness — the Course of their travels — they come to the large water
Nephis Brethren rebelleth against him he confoundeth them & buil
eth a ship — they call the place Bountiful — they Cross the large water
to the promised land &c — this is according to the account of Neph

First page of the printer's manuscript of the Book of Mormon, showing the introduction to 1 Nephi

hands. To be sure that no part of the manuscript would be lost, he instructed Oliver Cowdery to create a copy to take to the printer; the original would remain in a secure place. In our day, in which the copying of documents is quick and convenient, we can appreciate the tremendous amount of work expended by Oliver Cowdery (with some limited help from others) in transcribing, by hand, a copy of the Book of Mormon. But to do so assured the Prophet that the translation would not be lost. The "printer's manuscript" was not made all at once but was written as needed over the months of the typesetting.[17] The process of production extended from August 1829 into the spring of 1830.[18]

As the publication neared completion, Martin Harris became increasingly apprehensive. He was willing to do what the Lord required, but knowing the animosity against Joseph Smith in the area, he had reservations about whether the book would sell and whether he would lose his property if it did not. The Lord's response was not to be misunderstood: "Thou shalt not covet thine

The press used by E. B. Grandin to print the Book of Mormon. Now in the Museum of Church History and Art, Salt Lake City

own property, but impart it freely to the printing of the Book of Mormon, which contains the truth and the word of God. . . . Impart a portion of thy property, yea, even part of thy lands, and all save the support of thy family. Pay the debt thou hast contracted with the printer. Release thyself from bondage" (D&C 19:26, 34–35). The blessings that would result from Martin's efforts would be of greater value than his farm or any other earthly things: "Pray always, and I will pour out my Spirit upon you, and great shall be your blessing—yea, even more than if you should obtain treasures of earth" (D&C 19:38).[19]

As it turned out, Martin's concerns were well-founded. The Book of Mormon did not sell well enough for him to pay off Grandin from its profits, and eventually he had to sell 151 acres of his farm to settle the debt. That was a great sacrifice, and

Martin Harris rightly deserves to be honored for his contribution to this important part of the Restoration. It was a sacrifice that made the publication of the Book of Mormon possible.

On 26 March 1830, the Book of Mormon was finally available for public sale, containing "a record of a fallen people, and the fulness of the gospel of Jesus Christ to the Gentiles and to the Jews also; which was given by inspiration, and is confirmed to others by the ministering of angels, and is declared unto the world by them—proving to the world that the holy scriptures are true, and that God does inspire men and call them to his holy work in this age and generation, as well as in generations of old; thereby showing that he is the same God yesterday, today, and forever" (D&C 20:9–12).

The publication of the book culminated a sanctified work of preparation that had started twenty-four centuries earlier when Nephi began his record. Now the work of ancient prophets, the protecting watch of Moroni, the committed service of Joseph and Emma Smith, and the varied contributions of Oliver Cowdery, Martin Harris, the Smiths, the Knights, and the Whitmers had all come together through the attending grace of a loving Heavenly Father to produce a great miracle—the Book of Mormon. With the book now in print and available for the instruction of the honest in heart, the Lord could bring about the next aspect of his work of restoration: the Church was organized eleven days later.

Notes

1. Joseph Smith, *History of The Church of Jesus Christ of Latter-day Saints,* ed. B. H. Roberts, 2d ed. rev., 7 vols. (Salt Lake City: Deseret Book, 1957), 4:461.

2. Lucy Mack Smith, *Biographical Sketches of Joseph Smith the Prophet and His Progenitors for Many Generations* (Liverpool: S. W. Richards, 1853), 112–13. Significant primary sources for this period include *Biographical Sketches,* by the Prophet's mother, Lucy Mack Smith; Joseph Smith's history in Dean C. Jessee, ed., *The Papers of Joseph Smith,* 3 vols. (Salt Lake City: Deseret

Book, 1989–97), 1:283–301; and "Joseph Knight's Recollections of Early Mormon History," ed. Dean C. Jessee, *BYU Studies* 17, no. 1 (autumn 1976): 33–36.

3. Book of Mormon, 1830 edition, preface.

4. Jessee, *Papers of Joseph Smith,* 1:10.

5. Ibid.

6. *Latter Day Saints' Messenger and Advocate* 1, no. 1 (October 1834): 14; JS–H, footnote at verse 71; emphasis in the original.

7. "Joseph Knight's Recollections," 36.

8. See Lyndon W. Cook, ed., *David Whitmer Interviews: A Restoration Witness* (Orem, Utah: Grandin, 1991), 63–64.

9. Jessee, *Papers of Joseph Smith,* 1:295–96.

10. *The Saints' Herald* 29 (1 March 1882); in Cook, *David Whitmer Interviews,* 86.

11. Jessee, *Papers of Joseph Smith,* 1:296.

12. Smith, *Biographical Sketches,* 139.

13. Hiram Page was married to a Whitmer daughter. Oliver Cowdery later married another Whitmer daughter.

14. "The Testimony of Three Witnesses," Book of Mormon.

15. See Richard Lloyd Anderson, *Investigating the Book of Mormon Witnesses* (Salt Lake City: Deseret Book, 1981).

16. The copyright was obtained on 11 June 1829.

17. According to Professor Royal Skousen, about seventy pages of the original manuscript were used by the typesetters, perhaps because the copying was outpaced for a while by the typesetting.

18. The original manuscript is only about 25 to 30 percent extant today. Most fragments are housed in the LDS Church Archives in Salt Lake City. The printer's manuscript is in an excellent state of preservation and is virtually intact. It is housed in the RLDS Archives in Independence, Missouri.

19. See Milton V. Backman Jr. and Richard O. Cowan, *Joseph Smith and the Doctrine and Covenants* (Salt Lake City: Deseret Book, 1992), 24–25.

Chapter 14

The Book of Mormon in the Restoration

The Book of Mormon was destined to be not only the most important conversion tool for the last days (title page) but also the great, tangible sign of the Restoration (3 Ne. 21:1–7). It seems significant that before we had the Church, we had the Book of Mormon. Most religions in world history have produced their significant holy books long after the religion came into existence. Ours began with our holy book already in place. It defines our religion, rather than being an outgrowth of it. The Book of Mormon was a package of pure gospel that had been prepared many centuries in advance so the Church could begin on a sure doctrinal footing free of past traditions. Its content makes us independent of the creeds of medieval Christianity. But so also does its very existence, which shows that the latter-day Church and its teachings would not be a legacy inherited through the centuries.

Restoring Plain and Precious Truths

The Book of Mormon is a doctrinal keystone of the Restoration. In its pages, important truths are revealed that are central to the gospel in any age but that have been lost to the world over the centuries. The following is a brief survey of some of the

The Book of Mormon, 1830, first edition

important doctrinal concepts that the Book of Mormon brings into the world as part of its unique contribution to the Restoration.

The atoning mission of Jesus Christ. The Atonement is the very message of the Book of Mormon. It is the theme that binds together its historical narratives, its sermons, and its inspired commentary. "We talk of Christ, we rejoice in Christ, we preach of Christ, [and] we prophesy of Christ," Nephi recorded. "And we write according to our prophecies, that our children may know to what source they may look for a remission of their sins" (2 Ne. 25:26). The Book of Mormon has its focus in proclaiming and explaining the first principles and ordinances of Christ's gospel—faith, repentance, baptism, and the gift of the Holy Ghost (e.g., 3 Ne. 27:13–21). Nowhere are they presented better than in the Book of Mormon. Perhaps the greatest contribution of this "other testament of Jesus Christ" is the power and clarity with which it teaches us of Jesus and his work. Specific examples of unique contributions the Book of Mormon makes to our understanding of Christ's redemptive power might include the discussions of salvation through the merits of Christ (2 Ne. 2:8), the relationship between grace and works (2 Ne. 25:23; 31:19), and the salvation of little children (Moro. 8:8–22). In the Book of Mormon we are taught what it means to be a disciple of Christ (Mosiah 18:9–10), and we are instructed in the importance, the process, and the ultimate blessings of spiritual birth (Mosiah 5:6–9).

The nature and goals of Satan. In the Bible, the few references to Satan and his work tell us only little of his character and objectives but nothing of his origin. When we turn to the Book of Mormon, we learn something of where he came from, and we view his work and his objectives in clearer focus. Lehi learned from the plates of brass that the adversary was once "an angel of God" who fell from heaven. "Wherefore, he became a devil, having sought that which was evil before God. And because he had fallen from heaven, and had become miserable forever, he sought also the misery of all mankind." This obsession drives his perverse cruelty and his insatiable appetite for human sorrow. "For he seeketh that all men might be miserable like unto himself" (2 Ne. 2:17–18, 27).

The fall of Adam. The account in Genesis of Adam and Eve gives us very few insights into the Fall. Thanks to Paul, however, the New Testament enables us to understand its association with the gospel. But even so, the message, as preserved in the Bible today, is unclear. Overlaid with centuries of misinterpretation as the result of ancient and medieval speculation, the doctrine of the Fall was in need of a complete and radical restoration in the latter days.[1] The Book of Mormon teaches the Fall better than does any other book. The words of Lehi are illustrative:

> And now, behold, if Adam had not transgressed he would not have fallen, but he would have remained in the garden of Eden. And all things which were created must have remained in the same state in which they were after they were created; and they must have remained forever, and had no end.
>
> And they would have had no children; wherefore they would have

remained in a state of innocence, having no joy, for they knew no misery; doing no good, for they knew no sin. (2 Ne. 2:22–23)

The Book of Mormon thus teaches that the Fall, despite its immediate consequences, was a positive step in the progress of humankind. Without it, Adam and Eve would not have brought the human family into the world. Not knowing the natural opposites of life, they could not have experienced joy, nor could they have done good. But "all things have been done in the wisdom of him who knoweth all things. Adam fell that men might be; and men are, that they might have joy" (2 Ne. 2:24–25).

The Book of Mormon emphasizes Christ's atonement as the solution to the consequences of the Fall—death and sin (2 Ne. 9:6–10; Alma 11:40–42). "Since man had fallen he could not merit anything of himself; but the sufferings and death of Christ atone for their sins" (Alma 22:14). As Lehi taught, "the Messiah cometh in the fulness of time, that he may redeem the children of men from the fall" (2 Ne. 2:26).

The antiquity of the gospel. Traditional Christianity holds that the gospel was revealed to the world with Jesus Christ and that those who preceded his coming did not have available to them its blessings. The Book of Mormon, however, begins with a colony of Christians six hundred years *before* Jesus' birth. Later in its pages we read of another Christian group who lived perhaps two thousand years earlier than that. Those groups had Christianity revealed to them in plainness, and they knew, centuries before Christ's coming (Jacob 4:4–5), that his gospel was the only way to salvation and that "there is no other name given whereby salvation cometh" (Mosiah 5:8). The Book of Mormon teaches that this is true for those who lived before his mortal ministry as well as for those who lived afterward. Jesus' gospel was so immediate to the Book of Mormon prophets, even for those who lived long before his birth, that some of them spoke of his redeeming work in the past tense, "speaking of things to come as though they had already come" (Mosiah 16:6).

The role of prophets and the nature of revelation. Although the prophetic books in the Bible are marvelous collections of revelations, they tell us very little about the prophets themselves, their lives, and their struggles to fulfill the Lord's commands. The book of Jeremiah is a notable exception, recording details about the prophet's life and the challenges he faced. Jeremiah's contemporaries Lehi and Nephi set the pattern for the Book of Mormon prophets who followed them in giving us both a record of their prophecies and a narrative of their labors in the Lord's service. In the pages of the Book of Mormon we learn much about the nature of prophets and prophecy, about the feelings of the Lord's servants regarding their missions, and about their dedicated efforts to do what was required of them. No other book brings us closer to these things than does the Book of Mormon.

In the Book of Mormon we also see the processes by which revelation is received. Through appearances (Alma 8:14–18), dreams (1 Ne. 2:1), visions (1 Ne. 11–14), and quiet promptings (2 Ne. 32:7; Alma 14:11), the Lord's will was made known to his servants. Alma, struggling with a difficult issue in the Church, inquired of the Lord, received instructions, and wrote them down (Mosiah 26:13–33). Mormon, needing the answer to a doctrinal question, inquired of God and received knowledge (3 Ne. 28:37).

The Book of Mormon gives us a glimpse into the use of sacred instruments to facilitate revelation (1 Ne. 16:10, 26–29; Mosiah 8:13), concerning which we learn even more from the experiences of Joseph Smith.

Finally, in the Book of Mormon we learn that the central message of all of God's prophets has been Jesus Christ (Jacob 4:4; 3 Ne. 20:24).

The purpose and process of keeping sacred records. The Book of Mormon gives us not only a record of God's revelations and the history of a people but also the history of its own writing and

THE

BOOK OF MORMON:

AN ACCOUNT WRITTEN BY THE HAND OF MORMON, UPON PLATES TAKEN FROM THE PLATES OF NEPHI.

Wherefore it is an abridgment of the Record of the People of Nephi; and also of the Lamanites; written to the Lamanites, which are a remnant of the House of Israel; and also to Jew and Gentile; written by way of commandment, and also by the spirit of Prophesy and of Revelation. Written, and sealed up, and hid up unto the LORD, that they might not be destroyed; to come forth by the gift and power of GOD unto the interpretation thereof; sealed by the hand of Moroni, and hid up unto the LORD, to come forth in due time by the way of Gentile; the interpretation thereof by the gift of GOD; an abridgment taken from the Book of Ether.

Also, which is a Record of the People of Jared, which were scattered at the time the LORD confounded the language of the people when they were building a tower to get to Heaven: which is to shew unto the remnant of the House of Israel how great things the LORD hath done for their fathers; and that they may know the covenants of the LORD, that they are not cast off forever; and also to the convincing of the Jew and Gentile that JESUS is the CHRIST, the ETERNAL GOD, manifesting Himself unto all nations. And now if there be fault, it be the mistake of men; wherefore condemn not the things of GOD, that ye may be found spotless at the judgment seat of CHRIST.

BY JOSEPH SMITH, JUNIOR,

AUTHOR AND PROPRIETOR.

PALMYRA:

PRINTED BY E. B. GRANDIN, FOR THE AUTHOR.

1830.

The Book of Mormon, 1830, first edition, title page

extensive insights into its purpose. It is, in fact, a thoroughly self-conscious book that speaks often of itself and the objectives for which it was written. The title page identifies its author (Mormon), its subject matter ("the record of the people of Nephi, and also of the Lamanites"), its intended readership (Lamanites, Jews, and Gentiles), its authority ("written by way of commandment, and also by the spirit of prophecy and of revelation"), the time of its publication ("in due time"), and the source of its translation ("the gift of God"). But perhaps most importantly, it tells us the intent for which the book was written: "To show unto the remnant of the House of Israel what great things the Lord hath done for their fathers; and that they may know the covenants of the Lord . . .—And also to the convincing of the Jew and Gentile that JESUS is the CHRIST, the ETERNAL GOD, manifesting himself unto all nations."

The Book of Mormon describes the revelations that led to its composition over the course of many centuries (e.g., 1 Ne. 19:1–6; W of M), and it focuses throughout its pages on its intended latter-day readers and their needs. Its authors expressed the clear awareness of mission that directed them to prepare the book, which in turn gives it a sense of destiny not always apparent in the Bible. This sense of destiny is one of the Book of Mormon's greatest contributions to our understanding of the Bible. From it we see why God commands his prophets in any age to write his words and what the value of those sacred records is to their contemporaries and to future generations.

The history and destiny of the Bible. In addition to establishing and clarifying points of doctrine that relate to biblical teachings, the Book of Mormon tells us much concerning the Bible itself. Nephi learned in a vision that the Bible would contain "the covenants of the Lord, which he hath made unto the house of Israel" and "the fulness of the gospel of the Lord, of whom the twelve apostles bear record" (1 Ne. 13:23, 24). But "many plain and precious things" would be "taken away from the book," and "after these plain and precious things were taken away it goeth forth unto all the nations of the Gentiles," many of whom would "stumble" and be in an "awful state of blindness" because of the omissions (1 Ne. 13:28–29, 32). The plates of brass obtained by Nephi recorded the equivalent of the Old Testament to his time, before it went through the censoring process of what he called the "great and abominable church." Our Bible (the Old and New Testaments) would be smaller than the Old Testament record on those brass plates (1 Ne. 13:23).

The Book of Mormon foretells its own future as well. In it would be written "my gospel, saith the Lamb, and my rock and my salvation" (1 Ne. 13:36). Along with other books, it would come forth "by the power of the Lamb," and together those books would restore "the plain and precious things which have been taken away" from the Bible (1 Ne. 13:39–40). The Nephite record and the Bible would "be established in one" (1 Ne. 13:41), giving us "the testimony of two nations" (2 Ne. 29:8).

The Book of Mormon proves that the Christian tradition of a closed biblical canon is false—both by its own existence as well as by its teachings. The Lord told Nephi:

> And because that I have spoken one word ye need not suppose that I cannot speak another; for my work is not yet finished; neither shall it be until the end of man, neither from that time henceforth and forever.
>
> Wherefore, because that ye have a Bible ye need not suppose that it contains all my words; neither need ye suppose that I have not caused more to be written. . . .
>
> For behold, I shall speak unto the Jews and they shall write it; and I shall also speak unto the Nephites and they shall write it; and I shall also speak unto the other tribes of the house of Israel, which I have led away, and they shall write it; and I shall also speak unto all nations of the earth and they shall write it.
>
> And it shall come to pass that the Jews shall have the words of the Nephites, and the Nephites shall have the words of the Jews; and the Nephites and the Jews shall have the words of the lost tribes of Israel; and the lost tribes of Israel shall have the words of the Nephites and the Jews. (2 Ne. 29:9–10, 12–13)

The intent of the Book of Mormon is not to denigrate the Bible but to contribute to the restoration of what had once been "the fulness of the gospel of the Lord" that it contained (1 Ne. 13:24). One of its chief purposes is to testify of the truth of the Bible to Lehi's descendants, to the Gentiles, and to the Jews (1 Ne. 13:39–40; Morm. 7:8–9). The Book of Mormon thus stands as a witness for the Bible, "proving to the world that the holy scriptures are true" (D&C 20:11).

The destiny of the house of Israel. The writings of biblical prophets teach us much concerning the house of Israel, but nowhere are its mission and destiny explained better than in the Book of Mormon. Lehi and Nephi had deep sensitivities concerning the status of their family as a branch of Israel removed from the mother plant (1 Ne. 10:14; 15:12–16). It was a theme of great importance in their teachings and in those of their successors. In the words of the Book of Mormon from its beginning to its end, we gain a clearer understanding of the house of Israel and its role in God's plan than we do in any other book. Among its special contributions is the knowledge that God's covenant with Israel includes the promise of the gospel of Jesus Christ (3 Ne. 5:24–26), that Israel's restoration includes the restoration of the knowledge that Jesus is Israel's Redeemer (1 Ne. 10:14; 22:11–12), that the promised gathering of the Jews to Palestine will follow their conversion to Christ (2 Ne. 10:7–8; 3 Ne. 20:30–33), and that the Gentiles will save scattered Israel in the last days by bringing them Christ's gospel (1 Ne. 13:38–40; 15:13–14).

Apostasy and restoration. Near the beginning of the Book of Mormon, Nephi foresaw the destiny of his own people. In their land of promise, despite the personal coming of Christ and many other blessings, they would fall prey to their pride and the temptations of the devil, eventually to "dwindle in unbelief" (1 Ne. 12:19–23; see 1–23). The authors of the Book of Mormon recorded the process as it took place.

The Book of Mormon foretells the apostasy of early Christianity as well. Nephi foresaw that among the nations of the world, where the gospel will have been taught by Jesus and his apostles, a "great and abominable church" would arise. In addition to tampering with the Bible, it would take away "from the gospel of the Lamb many parts which are plain and most precious," as well as "many covenants of the Lord." It would do all this "that they might pervert the right ways of the Lord, that they might blind the eyes and harden the hearts of the children of men" (1 Ne. 13:26–27; see 4–32). The "great and abominable church" in this context seems to represent the apostate forces within the Lord's own Church, led by those in it who rejected the authority of the Twelve and sought to pattern their church after the image of the world.

The Book of Mormon also prophesies of the Restoration. Nephi wrote of the coming forth of the Book of Mormon and of other scriptures (1 Ne. 13:34–41). He foretold the Lord's restored Church in the latter days and the "marvelous work" that God would undertake to bring forth its truths. He wrote of "the power of the Lamb of God," which would be found among the Lord's Saints in that day (1 Ne. 14:7–14).

Lehi's teachings include a prophecy from the plates of brass that foretells the latter-day restoration. A "choice seer," whom we know to be Joseph Smith, would bring forth God's word, including the Book of Mormon, to the salvation of his people (2 Ne. 3:5–21).

The meaning of the law of Moses. Although the Old Testament preserves for us the law of Moses, it is to the New Testament that Bible readers must turn to understand the law's purpose. It was a "schoolmaster" to prepare Israel for the gospel (Gal. 3:24). But nowhere is its meaning explained better than in the Book of Mormon, whose authors understood that the law was "pointing [their] souls" to Christ (Jacob 4:5). The Nephite writers before Jesus' coming lived under the dispensation of Moses and were subject to the law of that dispensation. Yet they knew the gospel of Christ and had a clear perspective of the relationship between the gospel and the law of Moses. Amulek taught:

> Therefore, it is expedient that there should be a great and last sacrifice, and then shall there be, or it is expedient there should be, a stop to

the shedding of blood; then shall the law of Moses be fulfilled; yea, it shall be all fulfilled, every jot and tittle, and none shall have passed away.

> And behold, this is the whole meaning of the law, every whit pointing to that great and last sacrifice; and that great and last sacrifice will be the Son of God, yea, infinite and eternal.
>
> And thus he shall bring salvation to all those who shall believe on his name; this being the intent of this last sacrifice, to bring about the bowels of mercy, which overpowereth justice, and bringeth about means unto men that they may have faith unto repentance. (Alma 34:13–15)

But the ancient Israelites to whom the law had been revealed apparently lost its meaning and did not understand its purpose. For them, as the Book of Mormon prophet Abinadi taught, God revealed a system of "performances and ordinances" to keep them in remembrance of him:

> And now I say unto you that it was expedient that there should be a law given to the children of Israel, yea, even a very strict law; for they were a stiffnecked people, quick to do iniquity, and slow to remember the Lord their God;
>
> Therefore there was a law given them, yea, a law of performances and of ordinances, a law which they were to observe strictly from day to day, to keep them in remembrance of God and their duty towards him. (Mosiah 13:29–30)

But even "all these things were types of things to come" (Mosiah 13:31), a truth that is not taught in the Old Testament but is clear in the words of the Book of Mormon.

Proving to the World

With its emphasis on the most fundamental principles of the gospel—the mission of Christ, the nature of human existence, and the function of revelation and scripture—the Book of Mormon laid the foundation for the continuing doctrinal restoration that followed it. In rapid sequence, revelations now contained in the Doctrine and Covenants, the Joseph Smith Translation of the

Bible, and the Pearl of Great Price added to the magnificent revelation that we call the Book of Mormon.

The Book of Mormon is indeed the great sign of the Restoration. Its very existence challenges the world to test its credibility and the truthfulness of the story of its origin. It is thus no wonder that it, more than anything else in the Church's history, has been the target of critics of the Prophet Joseph Smith and his work. But those critics can do it no harm. It was, after all, "given by inspiration," "confirmed . . . by the ministering of angels" (D&C 20:10), and endorsed by the voice of Jesus Christ, saying, "As your Lord and your God liveth it is true" (D&C 17:6).

In proclaiming the Restoration and the Lord's work of the latter days, the Book of Mormon continues today the mission it began with its publication in March of 1830, "proving to the world . . . that God does inspire men and call them to his holy work in this age and generation, as well as in generations of old" (D&C 20:11). The Book of Mormon stands as an ensign of the restoration of the gospel through the Prophet Joseph Smith, held up to the world as evidence of God's love for his children today, bearing testimony that he is at work in our time and that those who carry the book to the nations of the earth are his true messengers.

Note

1. See, for example, Augustine's thoughts on the Fall, in Chapter 5, 46–48.

Chapter 15

The Restoration of the Priesthood

During the process of translating the Book of Mormon at his small home in Harmony, Pennsylvania, Joseph Smith and Oliver Cowdery for the first time began to learn what the Lord called "the fulness of the gospel of Jesus Christ," which was contained within the book's pages (D&C 20:9). While reading of the gospel among the ancient descendants of Lehi, they undoubtedly learned many new things concerning doctrines and procedures that are part of the Lord's work in every age. One topic of special interest to them was baptism. "No men in their sober senses," Oliver Cowdery recalled, "could translate and write the directions given to the Nephites, from the mouth of the Savior, of the precise manner in which men should build up his church, . . . without desiring a privilege of showing the willingness of the heart by being buried in the liquid grave." He continued: "We only waited for the commandment to be given, 'Arise and be baptized.'"[1]

The Aaronic Priesthood

That privilege came on 15 May 1829. Joseph Smith recorded that he and his scribe "went into the woods to pray and inquire of the Lord respecting baptism for the remission of sins" (JS–H 1:68). "On a sudden, as from the midst of eternity, the voice of the

Susquehanna River, Harmony, Pennsylvania, behind the home of Joseph and Emma Smith. Approximate site of the restoration of the Aaronic Priesthood

Redeemer spake peace to us, while the vail was parted and the angel of God came down clothed with glory, and delivered the anxiously looked for message, and the keys of the gospel of repentance!"[2] The Prophet later recalled, "He laid his hands upon my head and ordained me to be a priest after the order of Aaron and to hold the keys of this priesthood, which office was to preach repentance and baptism for the remission of sins and also to baptize."[3] The heavenly messenger stated: "Upon you my fellow servants, in the name of Messiah, I confer the Priesthood of Aaron, which holds the keys of the ministering of angels, and of the gospel of repentance, and of baptism by immersion for the remission of sins; and this shall never be taken again from the earth until the sons of Levi do offer again an offering unto the Lord in righteousness" (JS–H 1:69; D&C 13). Oliver Cowdery reported the angel's words as follows: "Upon you my fellow servants, in the name of Messiah I confer this priesthood and this authority, which shall remain upon earth, that the sons of Levi may yet offer an offering unto the Lord in righteousness!"[4]

The messenger identified himself as John the Baptist (JS–H 1:72). He commanded the two men to be baptized, giving instructions that Joseph Smith should first baptize Oliver Cowdery and that thereafter the scribe should baptize the Prophet. Joseph Smith next ordained Oliver Cowdery, after which the process was reversed, all in accordance with angelic instruction (JS–H 1:70–71). Through these actions, the priesthood of Aaron was restored to the world.

When Latter-day Saints speak of the Aaronic Priesthood, we speak of the same authority that Moses, under divine investiture, conferred on his brother Aaron (Ex. 28:1) and which was continued through Aaron's descendants to John the Baptist. This authority, sometimes also called the Levitical Priesthood, is the authority under which the law of Moses was administered in Old Testament times and by virtue of which John baptized Jesus Christ. As John stated, it encompasses the power of "the ministering of angels," "the gospel of repentance," and "baptism by immersion for the remission of sins" (JS–H 1:69). Joseph Smith received from him not only the priesthood but also the keys of that priesthood, meaning the power to preside over it, to pass it on to others, and to authorize others to use it.

John the Baptist, the son of Zacharias, was uniquely qualified to be the agent of the restoration of the Aaronic Priesthood. Joseph Smith taught that John was the "lawful heir"[5] to this authority, who "held the keys of the Aaronic Priesthood."[6] "He, having received the holy anointing, was the only lawful administrator."[7] "All the power and authority and anointing," the Prophet said, "descended upon the head of John the Baptist."[8] Thus the angelic visitor was not a randomly selected Levite sent to reveal the priesthood. He was the lawful heir to that authority by his descent from his ancestor Aaron. And because he was the last to hold the keys of the priesthood in ancient times, there could be no one more appropriate to bring those keys back to earth as part of the latter-day Restoration.

The Melchizedek Priesthood

John told Joseph Smith and Oliver Cowdery that the priesthood which he gave them did not include the authority to lay on hands for the gift of the Holy Ghost; that would come later (JS–H 1:70).[9] He also told them that he was acting under the direction of the ancient apostles Peter, James, and John, who held the keys of the priesthood of Melchizedek. Joseph Smith and Oliver Cowdery would receive that authority "in due time" (JS–H 1:72). The Melchizedek Priesthood is the highest order of priesthood that God grants to his children on earth. In a later revelation, Joseph Smith learned that its original name was "*the Holy Priesthood, after the Order of the Son of God.* But out of respect or reverence to the name of the Supreme Being, to avoid the too frequent repetition of his name, they, the church, in ancient days, called that priesthood after Melchizedek, or the Melchizedek Priesthood" (D&C 107:3–4). This priesthood encompasses every authority in the Church, presides over all of its functions, and empowers men to speak and act in the name of God.

We do not know the date when Peter, James, and John appeared on the earth to restore the Melchizedek Priesthood. The Prophet's writings and sermons are silent concerning the exact date, as also are the records of Oliver Cowdery. We do know that the restoration of the Melchizedek Priesthood happened after 15 May 1829 and before the Church was organized on 6 April 1830 (D&C 20:2–3, 38). Circumstantial evidence places the event within two weeks of the restoration of the Aaronic Priesthood. On 1 June 1829, the Prophet and his scribe arrived in Fayette, New York, to complete the translation of the Book of Mormon at the Whitmer home. It appears that the restoration of the higher priesthood had happened before that date.[10] In 1842 Joseph Smith stated that the event took place "in the wilderness between Harmony,

Susquehanna Valley, southern New York, near which the Melchizedek Priesthood was restored

Susquehanna county [Pennsylvania], and Colesville, Broome county [New York], on the Susquehanna river" (D&C 128:20). That would place the restoration of the Melchizedek Priesthood near the Pennsylvania–New York border, some miles upstream from the place where the Aaronic Priesthood had been restored.

With the restoration of the higher priesthood by those who held it anciently came also the restoration of the keys to preside over the Lord's work on earth. The keys of the priesthood belong to the apostleship. They are the "keys of the kingdom" (D&C 128:20) which Jesus had given his Twelve anciently and by which they, and now Joseph Smith and his successors, were authorized to speak and act in the name of Christ. The restoration of the apostleship also restored the keys of revelation. Joseph Smith taught that the Melchizedek Priesthood "is the channel through which all knowledge, doctrine, the plan of salvation and every important matter is revealed from heaven." It is "the channel through which . . . he has continued to reveal himself to the children of men to the present time and through which he will make known his purposes to the end of time."[11] "The apostles in ancient times held the keys of this priesthood—of the mysteries of the kingdom of God, and consequently were enabled to unlock, and unravel all things pertaining to the government of the church, the welfare of society, the future destiny of men, and the agency, power, and influence of spirits."[12] This priesthood "administereth the gospel and holdeth the key of the mysteries of the kingdom, even the key of the knowledge of God." In its ordinances, "the power of godliness is manifest" (D&C 84:19–20). Now those powers were restored to earth, into the hands of men who, like their fellow apostles anciently, would carry on the work of Christ.

One great blessing of the restoration of the Melchizedek Priesthood was the restoration of the gift of the Holy Ghost. Perhaps before the Prophet fully knew what it was, he was told about this gift by John the Baptist (JS–H 1:70). The gift of the Holy Ghost is a special blessing for those who through the covenant of baptism have taken upon themselves the name of Christ. It is their promise of the constant companionship of the Holy Spirit, provided they live their lives worthy of it. Many good persons outside Christ's church have received the influence of the Spirit in their efforts to serve the Lord according to the knowledge they have possessed. That influence is especially present among those who are searching for truth, and missionaries can attest that it is that influence of the Spirit and not their own skill that brings people to conversion. But the gift of the Holy Ghost promises more than the sometimes temporary promptings felt by seekers after truth. As Joseph Smith taught:

"There is a difference between the Holy Ghost and the gift of the Holy Ghost. Cornelius [a convert in Acts 10] received the Holy Ghost before he was baptized, which was the convincing power of God unto him of the truth of the gospel. But he could not receive the gift of the Holy Ghost until after he was baptized. And had he not taken this sign [or] ordinances upon him, the Holy Ghost, which convinced him of the truth of God, would have left him until he obeyed those ordinances and received the gift of the

Holy Ghost by the laying on of hands, according to the order of God."[13]

Thus the gift of the Holy Ghost is not only a special blessing but also a saving ordinance that signifies a covenant between God and individual Saints. Like baptism, it is required of those who would inherit the celestial kingdom (D&C 76:51–52). It gives them the assurance that God's latter-day work is true and that prophets guide his Church. And it enables them to retain that testimony in the face of life's challenges. Those who use this gift wisely and worthily are empowered to overcome the world by faith and to be sealed by the Holy Spirit of promise (D&C 76:53).

"I Have Chosen You"

Without the priesthood, sacred ordinances cannot be performed with legitimacy and are not recognized by God as binding, regardless of the motives of those who might seek to act in God's name. Because of this, a few months after the restoration of the priesthood the Lord revealed the truth that the Saints' previous baptisms were not valid and thus they would need to be baptized again under the authority of the newly restored priesthood (D&C 22:1–4). Joseph Smith taught that "all the ordinances, systems, and administrations on the earth are of no use to the children of men unless they are ordained and authorized of God." They must be performed by "a legal administrator. For none others will be acknowledged, either by God or angels."[14] This is a fundamental principle of true Christianity. Because of the importance of the priesthood, the coming of Peter, James, and John is one of the key events in the Lord's work of the last days, an indispensable part of the restoration of the gospel.

Having received the authority of God, Joseph Smith stood in the same position that was occupied by Peter in the ancient Church. Thus empowered, his works were authorized by heaven and were binding and valid. The same is true for all those who have received those same keys in succession from Joseph Smith to the present moment.

This authority is not a legacy inherited through the centuries of Christian history. The chain of priesthood that binds the restored Church to the primitive Church does not pass through the medieval church, the Reformation church, or the churches of Joseph Smith's day. The priesthood authority of The Church of Jesus Christ of Latter-day Saints is a new, undiluted revelation of the power that was held anciently by Jesus' apostolic witnesses. It was brought back by the very men who held it before, so that the priesthood in the last days would continue an unbroken succession of ordination from those who received it under the hands of Jesus Christ. "How have we come at the priesthood in the last days?" Joseph Smith asked. "It came down, down in regular succession. Peter, James, and John had it given to them, and they gave it up [to us]."[15]

When the Savior set apart his Twelve he told them, "Ye have not chosen me, but I have chosen you, and ordained you" (John 15:16). In saying that, he established the truth that divine authority is vested in men only by deliberate selection from God and only on God's terms. True authority cannot come in any other way—whether by believing in the Holy Bible, by receiving educational degrees, or by feeling sincerely that one has been called.

The Church of Jesus Christ of Latter-day Saints asserts its claim to being Christ's church because, among other reasons, its authority is not of men. It was revealed from God:

". . . Peter, and James, and John, whom I have sent unto you, by whom I have ordained you and confirmed you to be apostles, and especial witnesses of my name, and bear the keys of your ministry and of the same things which I revealed unto them;

"Unto whom I have committed the keys of my kingdom, and a dispensation of the gospel for the last times; and for the fulness of times, in the which I will gather together in one all things, both which are in heaven, and which are on earth" (D&C 27:12–13).

Notes

1. Oliver Cowdery, *Latter Day Saints' Messenger and Advocate* 1, no. 1 (October 1834): 15; see JS–H, footnote at verse 71.

2. Ibid.

3. Andrew F. Ehat and Lyndon W. Cook, eds., *The Words of Joseph Smith: The Contemporary Accounts of the Nauvoo Discourses of the Prophet Joseph* (Provo, Utah: Religious Studies Center, Brigham Young University, 1980), 327; spelling and punctuation modernized in some quotations.

4. Cowdery, *Messenger and Advocate* 1, no. 1 (October 1834): 16.

5. Ehat and Cook, *Words of Joseph Smith,* 65.

6. Ibid., 157.

7. Ibid., 235.

8. Ibid., 236.

9. "[I] was informed that this office did not extend to the laying on of hands for the giving of the Holy Ghost, that that office was a greater work and was to be given afterwards, but that my ordination was a preparatory work, or a going before." Ibid., 327; see also 332–33.

10. For a discussion of the evidence, see Larry C. Porter, "Dating the Restoration of the Melchizedek Priesthood," *Ensign,* June 1979, 5–10; and "The Restoration of the Priesthood," *Religious Studies Center Newsletter* 9, no. 3 (May 1995), 1–12.

11. Ehat and Cook, *Words of Joseph Smith,* 38–39.

12. *Times and Seasons* 3, no. 11 (1 April 1842): 745.

13. Ehat and Cook, *Words of Joseph Smith,* 108.

14. Ibid., 158.

15. Ibid, 9.

Chapter 16

The Church of Jesus Christ

After his ordination by heavenly messengers in the spring of 1829, Joseph Smith had sufficient priesthood authority to organize the Church of Jesus Christ. But the time was not yet right. It seems the Lord's timetable required that the Book of Mormon be published before the organization would take place. By the next spring, the time was right: the Book of Mormon was published on 26 March, and the Church was organized on 6 April.

Establishing the Church

The divine communication we call section 20 of the Doctrine and Covenants was given to accompany the organization of the Church and provide the framework for its character. Although that communication was established as a founding document on the day the Church was organized, it was received sometime before that date. The Prophet's history places it, undated, between section 18 (June 1829) and section 19 (March 1830).[1] Much of this document reads as if it were a general handbook of instruction for the Church, and indeed that is what it is. It may well have been recorded over an extended period of time, as the Lord revealed administrative matters to his prophet in preparing for the establishment of the Church. We know also that parts of it were added some time after the Church was organized, as the Restoration continued. But by 6 April 1830, enough of the document was in place that it could serve as the "constitution" of the new Church. That it was a revelation from heaven is confirmed in the Prophet's preface to it, contained in his history: "In this manner did the Lord continue to give us instructions from time to time, concerning the duties which now devolved upon us; and among many other things of the kind, we obtained of Him the following, by the spirit of prophecy and revelation; which not only gave us much information, but also pointed out to us the precise day upon which, according to His will and commandment, we should proceed to organize His Church once more here upon the earth."[2] The revelation set the pattern for all things to follow: in the Lord's Church, both the substance and the timing are determined by the Lord's will.

At the time of its formal organization, the Church consisted of three congregations in three locations in New York: the Manchester-Palmyra members were mainly the Smith family, the Colesville group was primarily the Knight family, and the Whitmers were most of the group in Fayette. It was decided that the formal organization would take place at the Whitmer home in Fayette, the same home in which the last part of the Book of Mormon was translated.[3] In obedience to the Lord's will, the Prophet set the date as 6 April 1830. According to David Whitmer, about forty or fifty people were in attendance,[4] but for the purpose of the legal incorporation of the Church, six were designated as original, founding members.[5] The Prophet's history records that after prayer, the congregation was invited to sustain him and Oliver Cowdery to preside over the Church. Joseph Smith then ordained Oliver Cowdery as an Elder of the Church, after which Oliver Cowdery similarly ordained Joseph Smith. "We then took bread, blessed it, and brake it with them; also wine, blessed it, and drank it with them. We then laid our hands on each individual member of the Church present, that they might receive the gift of the Holy Ghost, and be confirmed members of the Church of Christ."[6] When John the Baptist had appeared in May 1829, he

Reconstructed home of Peter Whitmer Sr. in Fayette, New York. Site of the completion of the Book of Mormon translation in June 1829 and the organization of the Church on 6 April 1830

said that the Aaronic Priesthood did not include the power to lay on hands for the gift of the Holy Ghost, but that they would receive that authority thereafter (JS–H 1:70). Because that ordinance was performed on the day the Church was organized, it is evident that the Melchizedek Priesthood had already been restored by then.

The Prophet continued: "The Holy Ghost was poured out upon us to a very great degree—some prophesied, whilst we all praised the Lord, and rejoiced exceedingly."[7] The new church was called "the Church of Christ" (D&C 20:1). In 1838 its full name was revealed: "The Church of Jesus Christ of Latter-day Saints" (D&C 115:4).[8]

At this founding meeting and in its accompanying revelation, Joseph Smith's early visions were acknowledged (D&C 20:5–8), and the content and historicity of the Book of Mormon were confirmed (vv. 8–12). Several basic beliefs were announced as the doctrinal foundation of the Church of Christ. These included latter-day revelation and the necessity of accepting it (vv. 11–15), the reality of God (v. 17), the Creation (v. 18), the Fall (v. 20), the mission of Christ (vv. 21–25), the universality of the plan of salvation (vv. 26–27), the unity of the Godhead (v. 28), the first principles and ordinances of the gospel (vv. 25, 29), the doctrines of justification and sanctification (vv. 30–31), and the possibility of falling from grace (vv. 32–34). As the Restoration continued, later revelations confirmed and developed each of these important points.

Because of the Bible, many of the theological principles mentioned in Doctrine and Covenants 20 were common to the churches of the time, and thus our belief in them was not unique. But the revelation establishes two significant points that place our Church in a category by itself and show its independence from the ideas of the world.

First, all that we know of the gospel we learn through what was revealed to Joseph Smith. "The Lord God has spoken," the Prophet recorded, "and we, the elders of the church, have heard and bear witness" (v. 16). "By these things"—that is, by the revelations of Joseph Smith—"we know that there is a God in heaven," and so forth (v. 17), confirming that latter-day revelation is the true source of the teachings of the Church.

Second, the revelations of the Restoration prove "to the world that the holy scriptures are true" (v. 11). It does not work the other way around. We do not use the Bible to prove to the world that our beliefs are true, but we use the restored gospel to prove what is in the Bible and to evaluate every manifestation of Christianity that derives from it (1 Ne. 13:39–40). To the extent that other churches' beliefs are based on the Bible, they will concur to some degree with our own. We welcome those points of convergence. Yet as much as we love the Bible, we acknowledge that our doctrine comes from modern revelation found only in The Church of Jesus Christ of Latter-day Saints. Thus there will always be profound differences between our Church and the other denominations of Christianity.

Ordinances and Offices

"We wish it to be understood distinctly," wrote Elder Parley P. Pratt of the Quorum of the Twelve Apostles in 1841, "that the organization of this Church came by express commandment and revelation from the Almighty—that all its offices, ordinances, and principles, were given by inspiration of the Holy Ghost, by the voice of God, or by the ministering of angels."[9] Like the doctrine, the policies and procedures of the new Church were established by divine command.

The instructional focus of Doctrine and Covenants 20 is on the sacred ordinances and priesthood offices of the Church. Ordinances are actions that symbolize and activate spiritual processes. When performed by holders of the Lord's priesthood, they are acknowledged by him as binding and legitimate. The instructions on baptism specify qualifications for membership. Those who are humble, desire to be baptized, have "broken hearts and contrite spirits," repent, "and are willing to take upon them the name of Jesus Christ, having a determination to serve him to the end, and truly manifest by their works that they have received of the Spirit of Christ unto the remission of their sins, shall be received by baptism into his church" (v. 37). Instructions for the ordinance itself were specified (vv. 71–74), and the words of the prayer were given.

In a series of brief verses that gave direction to the new Church, the revelation announced additional policies. Priesthood ordinations and the setting apart to offices were outlined (vv. 60, 65–67), and the principle of common consent was established (vv. 63, 65). The blessing of babies was enjoined (v. 70), and the ordinance of the sacrament was set forth (vv. 75–79), including the same prayers over the bread and the wine that had been published already in the Book of Mormon (Moro. 4–5). That the translated

Nephite prayers are the same as those in the Doctrine and Covenants is a further testimony that our Church today continues the Lord's work from other periods of history. A revelation in August 1830 gave additional instructions concerning the sacrament (D&C 27:2–4).

Some regulatory and administrative procedures were established on the day the Church was organized, including guidelines for ordination certificates (v. 64), expectations for the behavior of new members (vv. 68–69), guidelines for dealing with transgressors (v. 80), guidelines for conferences (vv. 61–62, 81), and the need for record keeping (vv. 82–84).

Organizational matters too were set in place, including the offices of the priesthood that would govern the Church. At the time, those offices included elders (vv. 38–45), priests (vv. 46–52), teachers (vv. 53–59), and deacons (vv. 57–59).

Although the apostleship had already been restored, as is confirmed in verses 2, 3, and 38, it is easy to see that on the day of the Church's establishment, its organization was very simple, and much more was to come. Indeed, the Church was "restored" on 6 April 1830, but "the same organization that existed in the Primitive Church" (Article of Faith 6) came later, as the growing needs of the Church warranted the continued development of its structure. The organizational document itself was updated with the later revelation of new administrative information.[10] For example, the material in verses 66 and 67, which mentions "traveling bishops," "high councilors," and "high priests," was not part of the original document but was added by the Prophet in preparing the 1835 Doctrine and Covenants. Further organizational revelations were received as the Church continued to grow, creating more structure and more priesthood offices.

From our vantage point many years after the founding of the Church, we can see that its dramatic growth has necessitated additional inspired changes in its structure and organization. The Prophet's successors have continued and will yet continue to adjust the organization and policies of the Church to meet the changing needs of its members. We who believe in the divinity of the Church and in the Lord's guidance of its leaders gladly receive all that he sees fit to reveal for it, according to his own timetable. The important thing is that regardless of specific details of the Church's structure or procedures, the fundamental principle of its existence in any generation is that it is acknowledged of God and possesses the keys of his priesthood in the apostleship, including the keys of continuing revelation.

The Blessing of the Church

Some in the world believe that organized religion is a hindrance to individual freedom and religious expression. The Church of Jesus Christ of Latter-day Saints is one of the most organized and structured of religions, possessing a well-defined system of authority and accountability. But far from being a hindrance, its structure is one of its greatest strengths and provides an abundance of blessings for its members.

The Church is the delivery system of the gospel. It is the mechanism by which the full benefits of the Lord's plan are carried into the lives of those who have taken upon themselves Christ's name. Because of the Restoration, we can see the authority of the priesthood at work in the Church. Because the priesthood is a power that can be passed on only by those who already possess it—under the direction of those who hold its keys—the Church as an institution safeguards the purity of the priesthood and the integrity of the process by which it is conveyed. Because of the institution of the Church, we know the only channels through which the Lord's authority is exercised, and we are not deceived by counterfeits. Priesthood ordinations, baptisms, the sacrament, callings to service, and temple ordinances are among the blessings of the Church that are watched over carefully by those who have been called to do so. And these blessings are dispensed freely to those whom they serve.

In the same way that the institution of the Church safeguards the priesthood, it also assures the purity of gospel doctrine. To the Prophet Joseph Smith and his successors, the Lord has given "the keys of the mystery of those things which have been sealed, even things which were from the foundation of the world, and the things which shall come from this time until the time of [Christ's] coming" (D&C 35:18). Because they possess the keys of revelation, it is the prerogative of prophets, seers, and revelators to interpret doctrine in behalf of the Church and to teach that doctrine to us. The organization of the Church provides the carefully maintained channels through which the Lord's message is conducted into the lives of individual members. General and local conferences, ward meetings, Church magazines, teachers' manuals, the Church Educational System, broadcasts, films, and publications all provide the means whereby Latter-day Saints can hear the gospel taught with one inspired voice, through the mouths of those who have been called of God to teach it.

The Church's structure also blesses us by providing us the opportunity to help meet the needs of others. Through missionary work and other callings, members accept the privilege of caring for others and blessing their lives through service. Through channels of accountability, the cares and concerns of individuals are passed on to priesthood leaders, who can make available the impressive human resources of the Church. The gospel inspires us to seek occasions for service, and the Church provides opportunities. When those who have callings at any level do their duty, no individual member is far from the blessings of the gospel. Those who have been served by their brothers and sisters in the Church, as well as those who have been privileged to render service, can be thankful for the restoration of the Church of Jesus Christ.

Notes

1. See Dean C. Jessee, ed., *The Papers of Joseph Smith,* 3 vols. (Salt Lake City: Deseret Book, 1989–97), 1:239–41, 300; and Joseph Smith, *History of The Church of Jesus Christ of Latter-day Saints,* ed. B. H. Roberts, 2d ed. rev., 7 vols. (Salt Lake City: Deseret Book, 1957), 1:64–72.

2. Smith, *History of the Church,* 1:64; Jessee, *Papers of Joseph Smith,* 1:300.

3. For a discussion of the location and related issues, see John K. Carmack, "Fayette: The Place the Church Was Organized," *Ensign,* February 1989, 14–19. In anticipation of the one-hundred-fiftieth anniversary of the establishment of the Church in 1980, a replica of the Whitmer home was built on the original location in Fayette, using original foundation stones.

4. Edward Stevenson to Orson Pratt, 23 December 1877; Edward Stevenson to John Taylor, 7 January 1878; Lyndon W. Cook, ed., *David Whitmer Interviews: A Restoration Witness* (Orem, Utah: Grandin, 1991), 14, 17.

5. The six were probably Joseph Smith Jr., Oliver Cowdery, Hyrum Smith, Samuel H. Smith, David Whitmer, and Peter Whitmer Jr. See Richard L. Anderson, "Who Were the Six Who Organized the Church on 6 April 1830?" *Ensign,* June 1980, 44–45; and October 1980, 71.

6. Smith, *History of the Church,* 1:78; cf. Jessee, *Papers of Joseph Smith,* 1:303.

7. Ibid.

8. In the mid-1830s the Church was frequently called the "Church of the Latter Day Saints." See Richard L. Anderson, "What Changes Have Been Made in the Name of the Church?" *Ensign,* January 1979, 13–14.

9. *Millennial Star* 1, no. 1 (1841): 8.

10. See Robert J. Woodford, "The Historical Development of the Doctrine and Covenants," 4 vols. (Ph.D. diss., Brigham Young University, 1974), 1:299–353.

Chapter 17

Revelations to Guide the Church

When the Lord opened the heavens with the First Vision in 1820, he began a process that has remained in his Church to the present day—the process of continuing revelation to his chosen servants. God's communication to his prophets is one of the foremost characteristics of true religion, and it is an aspect of the Church that has been a profound blessing to its members.

Joseph Smith was called to lay the foundation for the Lord's kingdom in the last days. To bring about that work, the Lord directed his prophet's actions and enlightened his mind, granting him the companionship of the Holy Ghost and a wisdom beyond his natural abilities. On occasion the Prophet also received revelations of a more formal kind, in which the voice of the Lord came to his mind in actual words.

Even before the Church was established, the Prophet recognized the importance of recording the revelations he received. The Church of Jesus Christ was to be a church founded on and directed by communication from God, and Joseph Smith knew that the revelations would be the standard that would regulate both its doctrine and its practice.

About twenty revelations had been recorded by 6 April 1830. The revelation that accompanied the organization of the Church,

THE EVENING AND THE MORNING STAR.

Vol. I. Independence, Mo. June, 1832. No. 1.

Revelations.

THE ARTICLES AND COVENANTS OF THE CHURCH OF CHRIST.

THE rise of the Church of Christ in these last days, being one thousand eight hundred and thirty years since the coming of our Lord and Savior Jesus Christ, in the flesh; it being regularly organized and established agreeable to the laws of our country, by the will and commandments of God in the fourth month and on the sixth day of the month, which is called April: Which commandments were given to Joseph, who was called of God and ordained an Apostle of Jesus Christ, an Elder of this Church; and also to Oliver, who was called of God an Apostle of Jesus Christ, an Elder of this Church, and ordained under his hand; and this according to the grace of our Lord and Savior Jesus Christ to whom be all glory both now and forever. Amen.

For, after that it truly was manifested unto this first Elder, that he had received a remission of his sins, he was entangled again in the vanities of the world, but after truly repenting God ministered unto him by an holy angel, whose countenance was as lightning, and whose garments were pure and white above all white-

The duty of the Elders, Priests, Teachers, Deacons and members of the Churc of Christ. An Apostle is an Elder, and it is his calling to baptize and to ord other Elders, Priests, Teachers and Deacons, and to administer the flesh and blo of Christ according to the Scriptures, and to teach, expound, exhort, baptize, and watch over the Church, and to confirm the Church by the laying on of the hands and the giving of the Holy Ghost, and to take the lead of all meetings. The El ders are to conduct the meetings as they are led by the Holy Ghost. The Priests' duty is to preach, teach, expound, exhort and baptize, and administer the Sacra ment, and visit the house of each member, and exhort them to pray vocally and in secret, and also to attend to all family duties; and ordain other Priests, Teacher and Deacons, and take the lead in meetings; but none of these offices is he to d when there is an Elder present, but in all cases is to assist the Elder The Teach ers' duty is to watch over the Church always, and be with them, and strengthen them, and see that there is no iniquity in the Church, neither hardness with eac other, neither lying nor back-biting nor evil speaking; and see that the Church meet together often, and also see that all the members do their duty; and he is t take the lead of meetings in the absence of the Elder or Priest, and is to be as sisted always, and in all his duties in the Church by the Deacons; but neither th Teacher nor Deacons, have authority to baptize nor administer the Sacrament, but

The "Articles and Covenants of the Church of Christ" (D&C 20),
Evening and Morning Star, June 1832

which is now section 20 of the Doctrine and Covenants, was viewed as the foundational latter-day revelation. It was sustained by the vote of the members as the "Articles and Covenants" of the Church in a conference in June 1830 and on some similar occasions thereafter.[1] The sustaining of that important document was the latter-day beginning of canonization, the process by which members of the Church formally accept a revelation and acknowledge it as binding, authoritative, and scripture. Perhaps because the Bible and the Book of Mormon predated the establishment of the Church and had already been pronounced true by revelation (D&C 17:6; 20:8–11), they were accepted as scripture from the start and did not need to be canonized by the Saints.

The Book of Commandments

At a conference of the Church in the fall of 1831, the decision was made to publish in a book the revelations that had been received to that date. The Lord revealed a "preface" to the book (now D&C 1) as well as an "appendix" (now D&C 133) in conjunction with the conference. About seventy revelations had been recorded by that time. Only a few of them had been published,[2] but others were circulating in handwritten copies, which created the likelihood that different versions would evolve. Oliver

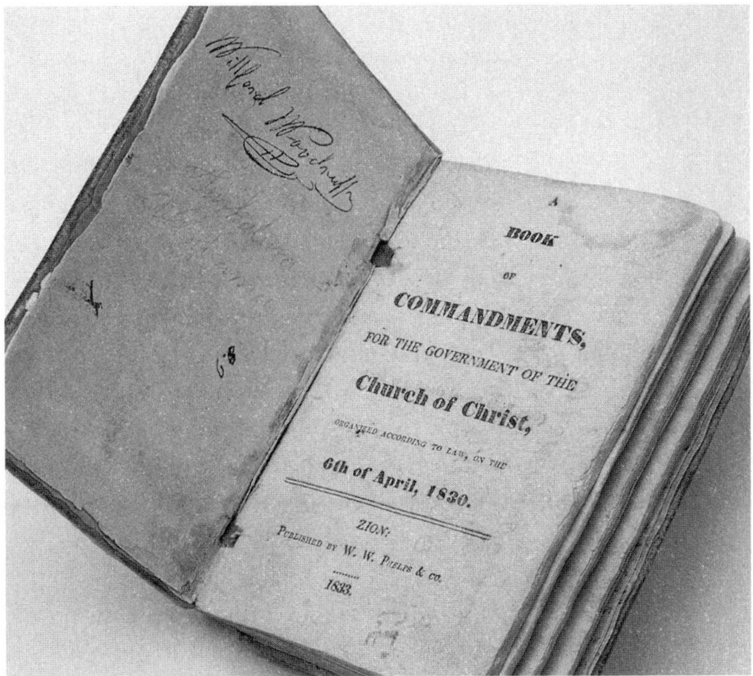

The Book of Commandments, 1833

Cowdery, the second elder of the Church, and W. W. Phelps, the Church's printer, were assigned to prepare the revelations for publication. The book was to be printed in Independence, Missouri, where Brother Phelps would soon set up a printing establishment. It would be called the Book of Commandments.

By the summer of 1833, the long process of typesetting had been underway for some months and was almost complete. Most of the pages had been printed. But on 20 July a mob broke into the printing shop, destroyed the press, and burned most of what had been printed. Church members rescued as many of the pages as they could, and from those pages about one hundred incomplete copies of the Book of Commandments were bound and published. It contained sixty-five of the revelations.

DOCTRINE AND COVENANTS

OF

THE CHURCH OF THE

LATTER DAY SAINTS:

CAREFULLY SELECTED

FROM THE REVELATIONS OF GOD,

AND COMPILED BY

JOSEPH SMITH Junior.
OLIVER COWDERY,
SIDNEY RIGDON,
FREDERICK G. WILLIAMS,

[Presiding Elders of said Church.]

PROPRIETORS.

KIRTLAND, OHIO.

PRINTED BY F. G. WILLIAMS & CO

FOR THE

PROPRIETORS.

1835.

The Doctrine and Covenants, 1835, first edition, title page

The Book of Commandments was never reprinted. As revelations continued to come to the Prophet, some were published in the Church's newspaper, the *Messenger and Advocate,* and thus received a measure of circulation among members of the Church. In time, however, it was decided that a new published collection was needed.

The Doctrine and Covenants

The first edition of the Doctrine and Covenants was published in Kirtland, Ohio, in 1835.[3] It contained 103 revelations.[4] At a conference in August that year, the revelations were canonized by the sustaining vote of the Church. The original members of the Quorum of the Twelve affixed their testimony to the collection of revelations and stated, in part: "We, therefore, feel willing to bear testimony to all the world of mankind, to every creature upon the face of the earth, that the Lord has borne record to our souls, through the Holy Ghost shed forth upon us, that these commandments were given by inspiration of God, and are profitable for all men and are verily true."[5]

The 1835 Doctrine and Covenants was in effect two books bound together in one cover. Included with the collection of revelations was another item called the "Lectures on Faith." These were doctrinal lessons presented by Church leaders in Kirtland, Ohio, in 1834 and 1835 at what was called the School of the Elders.[6] In a sense, they might be viewed as the equivalent of the Melchizedek Priesthood manual or the missionary training doctrinal manual of that day.

In 1844 a new edition of the Doctrine and Covenants, containing 111 sections, was published in Nauvoo, Illinois. The next edition was published in Salt Lake City, Utah, in 1876. It contained 136 sections and was divided for the first time into verses. It added more than twenty revelations that had been received in Joseph Smith's lifetime but had not been included in the Doctrine and Covenants before his death. The new Doctrine and Covenants was canonized at the general conference of the Church in October 1880. Official Declaration 1, the Manifesto on plural marriage, was canonized in 1890 and was printed with the Doctrine and Covenants beginning in 1908.

The 1921 edition was in use in the Church for sixty years. It introduced the familiar double columns, along with revised headings and footnotes. Beginning with the 1921 edition, the "Lectures on Faith" were no longer included in the Doctrine and Covenants.[7]

In 1981 another edition of the Doctrine and Covenants was published with new headings, footnotes, maps, and index.[8]

Sections 137 and 138 were added with that publication. Those two revelations had been known in the Church since they were received, but they had not been canonized until 1976. Official Declaration 2, the announcement of the revelation on priesthood, had been canonized in 1978 and was also included for the first time in the 1981 edition.

Perfecting the Church

Ecclesiastical matters became increasingly important after the Church was established formally on 6 April 1830. Organizational and administrative revelations came at the appropriate moments to meet the needs of Church growth and the changing circumstances of the Saints.

The first bishop was appointed early in 1831 (D&C 41:9). His calling began the process of revealing the duties of both the bishop over the whole Church, whom we now call the presiding bishop, and the bishops of local congregations (D&C 68:14–15; 72:10–12; 107:68–75, 87–88). Wards were first known in the Church in the 1840s in Nauvoo, where they were administrative divisions of the city. Over the course of time, they developed into the ecclesiastical units of the local level. Since the days of Joseph Smith, inspired prophets and apostles have continued to refine the bishops' role and the nature of the units over which they preside.

In 1831 the first high priests of the Church were ordained. An 1835 revelation designated the offices of elder and high priest as the two primary divisions of the Melchizedek Priesthood (see D&C 107:10–12).

The concept of the stake was revealed gradually, beginning in 1831, as the Church began dividing geographically between Zion, in Missouri, and Kirtland, Ohio. There would be a center place, and other organized areas would be the stakes of the tent of Zion (D&C 82:13–14; 101:21; 115:17–18). The first high council was called in 1834 to serve the Saints in the Kirtland area (D&C 102). Joseph Smith and his counselors in the First Presidency presided there. A presidency away from Church headquarters was called later that year, when David Whitmer, W. W. Phelps, and John Whitmer were called to preside over the Church in Missouri.[9] The term *stake* was not applied to these geographical areas until a few years later.

While these developments were taking place with local units, the general organization of the Church was being set in place. The role of the First Presidency unfolded in stages in 1832 and 1833, with Joseph Smith as president and Sidney Rigdon and Frederick G. Williams as counselors (D&C 81:1–2; 90:1–3, 6).[10] The calling and organization of the Twelve and the Seventy were made known in 1835 (D&C 107:22–27, 33–34, 38, 58, 93–98). Over the years, the Lord revealed more about their functions and the nature of their authority.

Although the Aaronic and Melchizedek Priesthoods had been restored in 1829, the duties of those priesthoods and the organization of their quorums were made known gradually in later years. A revelation in 1835 explained the structure of the quorums and their presidencies (D&C 107:10–14, 85–89).

For all those called to the Lord's priesthood, whether locally (as deacons, teachers, priests, elders, and high priests) or in the presiding quorums of general authorities (the Seventy, the Twelve, and the First Presidency), the Lord's message in the Doctrine and Covenants is the same, and it applies as well to each member of the Church in each calling: "Let every man learn his duty, and to act in the office in which he is appointed, in all diligence" (D&C 107:99).

In the years that have passed since the time of Joseph Smith, his successors in the presiding quorums of the Church have continued to perfect its organization and its function. The roles of each priesthood office have been refined as further experience and inspiration have guided God's servants. Continued growth and changing circumstances have brought about developments that were not needed in Joseph Smith's day but are vital parts of the

Church today. Missions, auxiliary organizations, units larger than stakes, and other administrative elements of the Church have all come in their due time, according to the Lord's wisdom. One of the hallmarks of Christ's Church is that as its needs change, he will inspire his chosen servants to refine it appropriately. The Doctrine and Covenants is a witness to that taking place in the early days of the Restoration.

Channels of Revelation

The Apostasy brought not only a cessation of revelation to the Church but also a loss of clear understanding concerning how persons can obtain revelation for the guidance of their own lives. Despite the scores of biblical examples of real prayer, many people have been taught that prayer consists of reciting memorized verses or that all the answers they would ever need are found in the pages of the Bible. Just as the Restoration establishes the Church and the priesthood as God's authorized channel for revealing his will to his people collectively, so it also gives all believers the keys by which they have access to the same divine source for their individual needs. The Restoration teaches us how to approach God and receive revelation for the conduct of our own lives.

Before moving to Harmony, Pennsylvania, to help Joseph Smith with the Book of Mormon translation, Oliver Cowdery had received a witness that Joseph Smith's work was of God and that he should assist with it.[11] But like many who have felt the influence of the Holy Ghost, he needed to be reassured of it, and he needed to learn the principles upon which inspiration would continue to be part of his life. The Lord said to him: "As often as thou hast inquired thou hast received instruction of my Spirit . . . I did enlighten thy mind; and now I tell thee these things that thou mayest know that thou hast been enlightened by the Spirit of truth" (D&C 6:14–15). Oliver was told, "Cast your mind upon the night that you cried unto me in your heart, that you might know concerning the truth of these things. Did I not speak peace to your mind concerning the matter?" (D&C 6:22–23).

As the Lord trained his disciples, he taught them that inspiration is neither easy nor automatic. His words to Oliver Cowdery concerning the Book of Mormon translation apply to all personal revelation: "You have supposed that I would give it unto you, when you took no thought save it was to ask me. But, behold, I say unto you, that you must study it out in your mind; then you must ask me if it be right, and if it is right I will cause that your bosom shall burn within you; therefore, you shall feel that it is right" (D&C 9:7–8).

It is instructive to note from the Lord's words that personal inspiration, following the necessary effort in study, prayer, and faith, would produce enlightenment, peace, and a feeling that something is right. These calm manifestations of the Spirit contrast sharply with some of the demonstrations of religiosity that were current in Joseph Smith's day and still remain in some branches of Christianity.

With respect to revelation for the Saints collectively, early sections of the Doctrine and Covenants teach that the only authorized channel is the head of the Lord's Church. "This generation shall have my word through you," the Lord said to Joseph Smith (D&C 5:10). "And this ye shall know assuredly—that there is none other appointed unto you to receive commandments and revelations until he be taken, if he abide in me" (D&C 43:3).

Just a few months after the Church was organized, one of the Eight Witnesses to the Book of Mormon, Hiram Page, stated that he had received a revelation concerning an important doctrinal matter. The Lord reminded the Church that the keys of revelation on such matters are in the hands of him who has been called to preside (D&C 28:1–7, 11–13). The Lord said concerning Hiram Page or anyone else who might feel called to reveal God's thoughts, "Behold, these things have not been appointed unto him" (D&C 28:12).

In a revelation a few months later, the Lord made the principle very clear: "It shall not be given to any one to go forth to preach my gospel, or to build up my church, except he be ordained by some one who has authority, and it is known to the church that he has authority and has been regularly ordained by the heads of the church" (D&C 42:11). This statement provided a foolproof safeguard for the purity of the new Church and protected its members against confusion about the true source of revelation and doctrinal authority. If a person is not called, sustained, and ordained by those who have been called, sustained, and ordained by the heads of the Church, that person has no authority to speak for God or for the Church (D&C 43:5–6).

Revelation to individuals through the gift of the Holy Ghost includes guidance concerning important personal decisions that affect their well-being. Foremost is a testimony of the gospel—a divinely revealed knowledge that God lives, that Jesus' atoning sacrifice has the power to save us from sin and death, and that the Church of Jesus Christ has been restored and is acknowledged of God.

The testimony of the Saints helps hold the Church together. Around the world, millions of Latter-day Saints have become active participants in the Restoration by receiving a testimony of its truthfulness. Because of that testimony, they acknowledge the authority and the inspiration of those who have been called of God to lead the Church, and they are willing to receive at their hands all that God has revealed in the past, all that he reveals now, and all that he will yet reveal in the future (Article of Faith 9). Such revelation has and will come through the president of the Church. As the Lord taught the Saints in 1830, others may enjoy the full benefits of the Holy Ghost to understand and teach what has been revealed for the Church already. But revelations to the Church will come through the Lord's prophets (D&C 28:1–2).

Notes

1. See Richard L. Anderson, "The Organization Revelations," in Robert L. Millet and Kent P. Jackson, eds., *The Doctrine and Covenants,* Studies in Scripture Series, vol. 1 (Salt Lake City: Deseret Book, 1989), 109–10.

2. Section 20, section 22, and part of section 27 were published in the (non-LDS) *Painesville Telegraph,* 19 April 1831.

3. For the history of the Doctrine and Covenants, see Robert J. Woodford, "Doctrine and Covenants Editions," in Daniel H. Ludlow, ed., *Scriptures of the Church* (Salt Lake City: Deseret Book, 1995), 280–84; or Daniel H. Ludlow, ed., *The Encyclopedia of Mormonism,* 5 vols. (New York: Macmillan, 1992), 425–27; and "The Doctrine and Covenants: A Historical Overview," in Millet and Jackson, *Doctrine and Covenants,* 3–22.

4. The last revelation is numbered 102, but erroneously two revelations had been numbered 66.

5. This testimony is found in the "Explanatory Introduction" of modern editions of the Doctrine and Covenants.

6. See Larry E. Dahl, "Lectures on Faith," in Ludlow, *Scriptures of the Church,* 410–16; or Ludlow, *Encyclopedia of Mormonism,* 818–21.

7. The introduction to the 1921 edition states: "Certain lessons, entitled 'Lectures on Faith,' which were bound in with the *Doctrine and Covenants* in some of its former issues, are not included in this edition. These lessons were prepared for use in the School of the Elders, conducted in Kirtland, Ohio, during the winter of 1834–1835; but they were never presented to nor accepted by the Church as being otherwise than theological lectures or lessons."

8. See Robert J. Matthews, "The New Publication of the Standard Works—1979, 1981," *BYU Studies* 22, no. 4 (fall 1982): 387–424.

9. Joseph Smith, *History of The Church of Jesus Christ of Latter-day Saints,* ed. B. H. Roberts, 2d ed. rev., 7 vols. (Salt Lake City: Deseret Book, 1957), 2:122–23.

10. See headnotes to sections 81 and 90; see also Lyndon W. Cook, *The Revelations of the Prophet Joseph Smith* (Provo, Utah: Seventy's Mission Bookstore, 1981), 170–72, 192.

11. Dean C. Jessee, ed., *The Papers of Joseph Smith,* 3 vols. (Salt Lake City: Deseret Book, 1989–97), 1:10; Lucy Mack Smith, *Biographical Sketches of Joseph Smith the Prophet and His Progenitors for Many Generations* (Liverpool: S. W. Richards, 1853), 128–29.

Chapter 18

Revelations to Glorify the Saints

In the Old Testament the word *Zion* appears about 150 times. In most instances it is synonymous with the word *Jerusalem* and has reference to that city and its people. In prophecies of the future, it is described in ideal terms. The word *Zion* does not appear in the New Testament. Through modern revelation, we learn that the concept of Zion as an ideal community of Saints was known among the Lord's people in ancient times, but the knowledge of it had been taken from the scriptures and lost from the world. It remained for the Restoration to bring it back, in all its fulness, so the Saints of the latter days would be privileged to establish Zion in preparation for Christ's coming.

But the Restoration reaches far beyond the building of Zion in the days of Joseph Smith. Its scope leads from his time into the Millennium, the ideal future day in which all the world will be Zion. From there we are taught of even greater things—the transcendent future blessings of those who inherit celestial glory. The revelations of the Doctrine and Covenants expand our horizons and point our vision into the eternities.

Building Zion

The earliest latter-day references to the establishment of Zion came in revelations during the spring of 1829 while the Book of Mormon was being translated. In separate revelations Oliver

Cowdery, Hyrum Smith, Joseph Knight Sr., and David Whitmer were each commanded, in almost identical words, to "seek to bring forth and establish the cause of Zion" (D&C 6:6; 11:6; 12:6; 14:6). Yet the revelations did not explain what Zion is nor make known the qualifications of those who would be part of it. Nor did the Book of Mormon translation reveal much concerning Zion. Outside of quotations from Isaiah, the word is found only about a dozen times in the Book of Mormon, and almost half of those are in the phrase "fight against Zion."[1] Very few of the Book of Mormon passages give enough context for us to develop an understanding of what Zion is and why the Saints should strive for it.

The restoration of the knowledge of Zion began in November and December 1830 with the restoration of the record of ancient Enoch through the Prophet Joseph Smith's inspired revision of the Bible. As we will see, the Joseph Smith Translation restored many things of significance, not the least of which was the knowledge that Enoch's people established Zion among them. Coming early in the Restoration, the account of Enoch and his society provided a model that Joseph Smith and the Saints of the latter days could follow.

The Doctrine and Covenants is the great book on Zion. In contrast to the few references to Zion in other scriptures, the Doctrine and Covenants uses the word in more than 180 places. It contains the Lord's revelations concerning its establishment, the covenants and obligations of those who would be its citizens, and its destiny from the Restoration into the Millennium. Because of those revelations, members of The Church of Jesus Christ of Latter-day Saints would have a clear focus on establishing Zion and being worthy to be part of it.

What is Zion? In the broadest sense, it is The Church of Jesus Christ of Latter-day Saints and its members throughout the world who earnestly strive to become "of one heart and one mind, and [dwell] in righteousness" with "no poor among them," as Joseph Smith learned in the record of Enoch (Moses 7:18). Though Zion is a place, the revelations teach us that it is also a community as well as a quality of the individuals in that community. Thus the references to Zion in the Doctrine and Covenants may be applied equally to a location as well as to the people of Zion anywhere. In our day, the character of Zion's people is more important than the geography of Zion's borders.

The restoration of the gospel included the revelation of the economic and social laws of Zion. Early in 1831 the Lord began to reveal the principles of consecration and stewardship. Saints who participated in a formally organized community consecrated all that they had to the Church. The bishop then gave them their portion, which was called an inheritance or a stewardship. It was theirs to use and develop. Surplus earnings from their stewardships were returned to the Church and used for public improvements and the inheritances of others.[2]

Relatively few Latter-day Saints were organized under this unique system of consecration. But the principles that guided it were to remain fundamental to the lives of all Church members, regardless of their economic conditions. Those principles include considering others' needs to be as important as our own (D&C 38:24–25; 82:19), unity (D&C 38:27), a commitment to "practise virtue and holiness" before the Lord (D&C 38:24), and a willingness to consecrate everything we have to God and his kingdom.[3]

The Prophet Joseph Smith learned that the center place of Zion, the New Jerusalem, will be located at Independence in Jackson County, Missouri, which is consecrated for the gathering of the Saints (D&C 57:1–3). There will be a temple there (D&C 84:4). Despite obstacles encountered by the early Saints in their efforts to establish that center place, the Lord has promised that it will one day be built and that its location has not changed (D&C 101:17, 20). In the meantime, stakes, which we can view as the extensions of Zion, will continue to be established throughout the world (D&C 101:21). The Saints are to gather to Zion (D&C

Temple site, Independence, Jackson County, Missouri. On the far right is the meetinghouse of the Church of Christ (Temple Lot). In the background at the right is the RLDS Stone Church

63:36) for a defense and a refuge (D&C 115:6). It will be their inheritance (D&C 38:19–20). But it can only be built on the principles of the law of the celestial kingdom (D&C 105:5), for its inhabitants must be the obedient (D&C 64:34–35) and the pure in heart (D&C 97:21).

The Restoration revealed the knowledge that Zion will be established and will flourish before Christ's coming (D&C 49:24–25). It will prosper (D&C 97:18) and be a place of peace and safety (D&C 45:66). Those of the world who renounce bloodshed will flee to it (D&C 45:68–69). Its inhabitants will be the Lord's people, the Lord will be their God (D&C 42:9), and his glory will be upon them (D&C 64:41). Zion will be an ensign to the world, and people of all nations will gather to it (D&C 64:42). The wicked will not come to it because the terror of the Lord will be upon it (D&C 45:67).

In accordance with the Lord's command, in the summer of

1831 the Prophet Joseph Smith went with other Church members to Jackson County to begin building the city of Zion at the appointed place. With the heavenly vision of the New Jerusalem in his heart, the Prophet knew that the Lord's promises concerning it would be fulfilled. But perhaps even the great seer, who saw the end from the beginning, was not shown the time sequence of Zion's redemption. The trials of the Saints in Missouri—beginning with their expulsion from Jackson County in 1833 and culminating in their expulsion from the state in 1838–39—caused him tremendous sorrow.[4]

When will Zion be redeemed? The revelations give us only broad hints. The Lord told his prophet that it would be "many years" before the Saints would receive their inheritance in Zion (D&C 58:44). One reason was opposition from the world. Another was the Saints' unreadiness; Zion could only be redeemed after chastening (D&C 100:13).

As the gospel spreads throughout the earth, Zion is being established wherever the Saints are found. In God's own due time, its center place will be built (D&C 136:18). The Lord's presence will go before the Saints to help them possess it (D&C 103:20). Its redemption will be as the deliverance of ancient Israel (D&C 103:15–18), meaning, it seems, that it will be brought about by acts of divine intervention rather than by human effort alone. The promises apply not only to the New Jerusalem but also to the pure in heart throughout the world, who build Zion wherever they are called to serve.

Enoch's city of Zion will return and join with the New Jerusalem (D&C 84:99–100; cf. Moses 7:63), and resurrected Saints will be with their Savior there (D&C 133:56). He will speak from Zion in the Millennium (D&C 133:20–21), and with the ultimate glorification of the earth, Zion will be the possession of the Saints in all eternity (D&C 38:20).

The Coming of the Lord

The Doctrine and Covenants reveals much concerning the events that will take place as the time approaches for Christ's second coming. The revelations on this topic are an important part of the Restoration, because they set forth in clarity what lies ahead for the Saints and the challenges they will face as they build God's kingdom on earth.

Through what we call natural disasters, the Lord will challenge the world to repent, while his servants will be at work all over the earth to claim those who desire to come unto Christ (D&C 88:84–85). The calamities that will take place will serve as signs to show that the coming of the Lord is near (D&C 45:35–38).[5] According to the revelations, the Saints will be able to recognize them and ascertain their message. The righteous will watch for the signs (D&C 39:23), and they will know them when they happen (D&C 68:11). Faithful Saints will be wise, they will receive the truth, they will take the Holy Spirit for their guide, and they will not be deceived (D&C 45:57). The forces of evil will not overcome them (D&C 38:9), but they will be preserved by God (D&C 101:12). Though in some instances they will barely escape, still the Lord will be with them (D&C 63:34), and they will be saved in Zion (D&C 115:6).

Modern revelation gives us a panoramic view of the Second Coming. Christ will come in glory (D&C 45:44) and in power (D&C 29:11). The mountains will flow at his presence (D&C 133:44), and the heavens and earth will shake (D&C 45:48). When he comes he will come in judgment (D&C 133:2), and the wicked will not survive (D&C 63:34).

At Jesus' coming, the Saints who have died since his resurrection will be resurrected themselves (D&C 45:45). They will then be caught up into the clouds to meet him (D&C 88:97–98), as will the Saints then living on earth (D&C 88:96). The Lord will be dressed in red when he appears, symbolizing the blood of those whom he will slay when he comes in judgment (D&C 133:46–51). All flesh will see him together (D&C 101:23). So great will be his glory that the sun will hide its face in shame at his presence, the moon will withhold its light, and the stars will be thrown from their places (D&C 133:49).

The Millennium—the thousand years of peace that will follow Jesus' coming—is presented in clear view in the Doctrine and Covenants. It will be the culmination of all our aspirations for Zion. In the Millennium, Zion will flourish to its fullest degree, with the center place at the New Jerusalem. When Christ returns, Satan will be bound (D&C 43:31). The earth will be glorified (D&C 101:25), and it will be translated, or transformed to a more sublime state.

Christ will dwell on earth a thousand years (D&C 29:11). He will be in the midst of his Saints, and he will be their king and lawgiver (D&C 45:59). They will be his people, and he will be their God (D&C 42:9). Those who have mourned will be comforted (D&C 101:14). There will be no sorrow; there will be no death (D&C 101:29). There will be no wickedness (D&C 29:9). In that day, all people will know the Lord (D&C 84:98), suggesting that they will be bound by covenant with him and will do his works. Everything that we ask will be given us (D&C 101:27). It will be a great day of revelation, for Christ will make known all things (D&C 101:32–34).

Men and women will continue to beget and bear children, who will be raised in a world dramatically unlike our own. A revelation explains that the children of the Saints in the Millennium will grow up without sin unto salvation (D&C 45:58). Although there will be no death, individuals will still need to undergo the process of resurrection, which for them will be a change from their translated state to a state of glory. The revelations teach that they will grow old, and then they will be "changed in the twinkling of an eye, and shall be caught up, and [their] rest shall be glorious" (D&C 101:30–31).

Translation room, John Johnson home, Hiram, Ohio, where much of the Joseph Smith Translation was revealed and where other important revelations were received, including the vision of the degrees of glory (D&C 76)

Eternal Glory

As a part of the restoration of the gospel for the last days, the Lord made known to the Prophet Joseph Smith what the ultimate destinies of God's children will be. Only a few revelations deal with that topic, yet those revelations open the heavens for us and shed light and knowledge not found anywhere else in scripture.

On 16 February 1832, Joseph Smith and his scribe, Sidney Rigdon, were engaged in the work of the translation of the Bible at the John Johnson home in Hiram, Ohio, where the Prophet was living at the time. In a great vision, which is now section 76 of the Doctrine and Covenants, the Lord revealed scenes of the ultimate destinies of the faithful and the unfaithful alike. What we learn about our final reward from that revelation and others is one of the major gifts of the Restoration.

Joseph Smith came to realize, before the vision was received, "that if God rewarded every one according to the deeds done in the body, the term 'heaven,' as intended for the Saints['] eternal home, must include more kingdoms than one."[6] Among the great contributions of this revelation is that it makes known that "heaven" consists of three separate degrees of glory, to be awarded according to faithfulness.

The celestial kingdom (D&C 76:50–70, 92–96) will be the inheritance of those "who shall come forth in the resurrection of the just"[7] (D&C 76:50). Its inhabitants will be those who receive "the testimony of Jesus," exercise faith, are baptized, overcome by faith, and are "sealed by the Holy Spirit of promise" (D&C 76:51–53). The Prophet learned later that the highest degree in the celestial kingdom will be for those who are sealed in "the new and everlasting covenant" of marriage (D&C 131:1–4; 132:15–21).

The Father will give "all things" into their hands; they will receive "of his fulness, and of his glory" (D&C 76:55–56). They will be "gods, even the sons of God—wherefore, all things are theirs, whether life or death, or things present, or things to come, all are theirs and they are Christ's, and Christ is God's" (D&C 76:58–59). They will live in the presence of the Father and the Son "forever and ever" (D&C 76:62). "These are they whose bodies are celestial, whose glory is that of the sun, even the glory of God, the highest of all" (D&C 76:70).

No one, except Jesus Christ, goes through life without sin. Thus no one can claim such a glorious reward on individual merits (D&C 76:61), and no one need suppose that one must be perfect in this life to return to the presence of God. Those who inherit the celestial kingdom will be "just" men and women who will be "*made* perfect through Jesus, . . . who wrought out this perfect atonement through the shedding of his own blood" (D&C 76:69; emphasis added).

Joseph Smith was taught that "he who is not able to abide the law of a celestial kingdom cannot abide a celestial glory" (D&C 88:22). The second degree of glory, the terrestrial kingdom

(D&C 76:71–80, 91, 97), will be inherited by those who do not accept God's law,[8] who do not accept[9] "the testimony of Jesus" in this life but do so "afterwards," who are the "honorable men of the earth, who were blinded by the craftiness of men" or who are "not valiant in the testimony of Jesus" (D&C 76:72–75, 79).

The inhabitants of the terrestrial glory are thus honorable persons who have the gospel but do not live it, or honorable persons who are not willing to accept the gospel before their final judgment. This glory, it seems, is the "heaven" to which so many good people all over the world look forward, and they will not be disappointed. Though they will not receive "of the fulness of the Father," they will receive "of the presence of the Son" and "of his glory" (D&C 76:76–77).

"He who cannot abide the law of a terrestrial kingdom cannot abide a terrestrial glory" (D&C 88:23). The telestial kingdom (D&C 76:81–90, 98–112), the least of the three degrees of glory, will be the inheritance of those who reject the gospel, the testimony of Jesus, the prophets, and the covenants (D&C 76:82, 101). This realm is reserved for those who are often identified in scripture as "the wicked" (e.g., Alma 11:41), who are liars, sorcerers, and adulterers (D&C 76:103). They will be "cast down to hell and suffer the wrath of Almighty God" (D&C 76:106), and they will not be freed "until the last resurrection" (D&C 76:85).

The great vision to Joseph Smith and Sidney Rigdon reveals that even those persons will be redeemed. Having rejected in life the benefits of the Atonement, they will suffer for their own sins until Christ's work is completed (D&C 76:106). Their suffering will bring both cleansing and, ultimately, a change of heart, for they "all shall bow the knee, and every tongue shall confess to him who sits upon the throne forever and ever" (D&C 76:110). Their final circumstances will be as varied as their behavior in life: "Every man shall receive according to his own works, his own dominion, in the mansions that are prepared" (D&C 76:111). In the eternal world they will enjoy the presence of neither the Father nor the Son, but "of the Holy Spirit," and "of the administering of angels who are appointed to minister for them" (D&C 76:86, 88). "And they shall be servants of the Most High; but where God and Christ dwell they cannot come, worlds without end" (D&C 76:112).

"He who cannot abide the law of a telestial kingdom cannot abide a telestial glory; therefore he is not meet for a kingdom of glory. Therefore he must abide a kingdom which is not a kingdom of glory" (D&C 88:24). The kingdom of no glory (D&C 76:30–38, 44–49) is reserved for those who are called "sons of perdition" (D&C 76:32). This outer darkness is for those who know and have partaken of God's power and yet allow themselves to be overcome, who deny the truth, defy God's power, deny the Holy Spirit "after having received it," deny Christ, "having crucified him unto themselves and put him to an open shame," and "deny the Son after the Father has revealed him" (D&C 76:31, 35, 43). For these there is "no forgiveness in this world nor in the world to come" (D&C 76:34).

The vision reveals that aside from those very few who will go to the kingdom of no glory, Christ's awesome atoning power will redeem all of humankind. "For all the rest shall be brought forth by the resurrection of the dead, through the triumph and the glory of the Lamb." Indeed, as the Prophet and his scribe testified, "This is the gospel, the glad tidings, which the voice out of the heavens bore record unto us—that he came into the world, even Jesus, to be crucified for the world, and to bear the sins of the world, and to sanctify the world, and to cleanse it from all unrighteousness; that through him all might be saved whom the Father had put into his power and made by him" (D&C 76:39–42).

Even the least of the degrees of glory, the telestial kingdom, "surpasses all [mortal] understanding" (D&C 76:89). Yet it pales in comparison with the terrestrial, as the brightness of a star pales next to that of the moon (D&C 76:81). And as the brightness of the moon pales in comparison with that of the sun, so also is the terrestrial glory eclipsed by the glory of the celestial kingdom, whose inhabitants will receive "the fulness of the Father" (D&C 76:71).

How glorious is God's eternal work, and how privileged we are to live in a day when the knowledge of it has been revealed. The understanding of our future possibilities—prepared through the atonement of Christ and based on our willingness to obey him—is one of the great gifts of the Restoration.

Notes

1. The phrase "fight against Zion," used by Book of Mormon authors, may have been borrowed from Isaiah 29:8.

2. See Richard O. Cowan, *The Doctrine and Covenants: Our Modern Scripture* (Salt Lake City: Bookcraft, 1984), 73–76; and Lyndon W. Cook, *Joseph Smith and the Law of Consecration* (Provo, Utah: Grandin Books, 1985).

3. See Spencer W. Kimball, "Becoming the Pure in Heart," *Ensign,* May 1978, 81.

4. See Dean C. Jessee, ed., *The Personal Writings of Joseph Smith* (Salt Lake City: Deseret Book, 1984), 308–9.

5. For a survey of some of the prophesied judgments, see Kent P. Jackson, "Prophecies of the Last Days in the Doctrine and Covenants and the Pearl of Great Price," in *The Heavens Are Open: The 1992 Sperry Symposium on the Doctrine and Covenants and Church History* (Salt Lake City: Deseret Book, 1993), 168–71.

6. Dean C. Jessee, ed., *The Papers of Joseph Smith,* 3 vols. (Salt Lake City: Deseret Book, 1989–97), 1:372.

7. "In an *evangelical sense,* righteous; religious; influenced by a regard to the laws of God; or living in exact conformity to the divine will"; Noah Webster, *An American Dictionary of the English Language* (New York: S. Converse, 1828; facsimile reproduction, San Francisco: Foundation for American Christian Education, 1980), s.v. "just."

8. The phrase "died without law" (D&C 76:72) seems to imply an unwillingness to accept the law, not a lack of opportunity. An 1836 revelation makes it clear that lack of opportunity in this life will not be a hindrance to an inheritance in the celestial kingdom (D&C 137:5–9).

9. The primary meaning of *receive* in Joseph Smith's day was "to accept." Webster, *Dictionary,* s.v. "receive."

Chapter 19

The Joseph Smith Translation of the Bible

One legacy of the Restoration is the love that Latter-day Saints have for the Old and New Testaments. In the broad spectrum of Christians, we align ourselves with those who believe in the Bible, have faith that its ancient writers were inspired, and reject the trends in modern society that devalue it and its teachings. In many circles today, the Bible has been removed from the position of honor that it once held. Its history has been explained away as myth, the divine perspective of its authors has been viewed as primitive, and the moral standard that it has held to the world for almost two thousand years has been rejected as archaic and oppressive. We can be grateful for the many good Christians who have held fast to this book, and we join with them in expressing our thanks to God for it.

Through the Restoration, we learn that the Bible did not arrive in the modern world in a pure state. Early in the Book of Mormon, Nephi informs us that before the Bible would be taken to the nations, it would be tampered with through the hands of a "great and abominable church" which would remove "precious things" from its texts (1 Ne. 13:23–29). Joseph Smith stated: "Many important points, touching the salvation of man, had been taken from the Bible, or lost before it was compiled."[1] On another occasion he said, "[There are] many things in the Bible which do not, as they now stand, accord with the revelation of the Holy Ghost to me."[2] And he believed in the Bible "as it ought to be, as it came from the pen of the original writers."[3] But "ignorant translators, careless transcribers, or designing and corrupt priests have committed many errors."[4]

The restoration of the gospel was in part the restoration of the Bible. It was the restoration of biblical history that had been lost through the processes just described. It was the restoration of biblical texts that had suffered the same fate. And more important, it was the restoration of biblical doctrine that had been either removed, distorted, or simply misinterpreted by a world that did not enjoy the fulness of the gospel.

The New Translation

Shortly after the Church was organized, the Prophet Joseph Smith undertook, in response to divine command, a careful reading of the Bible that eventually led to the restoration of many of the "precious parts" that Nephi had foretold would be taken from it.[5] In June 1830, the first revealed addition to the Bible was put in writing when the Prophet received and recorded a preface to the book of Genesis (now known as Moses 1). Over the next few years, he made changes, additions, and corrections as were given him by revelation as he studied the Bible. Collectively, these are called the Joseph Smith Translation (JST).

Joseph Smith had the authority to make changes in the Bible as God directed. In one revelation he is called "a seer, a revelator, [and] a translator" (D&C 107:92). He called his Bible revision a "translation," though it did not involve creating a new rendering from original Hebrew or Greek manuscripts. He never claimed to have consulted any text other than his English Bible, but he "translated" it in the sense of conveying its meaning in a new form. It appears that different categories of changes were involved in the process:[6]

Restoration of original text. Because we know through

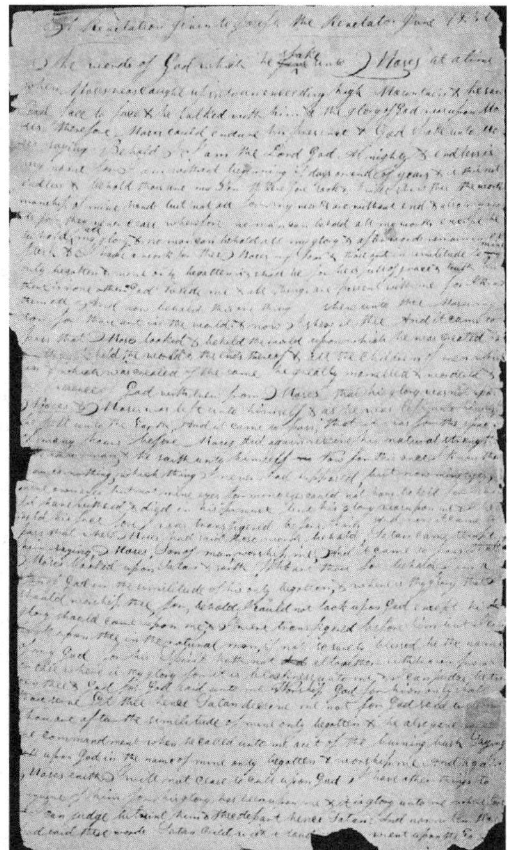

First page of the manuscript of the Joseph Smith Translation of the Old Testament, in the handwriting of Oliver Cowdery, 7¾ x 13 inches, containing Moses 1:1–19a

revelation that some things in the Bible were deleted or corrupted, we can be sure that the Joseph Smith Translation includes the restoration of words that were once in original manuscripts. In Moses 1:40–41, the Lord foretells the removal of material from an ancient record, as well as its restoration in the latter days.

Restoration of what was once said or done but which was never in the Bible. Perhaps the Joseph Smith Translation includes, for example, statements by prophets that were never recorded or teachings or events in Jesus' ministry that were not included originally by the biblical writers.[7]

Editing to make the Bible more understandable for today's readers. The Prophet's revisions include changing the word order to make a text read more easily or modernizing the language of the King James Version, as in the change from *saith* to *said* or from *that* and *which* to *who.*[8]

Editing to bring biblical wording into harmony with truth found in other revelations or elsewhere in the Bible. We believe that it was well within the scope of Joseph Smith's calling to change what needed to be changed in the Bible, regardless of the source of discrepancies or inaccuracies.

Working with his scribes,[9] the Prophet began with Genesis in June 1830 and continued with it for about twenty-four chapters until the following spring, when he interrupted that work to translate the New Testament (D&C 45:60–62). From March 1831 until February 1833, his translation efforts were concentrated on the New Testament. After that he returned to the Old Testament, which he finished in July 1833.[10] During the course of this work, changes were made in about thirteen hundred Old Testament verses and in about twenty-one hundred verses in the New Testament.[11] Many of the changes are simple rewordings of the existing King James Translation text. But other changes involve the addition of new material—in some cases substantial amounts—or even the deletion of existing words.

The Prophet considered the new translation finished by the summer of 1833, but he made changes in it periodically through the rest of his life. He sought to find the means to publish it in a book, but circumstances did not allow him to do so. Some excerpts were printed in Church periodicals under his direction, so sections of it were available during his lifetime. Still, when he was killed in 1844, he had not seen the realization of his desire to have the entire new translation appear in print.[12]

In 1851, Elder Franklin D. Richards of the Quorum of the Twelve Apostles was serving as president of the British mission in Liverpool. He recognized the need to make available for the

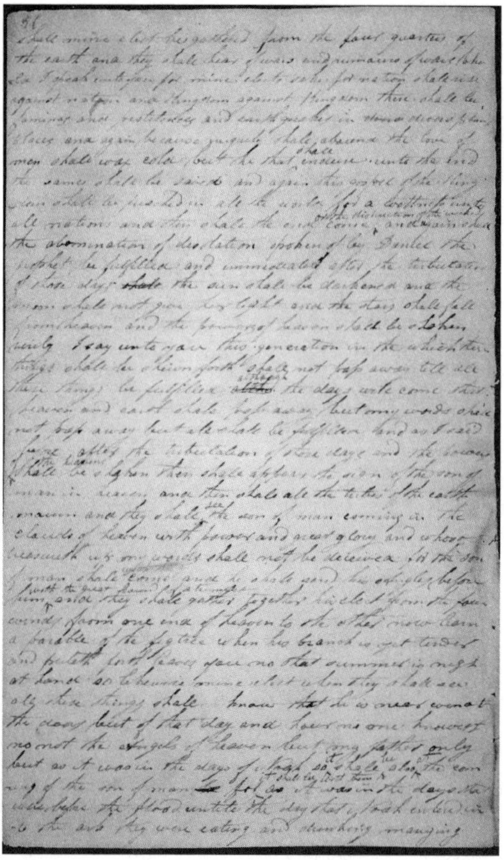

A page of the manuscript of the Joseph Smith Translation of the New Testament, in the handwriting of Sidney Rigdon, 7¾ x 13¼ inches, containing Joseph Smith–Matthew 1:27b–42b

British Saints some of Joseph Smith's revelations that had been published already in America, so he compiled a mission booklet entitled *The Pearl of Great Price.*[13] In it he included, among other important texts, some excerpts from the Prophet's new translation of the Bible: the first few chapters of Genesis, and Matthew 24.[14] Over the course of time, Elder Richards's compilation became a popular item of literature among members of the Church. Because most of the British Saints eventually emigrated to America, so also did the popularity of *The Pearl of Great Price*. In the 1870s the decision was made to prepare it for churchwide distribution.

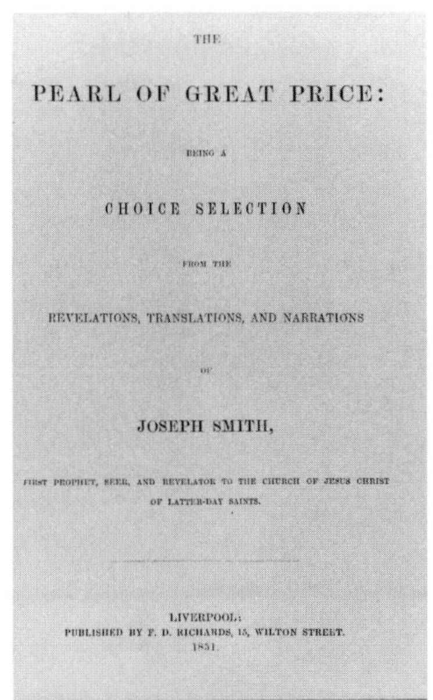

THE

PEARL OF GREAT PRICE:

BEING A

CHOICE SELECTION

FROM THE

REVELATIONS, TRANSLATIONS, AND NARRATIONS

OF

JOSEPH SMITH,

FIRST PROPHET, SEER, AND REVELATOR TO THE CHURCH OF JESUS CHRIST OF LATTER-DAY SAINTS.

LIVERPOOL:
PUBLISHED BY F. D. RICHARDS, 15, WILTON STREET.
1851.

1851 *Pearl of Great Price,* title page

The first Salt Lake edition was published in 1878. In the October 1880 general conference, it was presented to the assembled membership for a sustaining vote and was canonized as scripture and accepted as binding on the Church. Since then, the Pearl of Great Price has been one of the standard works, and the few chapters of the Joseph Smith Translation in it have been recognized not only as divine revelation—which they always were—but also as integral parts of our scripture and doctrine.

When Joseph Smith died, the manuscripts of the Joseph Smith Translation were in the possession not of the Church but of members of his family who remained in Illinois when the Saints moved west. In 1867, the Reorganized Church of Jesus Christ of Latter Day Saints published the new translation under the title, *Holy Scriptures.* The name *Inspired Version* was added in 1936. Because the Saints in Utah possessed neither the copyright nor the original manuscripts, the publication was not widely used in our Church.[15]

CONTENTS.

viii. CONTENTS.

INDEX TO WOODCUTS.

1851 *Pearl of Great Price,* contents pages

In 1979 the Church published a Latter-day Saint edition of the Bible in the English language, which included generous amounts of material from the Joseph Smith Translation in footnotes and in an appendix. Perhaps the most significant aspect of the new publication was that it made Joseph Smith's translation accessible to an extent that it had never been before. Since then, general authorities, Church curriculum writers, and scholars and students have drawn freely from it in their research and writing, bringing the translation to its rightful place alongside the other revelations of the Prophet Joseph Smith.

The Revelation of Biblical Truth

The Joseph Smith Translation is a revelation of profound importance and holds a significant place in the Restoration. Many of the characteristic beliefs of the Church derive from it, including many of the doctrines that set our religion apart from the rest of modern Christianity. Few Latter-day Saints appreciate what this great work has contributed to our faith. Following is a sample of some of the topics on which the Joseph Smith Translation reveals significant new truths. Several of these points are revealed nowhere else, and almost all of them are unknown in the doctrines of traditional Christianity. Collectively, they are a flood of doctrinal light and a great blessing of the Restoration.

The nature of deity. The Joseph Smith Translation is an additional witness to the corporeal nature of God: God has a body. Although the Bible teaches the same thing (Gen. 1:26–27; Ex. 33:11; Deut. 4:28; Acts 7:56), the revelation of this truth in clear and unmistakable terms in the Joseph Smith Translation establishes it beyond question. God created Adam "in the image of his own body" (Moses 6:9). God has a face, which can be seen (JST, Ex. 33:20). Enoch saw the Lord, "and he stood before my face, and he talked with me, even as a man talketh one with another, face to face" (Moses 7:4; cf. JST, John 1:18; 1 Tim. 6:15–16; 1 Jn. 4:12).

The scope of the Father's work. The Joseph Smith Translation gives us a faint glimpse into the extent of the Father's creative work, to which there is no end. We learn that he has created "worlds without number"—inhabited worlds that have run, or are running, the course of their existence, as ours is. God's creations are innumerable to us but are known individually to him. Yet in his wisdom, he has chosen to reveal to us only the things that pertain to our own earth (Moses 1:36). In all of his work, spanning as it does both time and space, there is one overriding purpose and motive. As he told Moses, "This is my work and my glory—to bring to pass the immortality and eternal life of man" (Moses 1:39; see also 1:33–39).

The mission of Jesus Christ. From the Joseph Smith Translation we learn much about Christ that is not taught in such clarity in the Bible. We learn that he had a pre-earthly existence in which he was chosen to execute the Father's plan. Already in that sphere he was called the Only Begotten of the Father. He had great power there and was able to cast Satan out for his rebellion

(Moses 4:2–3). We learn that he was the Creator, not only of this world but of all the Father's "worlds without number" (Moses 1:33). And throughout the New Testament, the Joseph Smith Translation adds insights that bring greater life and meaning to Jesus' mortal ministry, greater clarity to his words, and greater purpose to his mission (e.g., JST, Luke 3:5).

The plan of salvation. The Lord's plan of happiness is revealed in the Joseph Smith Translation in plain and clear terms, even in the Old Testament. We read of the necessity of faith, repentance, baptism, and the reception of the Holy Ghost. We learn that Jesus Christ is "the only name which shall be given under heaven, whereby salvation shall come unto the children of men" (Moses 6:52). We learn of the nature of Christ's atonement and how it responds both to Adam's transgression and to our own individual sins. And we are reminded that this redemption is "unto all men, through the blood of [the] Only Begotten" (Moses 6:62).

The character and motives of Satan. In passages that have no biblical counterpart, the Joseph Smith Translation gives us a clear picture of the circumstances that brought Satan to his fallen condition. In it we read that he refused to accept the Father's plan for our happiness but stepped forward with his own self-motivated propositions: he would be God's son, he would "redeem all mankind, that one soul shall not be lost," and the Father would give him His honor. From the Joseph Smith Translation we learn that this "plan," like everything else about Satan, was a lie—a campaign promise that he could not keep. He rebelled against God and was "cast down," drawing many after him. He then made it his purpose "to deceive and to blind men, and to lead them captive at his will, even as many as would not hearken unto [God's] voice" (Moses 4:1–4). In the Joseph Smith Translation we see the scriptures' clearest exposé of Satan's character. After trying unsuccessfully to tempt Moses, he "ranted upon the earth, and commanded, saying: I am the Only Begotten, worship me." When that also proved unsuccessful, Satan trembled, shaking the earth, and "cried with a loud voice, with weeping, and wailing, and gnashing of teeth" (Moses 1:12, 19–22). Moses recorded an account of these things about Satan and his motives, but none of it is found in the Bible.

The fall of Adam. The Joseph Smith Translation reveals some of the most important information we have concerning the fall of Adam and Eve. Adam said, "Blessed be the name of God, for because of my transgression my eyes are opened, and in this life I shall have joy, and again in the flesh I shall see God." Eve added, "Were it not for our transgression we never should have had seed, and never should have known good and evil, and the joy of our redemption, and the eternal life which God giveth unto all the obedient" (Moses 5:10–11).

The tone of these important words is foreign to the Bible that we have received through the centuries and to the beliefs of Augustine and others who established the Christian doctrine that has been passed down to our time.

The antiquity of the gospel. The Joseph Smith Translation teaches, through passages not contained in the Bible, that the gospel of Jesus Christ was revealed in the beginning of human history. Adam was a Christian and was baptized (Moses 6:51–62, 64–66). He and Eve taught the gospel of Christ to their children (Moses 5:9–12). Their descendants, such as Enoch and Noah, believed in Christ, worshiped the Father in his name, and preached faith in his atonement, repentance, baptism in similitude of his death and resurrection, and the laying on of hands for the gift of the Holy Ghost (Moses 7:10–11; 8:23–24). Abraham was also a Christian, knew the plan of salvation, and, as the Savior himself said, rejoiced to see the distant coming of Jesus Christ in the flesh (John 8:56; JST, Gen. 15:12). Moses knew Christ, understood the gospel, and knew of Christ's role as Creator and Redeemer (Moses 1:6, 32–33; 4:1–4). All the prophets testified of Jesus (JST, Matt. 4:18–19; Luke 16:16–17).

The doctrine of the priesthood. The Joseph Smith Translation teaches us things about the priesthood that cannot be learned from the Bible. Adam held what we today call the Melchizedek Priesthood (Moses 6:67), which is "the order of the Son of God, which order was without father, without mother, without descent, having neither beginning of days, nor end of life. And all those who are ordained unto this priesthood are made like unto the Son of God" (JST, Heb. 7:3). They shall "have power, by faith, to break mountains, to divide the seas, . . . to stand in the presence of God; to do all things according to his will, according to his command; . . . and this by the will of the Son of God which was from before the foundation of the world" (JST, Gen. 14:30–31).

The Joseph Smith Translation gives us information about the history of the priesthood that is entirely unknown in the Bible. We read that when Israel rebelled in the days of Moses, the Lord decreed: "I will take away the priesthood out of their midst; therefore my holy order, and the ordinances thereof, shall not go before them" (JST, Ex. 34:1).

The establishment of Zion. The early part of Genesis in the Joseph Smith Translation has a clear emphasis on teaching us the principles of the establishment of Zion. The focus is on the ministry of Enoch and his people, who successfully created a "City of Holiness, even ZION" (Moses 7:19). In the Old Testament, Enoch is mentioned in just six verses (Gen. 5:18–19, 21–24). In striking contrast, the account of Enoch and his people in the Joseph Smith Translation covers 116 verses (Moses 6:21, 25–8:2), making it by far the largest and most dramatic addition to the Bible in the Joseph Smith Translation. It is not insignificant that the account of Enoch was revealed so early in the Restoration (November to December 1830), when the Lord was beginning to lay the foundation for the establishment of Zion among his latter-day Saints.[16]

The doctrine of translation. In conjunction with the principles of the establishment of Zion, the Joseph Smith Translation reveals the doctrine of translation—the removal of sanctified persons from the earth. Genesis simply states, without explanation or context, that Enoch "walked with God: and he was not; for God took him" (Gen. 5:24). The Joseph Smith Translation shows that this was the culmination, for an entire society, of living the principles of Zion over many years. "And Enoch and all his people walked with God, and he dwelt in the midst of Zion; and it came to pass that Zion was not, for God received it up into his own bosom; and from thence went forth the saying, ZION IS FLED" (Moses 7:69; see also 21, 27). The Joseph Smith Translation also teaches that Enoch's city will return in the last days (JST, Gen. 9:21–23).

In a generation long after Enoch, as we learn only from the Joseph Smith Translation, another great leader established Zion and prepared his people to enter the presence of God. With faithfulness and the power of the priesthood, Melchizedek and his people "wrought righteousness, and obtained heaven, and sought for the city of Enoch which God had before taken, separating it from the earth" (JST, Gen. 14:34; see also 26–36).

The destiny of the house of Israel. The Joseph Smith Translation adds unique insights to our understanding of the family of Abraham. It restores Paul's words that Christ's mediation under the new covenant was "written in the law concerning the promises made to Abraham and his seed." "The promise which God made unto Abraham" was that Jesus was "the mediator of life" (JST, Gal. 3:20). The Joseph Smith Translation reveals a prophecy, not contained in the Bible, in which ancient Jacob foretold the destiny of the descendants of his son Joseph. Describing their great latter-day work to take the gospel to the rest of Israel, Jacob foretold the following: "For thou shalt be a light unto my people, to deliver them in the days of their captivity, from bondage; and to bring salvation unto them, when they are altogether bowed down under sin" (JST, Gen. 48:11). Joseph, seeing the distant future, foretold the ministry of "a choice seer" of his lineage who would "do a work" for his brethren of Israel. "And he shall bring them to the knowledge of the covenants" which God made with their fathers. He would both bring forth the Lord's word and also convince Israel of the Lord's word which they would already have. The records of Joseph and Judah would "grow together unto the confounding of false doctrines, and laying down of contentions, and establishing peace, . . . and bringing them to a knowledge of their fathers in the latter days; and also to the knowledge of my covenants, saith the Lord" (JST, Gen. 50:26–31). The choice seer to the house of Israel in this prophecy, which is entirely unknown to the Bible, was Joseph Smith.

The purpose of animal sacrifice. The Joseph Smith Translation teaches us that the origin of animal sacrifice was in the first generation of history and that its intent was to point worshipers to Christ. An angel told Adam that it was "a similitude of the sacrifice of the Only Begotten of the Father, which is full of grace and truth" (Moses 5:7).

The origin of the law of Moses. The Joseph Smith Translation provides a unique revelation concerning the law of Moses. After the golden calf incident, the Lord withdrew from Israel his sacred law—"my holy order, and the ordinances thereof" (JST, Ex. 34:1), "the everlasting covenant of the holy priesthood" (JST, Deut. 10:2). In place of that higher law and the blessings that pertain to it, the law of Moses was instituted as "the law of a carnal commandment; for I have sworn in my wrath, that they shall not enter into my presence, into my rest, in the days of their pilgrimage" (JST, Ex. 34:2).

The second coming of Jesus. Joseph Smith–Matthew in the Pearl of Great Price, an excerpt from the Joseph Smith Translation, is a great revelation concerning the last days and the coming of Jesus. Under inspiration, the Prophet reorganized the structure of Matthew 24 and added some new verses, thereby separating the prophecies about Jerusalem and the Early Church (JS–M 1:1–21a) from those about the last days (JS–M 1:21b–55). This inspired revision makes sense of a very difficult biblical chapter that otherwise cannot be understood fully.

Historical information. The Joseph Smith Translation adds some historical details that in some cases have doctrinal implications. Among others, new information on the following individuals is given: Adam, Eve, Enoch, and Melchizedek (cited above), Saul (JST, 1 Sam. 16:14–16), David (JST, 1 Kgs. 3:14; 11:4, 6, 33, 39), Solomon (JST, 1 Kgs. 3:1), Jesus (JST, Matt. 3:24–25 [at 2:23]; 4:1–9), the Twelve (JST, Matt. 6:25–27; Mark 14:36 [at 14:32]), and Judas (JST, Mark 14:28). These are only a few examples of individuals whose lives receive clarification in the Joseph Smith Translation

For the Salvation of God's Elect

With these impressive gospel contributions and others like them, the Joseph Smith Translation gives us the scriptures "even as they are in [God's] own bosom, to the salvation of [his] elect" (D&C 35:20). But these are not the only blessings that we receive through the Joseph Smith Translation. The new translation contributes to the development of the Latter-day Saint faith even in ways other than the changes that the Prophet made in the Bible.

First, many of the principal teachings and practices of the Church were put in place during the years 1830 through 1833, while the Prophet was most actively involved in translating the Bible. Almost 60 percent of the sections in the Doctrine and Covenants were revealed during those three years, and many of those revelations were the result of issues and questions raised during the Bible translation.

Second, the inspired effort that produced the Joseph Smith Translation was also the source of much of the doctrinal education of Joseph Smith himself. The work was its own reward because of all that he gained in the process of receiving and recording the new translation. The Prophet's impressive familiarity with the Bible, which is so evident in his later sermons and writings, was in large part the product of his work on the Joseph Smith Translation. That labor was an important aspect of his schooling in the doctrines of the kingdom. He learned the Bible well, but he learned even better the gift of prophecy that guided his labors to bring about this part of the doctrinal restoration. We, his students who have received the message of salvation through his ministry, continue to be blessed by all that he learned and taught.

Notes

1. Dean C. Jessee, ed., *The Papers of Joseph Smith,* 3 vols. (Salt Lake City: Deseret Book, 1989–97), 1:372.

2. Andrew F. Ehat and Lyndon W. Cook, eds., *The Words of Joseph Smith: The Contemporary Accounts of the Nauvoo Discourses of the Prophet Joseph* (Provo, Utah: Religious Studies Center, Brigham Young University, 1980), 211; spelling and capitalization modernized.

3. Ibid., 256.

4. Joseph Smith, *History of The Church of Jesus Christ of Latter-day Saints,* ed. B. H. Roberts, 2d ed. rev., 7 vols. (Salt Lake City: Deseret Book, 1957): 6:57.

5. The comprehensive treatment of the Joseph Smith Translation is Robert J. Matthews, *"A Plainer Translation": Joseph Smith's Translation of the Bible, a History and Commentary* (Provo, Utah: Brigham Young University Press, 1975).

6. For similar categorizations, see Robert L. Millet, "Joseph Smith's Translation of the Bible: A Historical Overview," in *The Joseph Smith Translation: The Restoration of Plain and Precious Things,* eds. Monte S. Nyman and Robert L. Millet (Provo, Utah: Religious Studies Center, Brigham Young University, 1985), 43–44; and Matthews, *"A Plainer Translation,"* 253.

7. It may be that this is what Joseph Smith had in mind when he stated, "From what we can draw from the scriptures relative to the teachings of heaven we are induced to think, that much instruction has been given to man since the beginning which we have not"; *Evening and Morning Star* 2, no. 18 (March 1834): 143.

8. It might also include "translating" archaisms or cultural oddities into modern counterparts. An example might be Romans 16:16, in which "Salute one another with *an* holy *kiss"* is changed to "Salute one another with *a* holy *salutation."*

9. The principal scribes were Oliver Cowdery, Sidney Rigdon, John Whitmer, and Frederick G. Williams.

10. See Matthews, *"A Plainer Translation,"* 96.

11. Ibid., 425.

12. Ibid., 40–48, 52–53.

13. For the history of the Pearl of Great Price, see H. Donl Peterson, *The Pearl of Great Price: A History and Commentary* (Salt Lake City: Deseret Book, 1987), 6–24.

14. Including also the last verse of Matthew 23. The 1851 *Pearl of Great Price* contained the following: the preface and the first six chapters of Genesis from the Joseph Smith Translation (now called "Selections from the Book of Moses"), Matthew 23:39–24:51 from the Joseph Smith Translation (Joseph Smith–Matthew), the book of Abraham, parts of five sections from the Doctrine and Covenants (no longer included), parts of the Prophet's 1838 history (Joseph Smith–History), the Articles of Faith, and a poem entitled "Truth" (no longer included but now hymn number 272 in the LDS hymnbook).

15. During the 1960s and 1970s, careful research into the manuscripts by Brigham Young University professor Robert J. Matthews confirmed for both churches that the RLDS *Inspired Version* was a faithful and accurate transcription of the original manuscripts.

16. See "Building Zion" in Chapter 18, 182–86.

Chapter 20

The Book of Abraham

The book of Abraham first came to light as a result of the purchase by the Church of some ancient Egyptian papyrus documents in 1835.[1] The documents consisted of "two papyrus rolls, besides some other ancient Egyptian writings with them."[2] During the latter half of that year, the Prophet Joseph Smith labored intermittently to translate the documents and publish their content to the world. His history states: "Much to our joy [we] found that one of the rolls contained the writings of Abraham, another the writings of Joseph of Egypt."[3]

The ongoing drama of the early days of the Church, combined with the press of Joseph Smith's other responsibilities, made it impossible for him to finish the translation as soon as he had hoped. But in the early part of 1842, in Nauvoo, he was able to devote his attention again to the records and finally publish the text of what we now call the book of Abraham.[4] It appeared in print in the 1 March and 15 March issues of the Church's newspaper, the *Times and Seasons*.[5] More material than we have now from the book of Abraham was anticipated after the first installments were published.[6] But the hope of receiving the remainder of Abraham's record, as well as that of Joseph, has not yet been realized.

The Prophet did not describe the revelatory process that produced the book of Abraham. Thus we do not have all the answers concerning the history of the papyrus documents that the Prophet

704

A TRANSLATION

Of some ancient Records that have fallen into our hands, from the Catecombs of Egypt, purporting to be the writings of Abraham, while he was in Egypt, called the Book of Abraham, written by his own hand, upon papyrus.

The Book of Abraham.

In the land of the Chaldeans, at the residence of my father, I, Abraham, saw that it was needful for me to obtain another place of residence, and finding there was greater happiness and peace and rest for me, I sought for the blessings of the fathers and the right whereunto I should be ordained to administer the same; having been myself a follower of righteousness, desiring also to be one who possessed great knowledge, and to be a greater follower of righteousness, and to possess a greater knowledge, and to be a father of many nations, a prince of peace; and desiring to receive instructions, and to keep the commandments of God, I became

that the priest made an offering unto the God of Pharaoh, and also unto the God of Shagreel, even after the manner of the Egyptians. Now the God of Shagreel was the Sun. Even the thank-offering of a child did the priest of Pharaoh offer upon the altar, which stood by the hill called Potiphar's Hill, at the head of the plain of Olishem. Now, this priest had offered upon this altar three virgins at one time, who were the daughters of Onitah, one of the Royal descent, directly from the loins of Ham. These virgins were offered up because of their virtue; they would not bow down to worship Gods of wood or of stone, therefore they were killed upon this altar, and it was done after the manner of the Egyptians.

4. And it come to pass that the priests laid violence upon me, that they might slay me, also, as they did those virgins, upon this altar; and that you might have a knowledge of this altar, I will refer you

The opening text of the book of Abraham,
Times and Seasons, 1 March 1842

possessed, their relationship to his published translation, the possibility that more documents once existed, the possibility of other extant but as yet undiscovered documents, and the connection between the extant fragments and the published text.[7] But what we know is sufficient for the present—that the book of Abraham is a revelation from God and that its translation was revealed to bless the world with gospel light.

The book of Abraham was included in Elder Franklin D. Richards's British mission booklet, *The Pearl of Great Price,* when it was first compiled in 1851. With the rest of that book, it was canonized as scripture by the sustaining vote of the Church in 1880.

A Doctrinal Restoration

As a major contributor to the restoration of the gospel, the profound effect of the book of Abraham on our religion comes from the unique material that it contains. The following items are some that add significantly to our understanding by revealing things that were misunderstood or entirely unknown to the world in 1835.

God and the order of the universe. Joseph Smith made reference to the "the system of astronomy" contained in Abraham's record.[8] The book of Abraham teaches us that there is order in the cosmos as manifested in stars, planets, and moons. But more important than any astronomical lesson is the lesson that the stars, planets, and moons teach us about things unseen. Abraham's great vision reveals the order of the universe's citizens, with God the Father in his position as the greatest of all the countless beings:

"And the Lord said unto me: These two facts do exist, that there are two spirits, one being more intelligent than the other; there shall be another more intelligent than they; I am the Lord thy God, I am more intelligent than they all. . . . My wisdom excelleth them all, for I rule in the heavens above, and in the earth beneath, in all wisdom and prudence, over all the intelligences thine eyes have seen from the beginning" (Abr. 3:19, 21; see also 1–24).

Later in the vision, Abraham saw Jehovah, or Jesus Christ. Though Christ was among "the intelligences that were organized before the world was" (Abr. 3:22), already in that premortal setting he was a transcendent being who was "like unto God" (Abr. 3:24). These truths counter centuries of Christian tradition about the origin and nature of God and Christ and lay the groundwork for other revelations to come.

The premortality of humankind. The book of Abraham gives us our best scriptural view into our premortal existence (Abr. 3:22–28). We learn, first of all, that we lived as intelligent beings before our earthly birth, which is a doctrine that was rejected by the Christian church of late antiquity. We were in the presence of the Father and the Son and received instruction from them concerning the course of our eternal existence. That we had agency—

the capacity to make rational choices and be accountable for them—is shown in the fact that even then we could be obedient or rebellious. From the book of Abraham we learn about what the Prophet Joseph Smith called the "Grand Council" in heaven.[9] We read of "noble and great ones" who were instructed by the Father and the Son in that setting.

The reason for life on earth. It is in Abraham's account of the Grand Council that we have the clearest statement in the scriptures concerning the purpose of humankind's mortal existence. The Father had a plan for us, to be carried out by the Son, that would bless the lives of those who would follow it. We would be tested on earth to see if we would "do all things whatsoever the Lord [our] God shall command [us]." If we would remain faithful in our premortal life, we would advance to mortality. If we would be faithful in that second, mortal, estate, we would "have glory added upon [our] heads for ever and ever" (Abr. 3:25–26). Joseph Smith later explained the principle that underlies this process: "All mind[s] and spirit[s] God ever sent into the world are susceptible of enlargement."[10] "The relationship we have with God places us in a situation to advance in knowledge. God has power to institute laws to instruct the weaker intelligences that they may be exalted with himself,"[11] "that they might have one glory upon another in all that knowledge, power, and glory. And so [he] took in hand to save the world of spirits."[12]

Satan's rebellion. In the Grand Council in heaven, as depicted in the book of Abraham, significant information concerning the origin of Satan is revealed. He was with those "noble and great ones" who were in the Father's presence before the creation of the earth. The book of Abraham teaches us that because God chose Christ instead of him, Satan became "angry, and kept not his first estate," meaning that he did not remain faithful in his premortal existence. He fell, and "many followed after him" (Abr. 3:27–28). None of this important information, which gives us insights into the character of the adversary, was available before the Restoration.

The Creation. The contribution of the book of Abraham includes new truths about the Creation. In the Abrahamic account, the Creation is accomplished by "the Gods." This reference continues the emphasis from the discussion of the premortal council. Christ said, "*We* will go down, . . . and *we* will take of these materials, and *we* will make an earth whereupon these may dwell" (Abr. 3:24, emphasis added; see Abr. 4–5). In contrast to the doctrines of medieval Christianity, the book of Abraham teaches that the earth would be made of already existing "materials," a subject on which Joseph Smith provided additional information: "The word create came from the word *bārā'*. [It] doesn't mean so; it means to organize, same as [a] man would use to build a ship. Hence we infer that God had materials to organize from—chaos, chaotic matter. Element had an existence from the time [God] had. The pure principles of element are principles that never can be destroyed; they may be organized and reorganized, but not destroyed."[13]

Abraham's life and priesthood. The book of Abraham contains historical material that is not found in the Bible, including important information about Abraham's family background. His "fathers" turned from their righteousness and became worshipers of pagan gods. The account of their efforts to sacrifice Abraham to their gods helps us view his history in the Bible in an entirely new light (see Gen. 22:1–18; Abr. 1:5–15). From the book of Abraham, we learn the reality and eternity of the priesthood and that it has been on the earth since the beginning. As "a follower of righteousness," Abraham sought and received the priesthood. He "became a rightful heir, a High Priest, holding the right belonging to the fathers." His priesthood "came down from the fathers, from the beginning of time, yea, even from the beginning, or before the foundation of the earth" (Abr. 1:2–4).

The Abrahamic covenant. The book of Abraham gives us

information in just a few verses that broadens our understanding of the Abrahamic covenant. We learn important things about the mission of Abraham's descendants, the future of the house of Israel, the principle of adoption, and Israel's relationship to the other nations of the earth. The Lord said to Abraham: "I will make of thee a great nation, and I will bless thee above measure, and make thy name great among all nations, and thou shalt be a blessing unto thy seed after thee, that in their hands they shall bear this ministry and Priesthood unto all nations. And I will bless them through thy name; for as many as receive this Gospel shall be called after thy name, and shall be accounted thy seed, and shall rise up and bless thee, as their father" (Abr. 2:9–10).

The Abundance of Peace and Truth

Because there is much we do not know about how we received the book of Abraham, it has been a frequent target of critics of the Church. But those who read its text in faith, with the intent of being taught the things of God, will respond as did the early Saints when they first understood its value: "Truly we can say, the Lord is beginning to reveal the abundance of peace and truth."[14]

The book of Abraham was brought forth to be one of the primary tools of the Restoration, revealing much about the nature of God, the nature of human existence, the nature of God's eternal plan for his children, and the power of the covenants and ordinances by which we become his heirs. It ties us with our premortal existence and thus also with our eternity.

It may be that only the temple brings us nearer to our roots. It seems perhaps significant that the records of Abraham and Joseph came to light and were on the Prophet's mind while the Kirtland Temple was under construction, in preparation for the revelation of its blessings. Perhaps it is also noteworthy that the Prophet published what we have of the book of Abraham while the Nauvoo Temple was being built, in the months that preceded the first endowment ordinances of modern times. The records of Abraham and Joseph may have played a part in the restoration of these sublime things. Elder Bruce R. McConkie suggested that the temple ordinances "were given in modern times to the Prophet Joseph Smith by revelation, many things connected with them being translated by the Prophet from the papyrus on which the book of Abraham was recorded."[15]

We do not know the content of the rest of the Abrahamic record, but we look forward to receiving it when the time is right. Nor do we know what is contained in the record of ancient Joseph. We can be certain, however, that in the Lord's time, all things will be revealed that are of importance to his children—either while the world continues or after the coming of Christ.

Notes

1. For an account of the history behind the book of Abraham, see H. Donl Peterson, *The Story of the Book of Abraham: Mummies, Manuscripts, and Mormonism* (Salt Lake City: Deseret Book, 1995).

2. W. W. Phelps to Sally Waterman Phelps, 19–20 July 1835, "Writing to Zion: The William W. Phelps Kirtland Letters (1835–1836)," ed. Bruce A. Van Orden, *BYU Studies* 33, no. 3 (1993): 555.

3. Joseph Smith, *History of The Church of Jesus Christ of Latter-day Saints,* ed. B. H. Roberts, 2d ed. rev., 7 vols. (Salt Lake City: Deseret Book, 1957), 2:236.

4. Peterson, *Story of the Book of Abraham,* 158.

5. *Times and Seasons* 3, no. 9 (1 March 1842): 703–6; 3, no. 10 (15 March 1842): 719–22; 3, no. 14 (16 May 1842): 783. Facsimile 1 was published in the 1 March 1842 issue, Facsimile 2 in the 15 March issue, and Facsimile 3 in the 16 May issue.

6. Elder John Taylor wrote the year before the Prophet's death: "We had the promise of Br. Joseph, to furnish us with further extracts from the Book of Abraham. These with other articles that we expect from his pen . . . we trust will make the paper sufficiently interesting." *Times and Seasons* 4, no. 6 (1 February 1843), 95.

7. Some of these questions are explored in Peterson, *Story of the Book of Abraham.*

8. Dean C. Jessee, ed., *The Papers of Joseph Smith,* 3 vols. (Salt Lake City: Deseret Book, 1989–97), 2:45.

9. Andrew F. Ehat and Lyndon W. Cook, eds., *The Words of Joseph Smith: The Contemporary Accounts of the Nauvoo Discourses of the Prophet Joseph* (Provo, Utah: Religious Studies Center, Brigham Young University, 1980), 345, 367; spelling and punctuation modernized in some quotations.

10. Ibid., 341.

11. Ibid., 346.

12. Ibid., 352.

13. Ibid., 359.

14. Smith, *History of the Church,* 2:236.

15. Bruce R. McConkie, *Mormon Doctrine,* 2d ed. (Salt Lake City: Bookcraft, 1966), 779.

Chapter 21

The Restoration of Keys

Joseph Smith received both the Aaronic and the Melchizedek Priesthoods some months before the Church was organized. With those priesthoods, he also received the *keys*—the right to preside in them and to pass them on to others. But those were not the only keys the Prophet would receive. In due time, the Restoration brought back to earth other keys, which empowered him and his successors to carry on specific priesthood responsibilities.

In December 1830, only eight months after the organization of the Church, the Lord instructed his Saints in New York to migrate to Ohio (D&C 37:3). "There I will give unto you my law," he said, "and there you shall be endowed with power from on high" (D&C 38:31–32). The law that they received in Ohio was section 42 of the Doctrine and Covenants, which revealed information on Church government, moral behavior, the establishment of Zion, and the law of consecration.

The endowment "with power from on high" began to come a few years later when the Kirtland Temple was built. On 3 April 1836, Joseph Smith and Oliver Cowdery, the president and assistant president of the Church, were praying in the newly dedicated Kirtland Temple. The Prophet reported, "The veil was taken from our minds, and the eyes of our understanding were opened" (D&C 110:1). Jesus Christ came to acknowledge and receive his holy house (D&C 110:2–10). Then three others appeared in succession—Moses, Elias, and Elijah—each bringing spiritual blessings to the Church.[1]

Moses and the Gathering of Israel

Joseph Smith recorded the coming of Moses: "The heavens were again opened unto us; and Moses appeared before us, and committed unto us the keys of the gathering of Israel from the four parts of the earth, and the leading of the ten tribes from the land of the north" (D&C 110:11). Moses' earthly career was a mission of great importance to the house of Israel. Through his service, God made a people out of the spiritually scattered and lost Israelites, restored to them the knowledge of who they were, delivered them from bondage, revealed a law to them, established their government under priesthood and prophetic authority, bound them to him under sacred covenants, and set them on a course that would lead them to their promised land.

All of those blessings constituted the gathering and the restoration of Israel. Moses was the bearer of the keys associated with those events, and his name will be forever associated with that mission. It is fitting that as part of the latter-day restoration of the gospel, he conferred them on his modern counterpart Joseph Smith, whose calling was to continue that work in our time.

It is not difficult to see close parallels between the mission of Moses and that of Joseph Smith (JST, Gen. 50:24–36). Through the work of Joseph Smith, God would make a people out of those who were spiritually scattered and lost, restore to them the knowledge of who they were, deliver them from spiritual bondage, reveal a law to them, establish their government under priesthood and prophetic authority, bind them to him under sacred covenants, and set them on a course that would lead to the establishment of Zion. In the work of Joseph Smith and his successors, we see the fruit of the keys that were restored by Moses.

Moses' keys are the keys of missionary work for Israel but also for those whom the scriptures call the Gentiles, who become members of the covenant family when they accept the gospel. The mission of the Church in the latter days, assisted by the keys that Moses restored, is to all: "The voice of warning shall be unto all people, by the mouths of my disciples, whom I have chosen in these last days. And they shall go forth and none shall stay them, for I the Lord have commanded them" (D&C 1:4–5).

Missionary work had been underway since the beginning of the Restoration. Moses' keys put the seal on that labor and enabled the work of gathering to continue at an even greater pace. A year after he appeared, the restored gospel was taken for the first time to countries outside North America, resulting ultimately in the conversion of thousands. The gathering to the covenants of the gospel has continued since the days of Joseph Smith. The millions who are now members of the Lord's Church are testimony to the power of the keys that Moses restored.

Elias and the Abrahamic Covenant

After Moses departed from Joseph Smith and Oliver Cowdery, "Elias appeared, and committed the dispensation of the gospel of Abraham, saying that in us and our seed all generations after us should be blessed" (D&C 110:12). Though the identity of the messenger is not clear, the nature of his keys seems to be more certain. Elias brought to the Church "the dispensation of the gospel of Abraham." The words "in us and our seed all generations after us should be blessed" are reminiscent of biblical promises pertaining to God's covenant with the ancient Patriarchs (e.g., Gen. 22:18) and reflect the promises that were revealed in the book of Abraham only months before Elias's coming (Abr. 2:9–11). It appears, then, that the messenger Elias restored keys pertaining to the covenant of Abraham, keys through which worthy men and women join in that covenant to create eternal family units.

Faithful Saints, by virtue of those keys, are married not only for time but also for eternity. Their children are sealed to them, as they are to their faithful ancestors before them (D&C 132:19–20,

Kirtland Temple, Kirtland, Ohio. These Melchizedek Priesthood pulpits in the main floor assembly room were the site of the appearance of Jesus, Moses, Elias, and Elijah on 3 April 1836 (D&C 110). Photo, 1935

30–31). In ways that have not been revealed, their exaltation brings them "a continuation of the seeds forever and ever" that will "continue as innumerable as the stars" (D&C 132:19, 30).[2]

Because the name *Elias* is often used in scripture as a title to represent a forerunner—a messenger who goes ahead to prepare the way for a greater revelation—we do not know if the name is used as a title of the messenger in this manifestation, or if the angelic visitor who appeared in the Kirtland Temple was a man by that name. Perhaps the Elias who restored the keys of the Abrahamic covenant was Abraham himself, or a contemporary of Abraham, or someone of his lineage who held the keys.

Elijah and the Sealing Keys

The final angelic key holder who appeared to Joseph Smith and Oliver Cowdery on that occasion was Elijah. He said:

"Behold, the time has fully come, which was spoken of by the mouth of Malachi—testifying that he [Elijah] should be sent, before the great and dreadful day of the Lord come—to turn the hearts of the fathers to the children, and the children to the fathers, lest the whole earth be smitten with a curse—therefore, the keys of this dispensation are committed into your hands; and by this ye may know that the great and dreadful day of the Lord is near, even at the doors" (D&C 110:14–16).

This was not the first time Joseph Smith had been instructed concerning the mission of Elijah. When Moroni appeared to him on 21–22 September 1823, Moroni taught him by quoting Malachi 4:5–6, which foretells Elijah's coming (JS–H 1:38–39; D&C 2:1–3). Moroni's version changes the verses from those in the Bible to emphasize Elijah as a restorer of priesthood power. The resurrected Christ quoted the same verses to Lehi's children (3 Ne. 25:5–6), and Joseph Smith discussed them on several occasions.[3]

Elijah restored the keys of the sealing power.[4] Most often we consider this power in the context of the redemptive work for the dead and the "welding link" that temple work creates "between the fathers and the children" (D&C 128:18; see also 17). According to Joseph Smith, Elijah's keys "turn the hearts of the children to the *covenant* made with their fathers,"[5] they "*reveal* the covenants of the fathers to the children and of the children to the fathers, *that they may enter into covenant with each other,*"[6] and they "*seal* the hearts of the fathers to the children—and the children to the parents."[7]

But Elijah's keys do even more; they seal and validate *all* ordinances of the priesthood so that ordinances performed on earth are binding in heaven as well. Joseph Smith taught: "Elijah was the last prophet that held the keys of this priesthood, and who will, before the last dispensation, restore the authority and deliver the keys of this priesthood in order that all the ordinances may be attended to in righteousness. . . . Why send Elijah? Because he holds the keys of the authority to administer in all the ordinances of the priesthood. And without the authority is given, the ordinances could not be administered in righteousness."[8] Moreover, "the spirit, power, and calling of Elijah is that ye have power to hold the keys of the revelations, ordinances, oracles, powers, and endowments of the fulness of the Melchizedek Priesthood and of the kingdom of God on the earth, and to receive, obtain, and perform all the ordinances belonging to the kingdom of God."[9]

The appearance of Moses, Elias, and Elijah in the Kirtland Temple repeated in many ways the similar event that the ancient apostles Peter, James, and John experienced, as recorded in the New Testament (Matt. 17:1–9). At that time, as in 1836, the Lord was beginning a new dispensation of his Church, and ancient holders of priesthood power came to pass on the keys of their ministry to enable the Lord's work to be carried forward. In the latter days, this transmittal of keys was an indispensable step in the process of the Restoration.

Keys, Honors, Majesty, and Glory

Because the Prophet Joseph Smith was very circumspect regarding spiritual events, we are not privileged to know everything he knew and experienced. We know, however, that other ancient prophets appeared to him and conveyed to him the keys of their callings so the Church in our day would be able to fulfill its divinely appointed role: "Now, what do we hear in the gospel which we have received? A voice of gladness! A voice of mercy from heaven; and a voice of truth out of the earth; glad tidings for the dead; a voice of gladness for the living and the dead; glad tidings of great joy. . . . And the voice of Michael, the archangel; the voice of Gabriel, and of Raphael, and of divers angels, from Michael or Adam down to the present time, all declaring their dispensation, their rights, their keys, their honors, their majesty and glory, and the power of their priesthood" (D&C 128:19, 21).

The Restoration would be comprehensive, because in this, the final dispensation of the gospel, "all things which are in Christ Jesus, whether in heaven or on the earth, shall be gathered together in him, and . . . all things shall be restored, as spoken of by all the holy prophets since the world began: for in it will take place the glorious fulfillment of the promises made to the fathers, while the displays of the power of the Most High will be great, glorious, and sublime."[10]

In the spring of 1844, a few weeks before his death, Joseph Smith passed on the keys that he had received to the Quorum of the Twelve Apostles. President Wilford Woodruff, who was there, remembered the Prophet's words as follows: "I have sealed upon your heads all the keys of the kingdom of God. I have sealed upon you every key, power, principle that the God of heaven has revealed to me. Now, no matter where I may go or what I may do, the kingdom rests upon you. . . . But, ye apostles of the Lamb of God, my brethren, upon your shoulders this kingdom rests; now you have got to round up your shoulders and bear off the kingdom."[11]

"Said he, during that period, 'I now rejoice. I have lived until I have seen this burden, which has rested on my shoulders, rolled on to the shoulders of other men; now the keys of the kingdom are planted on the earth to be taken away no more for ever.' But until he had done this, they remained with him; and had he been taken away they would have had to be restored by messengers out of heaven. But he lived until every key, power and principle of the holy Priesthood was sealed on the Twelve and on President Young, as their President."[12]

Fully empowered with all the keys of the priesthood, the Twelve were able to go forward in the work that God had begun through Joseph Smith. Though all who have been ordained to the Quorum of the Twelve bear all the keys, they are fully activated in the person of the senior apostle, who is the president of the Church. As new members of the Twelve are called, they receive those same keys, and thus the Lord's power is continued in his

Church in the fifteen men who compose the First Presidency and the Quorum of the Twelve. The latter-day Church has never been without the keys since they were first restored.

Notes

1. For a review of the events that led up to these manifestations, see Milton V. Backman Jr., *The Heavens Resound: A History of the Latter-day Saints in Ohio, 1830–1838* (Salt Lake City: Deseret Book, 1983), 284–308.

2. These blessings are discussed in Chapter 22, 230–34.

3. Joseph Smith, *Joseph Smith's Commentary on the Bible,* comp. and ed. Kent P. Jackson (Salt Lake City: Deseret Book, 1994), 69–74.

4. See Charles R. Harrell, "Turning the Hearts of the Fathers and the Children," in Robert L. Millet and Kent P. Jackson, eds., *The Doctrine and Covenants,* Studies in Scripture Series, vol. 1 (Salt Lake City: Deseret Book, 1989), 57–63.

5. Andrew F. Ehat and Lyndon W. Cook, eds., *The Words of Joseph Smith: The Contemporary Accounts of the Nauvoo Discourses of the Prophet Joseph* (Provo, Utah: Religious Studies Center, Brigham Young University, 1980), 242; emphasis added.

6. Ibid., 241; emphasis added.

7. Ibid., 336; emphasis added.

8. Ibid., 43.

9. Ibid., 329.

10. *Times and Seasons* 1, no. 12 (October 1840): 178.

11. *Millennial Star* 51 (1889): 546–47; see also *Times and Seasons* 5, no. 20 (1 November 1844): 698–70.

12. In *Journal of Discourses,* 26 vols. (London: Latter-day Saints' Book Depot, 1855–86), 13:164 (12 December 1869).

Chapter 22

The Holy Temple

The revelation of God's house and its sacred activities did not come to Joseph Smith all at once but rather in stages, beginning in 1831 with the command to build a temple in Independence, Missouri (D&C 57:3; 58:57). In time, the Lord enlightened his prophet with other insights, including an understanding of the construction and purpose of the temple in Kirtland. The temple revelations culminated in Nauvoo in the knowledge of vicarious work for the dead, the endowment, and sealings.

The idea of the temple was something completely foreign to the religious culture of Joseph Smith's day, entirely unknown to the Christian world and its traditions. Today it still sets us apart profoundly from all other Christian churches. It was a revelation of divine truth that is one of the greatest contributions of the Restoration.

The Kirtland Temple

The commandment to build a temple in Kirtland, Ohio, was received in late 1832 (D&C 88:119–21). Construction was begun in June the following year. It is not clear what the Prophet knew about temple work when the construction started, but he and the Saints labored with energy and commitment, knowing that it was the Lord's will and having the assurance that great blessings lay in store for them when it was completed. An 1833 revelation

Kirtland Temple,
Kirtland, Ohio.
The first temple of
the latter-day Church

provided the basics of its design (D&C 95:11–17). The temple, which still stands today, has two large meeting rooms, one on the main floor and one directly above it. In each of those rooms, the east and west sides contain a series of pulpits—for the Aaronic Priesthood on the east end of the room and for the Melchizedek Priesthood on the west end. On the third floor are several smaller rooms.

The temple was dedicated on 27 March 1836, accompanied by a tremendous spiritual outpouring.[1] The dedicatory prayer was offered by the Prophet Joseph Smith. It was prepared and written in advance, having been given by revelation. We have it now as section 109 of the Doctrine and Covenants.

One week later, on 3 April, while Joseph Smith and Oliver Cowdery were praying in the Melchizedek Priesthood pulpit area in the main-floor room of the temple, the Lord Jesus Christ appeared to them:

> His eyes were as a flame of fire; the hair of his head was white like the pure snow; his countenance shone above the brightness of the sun; and his voice was as the sound of the rushing of great waters, even the voice of Jehovah, saying: . . .
>
> Let the hearts of your brethren rejoice, and let the hearts of all my people rejoice, who have, with their might, built this house to my name.
>
> For behold, I have accepted this house, and my name shall be here; and I will manifest myself to my people in mercy in this house. . . .
>
> Yea the hearts of thousands and tens of thousands shall greatly rejoice in consequence of the blessings which shall be poured out, and the endowment with which my servants have been endowed in this house.
>
> And the fame of this house shall spread to foreign lands; and this is the beginning of the blessing which shall be poured out upon the heads of my people. (D&C 110:3, 6–7, 9–10)

After the Savior appeared, the three ancient prophets—Moses, Elias, and Elijah—came and restored their keys to Joseph Smith and the Church (D&C 110:11–16).

The Kirtland Temple's primary function was as a meetinghouse. But it was there that the Lord began to make known in small measure the purposes of temples and the sacred ordinances that pertain to them. Some ordinances were revealed and administered in the process of its preparation and construction.[2] The spiritual experiences and the restoration of the keys at Kirtland played a significant role in the Saints' preparation for greater things, but the temple blessings that we know today were not revealed in their fulness until some years later, after the Church had relocated to Nauvoo, Illinois.

During the turbulent 1830s, the Saints understood the need for temples to be built wherever God's kingdom was established. A site was dedicated at Independence in 1831, but because of persecution, the Saints were unable to build the Lord's house there (D&C 124:49, 51, 53). After Joseph Smith and most of the Church had left Kirtland and its temple in 1838, a site was dedicated at Far West, Missouri. But the Saints did not find enough peace from persecution to build another temple until they had become established in Nauvoo.

The Redemption of the Dead

In January 1836 in the Kirtland Temple, the Prophet learned in a vision that "all who have died without a knowledge of this gospel, who would have received it if they had been permitted to tarry, shall be heirs of the celestial kingdom of God" (D&C 137:7). Two and one-half years later in Far West, the Prophet stated: "All those who have not had an opportunity of hearing the gospel, and being administered to by an inspired man in the flesh, must have it hereafter, before they can be finally judged."[3]

We do not know when the Lord revealed the doctrine of the redemption of the dead. Perhaps like some other doctrines it came gradually over the course of time. Joseph Smith's first public discourse on the topic was on 15 August 1840, a year after the Saints had settled in Nauvoo.[4] After that he spoke about it frequently, originally in the context of baptism but later, after the endowment had been made known, in the context of the higher ordinances as well.[5]

True religion teaches that all who will be heirs of the celestial kingdom must accept the doctrines of Christ and submit themselves to the sacred ordinances of his gospel (e.g., Mark 16:15–16; John 3:3–5). Those who did not have the opportunity in life to know the Lord and his Church will be given every opportunity to hear the saving message and accept it in the world of spirits after death. The Lord's missionaries there are the spirits of departed Saints. They are teaching the gospel in the spirit world as other missionaries are here. On earth, faithful Saints have the privilege of officiating vicariously for departed persons by receiving for them the ordinances, including baptism and the ordinances of the temple. A tremendous power that accompanied the restoration of Elijah's keys turns the hearts of the children to identify their departed ancestors and provide the ordinances in their behalf

(D&C 27:9). Conversion takes place in the spirit world, but the ordinances are performed vicariously on earth among mortals. The sealing power of Elijah's keys makes those ordinances binding both on earth and in heaven.[6]

Joseph Smith taught: "[God] knows the situation of both the living, and the dead, and has made ample provision for their redemption, according to their several circumstances, and the laws of the kingdom of God, whether in this world, or in the world to come. . . .

"When speaking about the blessing pertaining to the gospel, and the consequences connected with disobedience to its requirements, we are frequently asked the question, what has become of our Fathers? will they all be damned for not obeying the gospel, when they never heard it? certainly not. But they will possess the same privilege that we here enjoy, through the medium of the *everlasting* priesthood, which not only administers on earth but in heaven."[7]

"Let the dead speak forth anthems of eternal praise to the King Immanuel," Joseph Smith wrote, "who hath ordained, before the world was, that which would enable us to redeem them out of their prison; for the prisoners shall go free" (D&C 128:22).

The first baptisms for the dead were performed in the Mississippi River in the late summer of 1840. By the end of the next year, a temporary font was constructed in the Nauvoo Temple and the baptisms were being administered there—even though the building remained under construction for more than four more years.

Endowments and Sealings

The word *endowment* denotes an extraordinary gift or blessing. In modern contexts, the word is used often with reference to gifts that continue to produce benefits long after the initial giving is finished. What we call the *temple endowment* or *endowment of the holy priesthood* is precisely such a gift, as it provides blessings that reach far beyond the initial experience.

Because the service of the Lord's house is sacred, it is not discussed outside the temples except in the most general of terms. Modern prophets have taught us that the endowment is both an instructional session and a series of ordinances. President Spencer W. Kimball stated that it "comprises a course of instruction relating to the eternal journey of man and woman from the preearthly existence through the earthly experience and on to the exaltation each may attain."[8] President Ezra Taft Benson elaborated: "In the course of our visits to the temple, we are given insights into the meaning of the eternal journey of man. We see beautiful and impressive symbolisms of the most important events—past, present, and future—symbolizing man's mission in relationship to God. We are reminded of our obligations as we make solemn covenants pertaining to obedience, consecration, sacrifice, and dedicated service to our Heavenly Father."[9]

The first endowments were administered on 4 May 1842 to members of the Twelve and other faithful persons. Because the Nauvoo Temple was still under construction, Joseph Smith conducted the ordinances in the upstairs room of his red brick store, which served as his office and the headquarters of the Church. In revealing and administering the sacred temple ordinances "for the first time in these last days," the Prophet set forth "all those plans and principles by which any one is enabled to secure the fullness of those blessings which have been prepared for the Church of the First Born, and come up and abide in the presence of the Eloheim in the eternal worlds."[10] The sacred endowment ceremony was now restored and made available to the Church. Its ordinances were administered and validated by the keys that Elijah restored, binding not only on earth but in heaven.

On 12 July 1843, the Prophet dictated to a scribe a revelation that he had received, at least in part, more than a decade earlier. It is now section 132 of the Doctrine and Covenants. The revelation probably came during the course of his work on the new translation of the Bible early in 1831, when he read with prophetic eyes

Red brick store, Nauvoo, Illinois, where the first endowments were received and where the Relief Society was organized. Photo, before 1880

the accounts of the Patriarchs in the book of Genesis. As a recent apostle has stated, the focus of those accounts is "family, family, family; and not only family, it is celestial marriage and the continuation of the family unit in eternity. You have to understand the gospel to catch that vision."[11] Those biblical narratives emphasize the profound significance of marrying within the covenant. But more importantly, they set forth repeatedly the blessings that come to a faithful woman and man who stand in a covenant relationship with each other and with God.

In responding to questions asked by Joseph Smith, the Lord stated: "Prepare thy heart to receive and obey the instructions which I am about to give unto you" (D&C 132:3).[12] In one of the most far-reaching of revelations ever dispensed from heaven, the Lord set forth the doctrine of the eternity of the marriage covenant as well as the nature of plural marriage. It appears that the legitimacy of polygamous marriages in the Bible was the Prophet's foremost question (see D&C 132:1), but a large part of the revelation deals with the eternity of marriage, the eternity of the relationship between parents and children, and the conditions and covenants that make those blessings possible.

The Lord stated:

> If a man marry him a wife in the world, and he marry her not by me nor by my word, and he covenant with her so long as he is in the world and she with him, their covenant and marriage are not of force when they are dead. . . .
>
> If a man marry a wife by my word, which is my law, and by the new and everlasting covenant, and it is sealed unto them by the Holy Spirit of promise, by him who is anointed, unto whom I have appointed this power and the keys of this priesthood; . . . it shall be done unto them in all things whatsoever my servant hath put upon them, in time and through all eternity; and shall be of full force when they are out of the world; and they shall pass by the angels, and the gods, which are set there, to their exaltation and glory in all things, as hath been sealed upon their heads, which glory shall be a fulness and a continuation of the seeds forever and ever.
>
> Then shall they be gods, because they have no end; therefore shall they be from everlasting to everlasting, because they continue; then shall they be above all, because all things are subject unto them. . . .
>
> Abraham received promises concerning his seed, and of the fruit of his loins—from whose loins ye are, namely, my servant Joseph—which were to continue so long as they were in the world; and as touching Abraham and his seed, out of the world they should continue; both in the world and out of the world should they continue as innumerable as the stars; or, if ye were to count the sand upon the seashore ye could not number them.
>
> This promise is yours also, because ye are of Abraham, and the promise was made unto Abraham; and by this law is the continuation of the works of my Father, wherein he glorifieth himself. (D&C 132:15, 19–20, 30–31)

This was a revelation of such importance that its consequences stretch into the eternities, touching the lives of an infinite number of souls. The keys of these Abrahamic blessings, including eternal marriage and eternal increase, were restored by Elias on 3 April 1836 in the Kirtland Temple. With those keys and with the sealing keys restored by Elijah at the same time, Joseph Smith and others who would hold them would have the power to create eternal families, sealing upon worthy couples all the blessings of exaltation that God ever promised.

This was the capstone of the Restoration—the crowning doctrine and the crowning power dispensed by a loving God to his weak and humble children. Through his immeasurable grace and mercy, brought to bear in the atonement of Christ, he has promised his faithful children joint heirship with his perfect Son Jesus. To those who remain true and faithful to the ordinances and covenants that they receive, he has promised *all* that he has (D&C 84:37–38).

In response to the revelation, the Prophet and others to whom he gave authority began sealing worthy, endowed couples in the "new and everlasting covenant" of marriage. Elder Wilford Woodruff of the Twelve recorded his own experience in the fall of 1843. He and his wife were visiting at the home of Elder John Taylor, a fellow apostle, "conversing about the principle[s] of the celestial world, or some of them. Brother Hyrum Smith was in with us and presented some ideas of much interest to me concerning baptism for the dead, the resurrection, redemption, and exaltation in the new and everlasting covenant that reacheth into the eternal world. He sealed the marriage covenant between me and my wife, Phebe W. Carter, for time and eternity."[13]

The Nauvoo Temple

During the time that the Lord's house was under construction in Nauvoo, the Prophet Joseph Smith prepared the Saints in a variety of ways not only for temple ordinances but also for the greater commitment to discipleship that would be required by future developments. During the early part of 1842, for example, the book of Abraham was published in the Church's Nauvoo newspaper, the *Times and Seasons.*[14] "Church History" was published at about the same time,[15] as was the "History of Joseph Smith."[16] The first of these, sometimes called the "Wentworth Letter," includes an account by Joseph Smith of the First Vision and the coming forth of the Book of Mormon. The second is the Prophet's fuller account of those early experiences that we now have as Joseph Smith–History in the Pearl of Great Price. Also during those Nauvoo years, the Prophet's great public sermons extended the Saints' doctrinal horizons.

One significant development during this period was the establishment of the Nauvoo Relief Society for the women of the Church. In the spring of 1842 at a meeting in the upper room of his red brick store, Joseph Smith met with a group of women who had organized to assist with the building of the temple by providing clothing and provisions for construction workers. The Prophet established them as an organization of the Church and redefined their mission to include looking out for the poor, helping to strengthen the virtue of the community, and saving souls. "I now turn the key to you in the name of God," he said, "and this Society shall rejoice and knowledge and intelligence shall flow down from this time."[17] Beginning as a small group in Nauvoo and then being reestablished in Utah in the 1860s, the Relief Society is now a worldwide organization that includes all the women of the Church. It continues true to its calling to bless the lives of Latter-day Saints through service.

Construction on the Nauvoo Temple was begun in the fall of 1840, and the ceremonial laying of the cornerstones took place on 6 April 1841. Joseph Smith moved the work forward despite continued persecution, expanded administrative obligations, explosive population growth (fueled by the arrival of thousands of European converts), and other developments and concerns that occupied him. When he was killed in June 1844, the temple was still two years from completion.

Sensing the shortness of his own mission and knowing the

Nauvoo Temple, Nauvoo, Illinois. Photo (daguerreotype), 1840s

importance of the sacred ordinances, Joseph Smith passed on to the Twelve the ministry of the temple. The apostles received their endowments and their sealings with their wives, and they were instructed, prepared, and empowered so they could administer the ordinances as God's authorized servants. Less than three months after the Prophet's martyrdom, Elder Orson Hyde of the Twelve stated: "We were in council with Brother Joseph almost every day for weeks. . . . He conducted us through every ordinance of the holy priesthood, and when he had gone through with all the ordinances, he rejoiced very much and says, 'Now if they kill me, you have got all the keys and all the ordinances, and you can confer them upon others.'"[18] President Wilford Woodruff later recalled: "In the winter of 1843–4, Joseph Smith, the Prophet of God, called the Twelve Apostles together in the City of Nauvoo, and spent many days with us in giving us our endowments, and teaching us those glorious principles which God had revealed to him."[19]

As sections of the temple were finished after the Prophet's death, they were made available for the ordinances. By the time the main body of the Church evacuated Nauvoo in February 1846, bound for a new home in the West, more than five thousand had received their endowments from the apostles in the temple. The Lord had been true to his promise given in 1841: "I grant unto you a sufficient time to build a house unto me" (D&C 124:31). Three months after the main exodus from Nauvoo, the temple was finally dedicated—on 1 May 1846. Two and one-half years later it was in ruins, the result of abandonment, vandalism, and arson.

The highest, the noblest, and the best of our religion are embodied in the temple and its ordinances and covenants. That is true not only because the highest priesthood ordinances are performed there but also because the highest yearnings of our souls find fulfilment there—our yearnings for oneness with God and with those whom we love, whether living or departed. Thus it should not be surprising that wherever the Saints have been established, temples have been established as well. Just four days after President Brigham Young arrived in the Salt Lake Valley with the first of the pioneers, he designated a site for the construction of a temple. And so it has continued all over the world since then.

Notes

1. See Milton V. Backman Jr., *The Heavens Resound: A History of the Latter-day Saints in Ohio, 1830–1838* (Salt Lake City: Deseret Book, 1983), 294–300. See Elder Orson Pratt's recollections in *Journal of Discourses,* 26 vols. (London: Latter-day Saints' Book Depot, 1855–86), 18:132.

2. Joseph Smith, *History of The Church of Jesus Christ of Latter-day Saints,* ed. B. H. Roberts, 2d ed. rev., 7 vols. (Salt Lake City: Deseret Book, 1957), 2:379–80, 382.

3. *Elders' Journal* 1, no. 3 (July 1838): 43.

4. Smith, *History of the Church,* 4:231; Andrew F. Ehat and Lyndon W. Cook, eds., *The Words of Joseph Smith: The Contemporary Accounts of the Nauvoo*

Discourses of the Prophet Joseph (Provo, Utah: Religious Studies Center, Brigham Young University, 1980), 49 n. 1 (15 August 1840).

5. Joseph Smith, *Joseph Smith's Commentary on the Bible,* comp. and ed. Kent P. Jackson (Salt Lake City: Deseret Book, 1994), 69–73, 169–70, 195, 201–4.

6. The doctrine of the redemption of the dead was revealed clearly in the days of Joseph Smith. But in 1918 a marvelous vision to President Joseph F. Smith provided additional details on the process; see D&C 138.

7. *Times and Seasons* 3, no. 12 (15 April 1842): 760.

8. "The Things of Eternity—Stand We in Jeopardy?" *Ensign,* January 1977, 6; see also James E. Talmage, *The House of the Lord,* rev. ed. (Salt Lake City: Deseret Book, 1969), 83–84.

9. Ezra Taft Benson, *The Teachings of Ezra Taft Benson* (Salt Lake City: Bookcraft, 1988), 251.

10. Smith, *History of the Church,* 5:2.

11. Bruce R. McConkie, "The Promises Made to the Fathers," in Kent P. Jackson and Robert L. Millet, eds., *Genesis to 2 Samuel,* Studies in Scripture Series, vol. 3 (Salt Lake City: Deseret Book, 1989), 55.

12. See Robert L. Millet, "A New and Everlasting Covenant," in Robert L. Millet and Kent P. Jackson, eds., *The Doctrine and Covenants,* Studies in Scripture Series, vol. 1 (Salt Lake City: Deseret Book, 1989), 512–26.

13. Wilford Woodruff diary, 11 November 1843; *Wilford Woodruff's Journal,* ed. Scott G. Kenney, 9 vols. (Salt Lake City: Signature Books, 1983–85), 2:326–27; punctuation and spelling modernized.

14. *Times and Seasons* 3, no. 9 (1 March 1842): 703–6; 3, no. 10 (15 March 1842): 719–22; 3, no. 14 (16 May 1842): 783.

15. *Times and Seasons* 3, no. 9 (1 March 1842): 706–10.

16. *Times and Seasons* 3, no. 10 (15 March 1842): 726–28; 3, no. 11 (1 April 1842): 748–49.

17. Ehat and Cook, *Words of Joseph Smith,* 118.

18. *Times and Seasons* 5, no. 17 (15 September 1844), 651; punctuation modernized.

19. Wilford Woodruff, "Epistle to the Church," 10 October 1887, in James R. Clark, ed., *Messages of the First Presidency of The Church of Jesus Christ of Latter-day Saints,* 6 vols. (Salt Lake City: Bookcraft, 1966–75), 3:134.

Chapter 23

Joseph Smith the Seer

The mission of the Prophet Joseph Smith included, among other things, the revelation of new scripture. The Book of Mormon, the Doctrine and Covenants, the Pearl of Great Price, and the Joseph Smith Translation provided an explosion of gospel knowledge—each contributing in unique ways to the opening of the heavens with the restoration of lost truth. Any one of them individually would be a miracle of profound consequence. Collectively, they flood the world with gospel light as never before. And they stand unitedly as a witness to the latter-day restoration of the gospel through the Prophet Joseph Smith.

Not all that God revealed through Joseph Smith is found in scriptural records. His sermons and writings contain inspired insights of tremendous worth. He was a great seer, which the book of Moses defines as one who sees things that are "not visible to the natural eye" (Moses 6:36). He was blessed with doctrinal knowledge that gave him a clearer understanding of truth than any other man of modern times. By the power of the Holy Ghost, he "understood the fulness of the gospel from beginning to end and could teach it."[1] And because he had that power, we can trust his teachings to lead us in the way of salvation.

Joseph Smith taught that "a prophet is not always a prophet—only when he is acting as such,"[2] and he reminded the Saints that he was only a man and was imperfect.[3] But when he taught the principles of the gospel in his prophetic role, his doctrine can be trusted as "scripture, . . . the will of the Lord, . . . the mind of the Lord, . . . the word of the Lord, . . . the voice of the Lord, and the power of God unto salvation" (D&C 68:4). "When did I ever teach anything wrong from this stand?" he asked. "I never told you I was perfect, but there is no error in the revelations which I have taught."[4] "The doctrine I teach is true."[5]

The Prophet understood well that it was his mission not only to receive God's word by revelation but also to teach what he knew. "'Tis my duty to teach the doctrine,"[6] he stated, and "it is my meditation all the day, and more than my meat and drink, to know how I shall make the Saints of God to comprehend the visions that roll like an overflowing surge before my mind."[7] Sharing with others that "overflowing surge" of revelation was part of his great legacy to the human family.

Doctrinal Writings

Joseph Smith was a teacher in writing as well as from the pulpit. Whether in private correspondence or in open publications, he used writing as a medium through which to proclaim the gospel message. His written words are preserved primarily in diaries, letters, and newspaper articles.[8]

The Prophet's diaries, kept to record the history of the Restoration, are a source of his teaching for later generations. Some of his diary entries were dictated by him to scribes. Other diaries were kept in his name by scribes who observed his activities and recorded what he did and said. Both kinds contain significant information in his words about Church government, Church history, and doctrinal instruction. The material contained in these sources is an important part of the Restoration.[9]

In private correspondence, Joseph Smith used doctrinal principles, often illustrated with scriptural examples, to give encouragement and instruction. When he wrote to family members or Saints, his letters became an opportunity to teach and explain.

When he wrote to persons who were not members of the Church, his letters were missionary tools that introduced the principles of the gospel.[10]

The Prophet used the Church's periodicals as another means of teaching the gospel. During the early history of the Church, we had religious newspapers that contained articles on a variety of gospel subjects. These periodicals functioned much as our Church magazines do today. In the *Evening and Morning Star* (Independence, 1832–33; Kirtland, 1833–34), the *Latter Day Saints' Messenger and Advocate* (Kirtland, 1834–37), the *Elders' Journal* (Kirtland, 1837; Far West, 1838), and the *Times and Seasons* (Nauvoo, 1839–44), articles and editorials by Joseph Smith communicated important gospel topics to the Saints. They are a significant window into his prophetic thought.[11]

Doctrinal Sermons

Joseph Smith had taught the gospel openly since the beginning of the Restoration. But before the Nauvoo period, his public discourses seemed to play a smaller role in his ministry than did some other aspects of his calling—organizing and administering the Church, building buildings, translating and printing sacred books, and caring for the temporal needs of the Saints. The Prophet had delegated much of the public speaking to his counselor in the First Presidency, the gifted orator Sidney Rigdon, who had been called by revelation to be his spokesman (D&C 35:23; 100:9–11). But when Joseph Smith emerged in the spring of 1839 from his imprisonment in the Liberty, Missouri, Jail, he brought with him a new urgency to make known to the world the things of God. During his Nauvoo years, from May 1839 until his death in June 1844, that urgency guided and energized his life.[12]

Among other important things the Nauvoo period is known for, it was the time when the Prophet himself taught powerful doctrinal principles in public sermons, some before small groups but many before thousands in outdoor meeting places.[13] As he spoke, the great seer opened the windows of heaven and stretched his listeners' gospel understanding with truths they had never heard before.

Joseph Smith "said he was not like other men. . . . He had to depend entirely upon the living God for every thing he said" when he spoke publicly.[14] Indeed, his discourses were revelatory events, and they were a principal means by which the Lord gave new gospel light to the Church during the last years of the Prophet's life. Those who heard him speak knew they were witnessing something extraordinary. One listener recorded in his journal: "We felt a desire to behold the Prophet Joseph. On the following day (Sunday), we proceeded to the temple (then in an unfinished state) to hear him preach. We were gratified in seeing and hearing him on that occasion, and we soon felt and knew we were listening to one that had not been taught of men—so different were all his thoughts and language."[15] Another wrote: "I have listened to his clear and masterly explanations of deep and difficult questions. To him all things seemed simple and easy to be understood, and thus he could make them plain to others as no other man could."[16]

To Know the Character of God

Joseph Smith stated: "But few understand the character of God. They do not know, they do not understand their relationship to God. . . . What kind of a being is God? Turn your thoughts in your hearts and say, have any of you seen or heard him or communed with him? This is a question that may occupy your attention."[17]

The endeavor to know God, according to the Prophet, is a matter of great importance for the world: "If men do not comprehend the character of God, they do not comprehend themselves. What kind of a being is God? Eternal life [is] to know God. If man does not know God, [he] has not eternal life."[18]

The true understanding of God's character had been removed from Christianity through the Apostasy and further obscured by

The Prophet Joseph Smith (1805–44), portrait by Sutcliffe Maudsley, Nauvoo, 1844

the philosophies that guided the creation of traditional Christian thought. And despite the efforts of good people through the centuries to find the God of scripture, nothing short of a latter-day restoration of truth—direct from heaven—could bring back the fulness of the knowledge that was lost. During the last years of his life, and especially during the last months, much of Joseph Smith's public teaching was dedicated to making known to the world "what kind of being" God is. It is not insignificant that his greatest doctrinal contribution in those days was to teach us the true nature of God. That process, which had begun with the First Vision more than two decades earlier, culminated in the great doctrines he taught in the spring of 1844.

In the funeral sermon for a man named King Follett at general conference on 7 April, and in the final public sermon of his life on 16 June, Joseph Smith unveiled to us the God of heaven and taught us of our true relationship to him.[19] Following are some of the things that the Lord made known to his prophet about God and man, as recorded by scribes from his sermons, mostly near the end of his life.

The Father, the Son, and the Holy Ghost are three separate beings. "Any person that has seen the heavens opened knows that there are three personages in the heavens holding the keys of power."[20] "Every one [is] a different or separate person, and so [are] God and Jesus Christ and the Holy Ghost separate persons. But they all agree in one or the selfsame thing."[21]

This was not a new doctrine in 1844; in fact, it was a great message of the First Vision in 1820. But its significance is enormous because, like other things Joseph Smith learned by revelation about God, it disagrees so radically with the received Christian doctrine of the Trinity. "I have always declared God to be a distinct personage. Jesus Christ [is] a separate and distinct person from God the Father; the Holy Ghost is a distinct personage or spirit. And these three constitute three distinct personages and three Gods."[22]

The Father and the Son have bodies of flesh and bones. "The Father has a body of flesh and bones as tangible as man's; the Son also" (D&C 130:22). "There is no other God in heaven but that God who has flesh and bones."[23]

In the First Vision, young Joseph Smith certainly was able to see and understand that God and man are in the same shape or form, just as the Bible teaches (Gen. 1:26–27). At some point in his life, he learned the additional truth that God is not a spirit but that he has a body that is tangible. Without question, the material nature of God's body is a dramatic departure from Christian tradition, which holds God to be "a most pure spirit, invisible, without body, parts, or passions, immutable, immense, . . . incomprehensible."[24]

Perhaps an even more dramatic departure from tradition, however, is the knowledge that God's body is of flesh and bones, which, if one were to consider the matter thoughtfully, tells us something of our relationship to deity. Because God has a material body, then obviously "the idea that the Father and the Son dwell in a man's heart is an old sectarian notion, and is false" (D&C 130:3).

The Holy Ghost has a body of spirit. "The Son has a tabernacle and so has the Father. But the Holy Ghost is a personage of spirit without tabernacle."[25] Although "tabernacle" in this statement from the Prophet means physical body, the Holy Ghost is not without a body; he has a body of spirit. Joseph Smith taught: "There is no such thing as immaterial matter. All spirit is matter, but it is more fine or pure, and can only be discerned by pure eyes; we cannot see it; but when our bodies are purified we shall see that it is all matter" (D&C 131:7–8). Further, "the Holy Ghost is yet a spiritual body and [is] waiting to take to himself a body, as the Savior did."[26] And "the Holy Ghost is now in a state of probation, which if he should perform in righteousness, he may pass through the same or a similar course of things that the Son has."[27]

God is a man. "God, that sits enthroned, is a man like one of yourselves. That is the great secret. If the veil were rent today and the great God, who holds this world in its sphere or its orbit, [and] the planets—if you were to see him today you would see him in all the person, image, [and] very form of man. For Adam was created in the very fashion of God."[28] For Latter-day Saints, this is a literal description with profound implications.

God was once as we are now. "God [is] a man like one of us, even like Adam. [He was] not God from all eternity; [he was] once on a planet with flesh and blood, like Christ."[29] "I want you to understand God and how he comes to be God. We suppose that God was God from eternity. I will refute that idea, or I will do away or take away the veil so you may see. It is the first principle to know that we may converse with him and that he once was a man like us. . . . The Father was once on an earth like us."[30]

This is a revolutionary doctrine, and as the Prophet told us, it draws back the veil so we can see as never before. Obviously, it places tremendous distance between Latter-day Saint theology and that of the rest of Christianity. The knowledge that God "once was a man like us," that we indeed are created in his image, and that he has a body of flesh and bones, should give us cause to ponder our own nature and contemplate who we really are.

Based on Jesus' statement in John 5:19 that he, Jesus, does not do anything except what he sees the Father do, Joseph Smith presented the Savior's words as follows: "I do the things I saw my Father do before worlds came rolling into existence. I saw my Father work out his kingdom with fear and trembling, and I must do the same."[31] " 'The work that my Father did do I also.' And these are the works: he took himself a body and then laid down his life that he might take it up again"—the birth, death, and resurrection of God. "We then also took bodies to lay them down, to take them up again."[32]

There are other Gods. Because God was once a man in a probationary status similar to our own, it follows that he was neither the first nor the only divine being in the cosmos.

This knowledge, according to the Lord's prophet, "sets one free to see all the beauty, holiness, and perfection of the Gods." Joseph Smith said, "All I want is to get the simple truth, [the] naked and the whole truth. . . . If Jesus Christ was the Son of God and . . . God the Father of Jesus Christ had a father, you may suppose that he had a father also. Where was there ever a son without a father? Where ever did [a] tree or anything spring into existence without a progenitor? And everything comes in this way. . . . Hence if Jesus had a father, can we not believe that he had a father also?"[33]

These words draw back the veil even more and give us a far brighter view of reality—not only the reality of our own world and experience but a reality that far transcends the scope of all that we can perceive. A grand celestial process is at work.

Although our God had predecessors, he is still to us the only God. "I want to set it in a plain, simple manner," Joseph Smith said. "There is but one God pertaining to us, in all, through all."[34] The scriptures teach truly that he is the only God, because the whole scope of our own existence and progression is under his divine government, and in all things we are dependent on him. We do not know all that there is to know, because not all reality in the universe pertains to us. As the Lord told Moses, "Only an account of this earth, and the inhabitants thereof, give I unto you" (Moses 1:35). This general principle, which governs all that God chooses to make known, tells us that there are, for the present, divinely established bounds to our perceptions.

We are eternal beings. "The spirit of man is not a created being. It existed from eternity and will exist to eternity."[35] Ancient and modern scriptures contain numerous references to eternal destinies and eternal rewards, and thus we can understand, to some degree, an eternal future. But because all that we know has a beginning, it is difficult for us finite mortals to comprehend an eternal past. Through the Prophet Joseph Smith, the Lord revealed more about our origin than we could have imagined without the bright light of modern revelation: "The soul, the immortal spirit,"[36] "the soul, the mind of man, where did it come from?"[37] "They say God created it in the beginning. The idea lessens man, in my estimation. [I] don't believe the doctrine [and] know better; God told me so. . . . We say that God was self-existent. . . . Who told you that man did not exist upon the same principle? . . . The mind of man, the intelligent part,"[38] "is as immortal as God himself."[39]

These divinely inspired words add a missing dimension to our understanding of who we are. Some part of us, recorded by the Prophet's scribes as "the spirit," "the soul," "the immortal spirit," "the mind of man," "the intelligent part," and "intelligence," is as eternal as God himself. According to Joseph Smith, God did not make it; it always existed: "Intelligence is eternal, and it is self-existing."[40] It is "a spirit from age to age, and [there is] no creation about it."[41]

But there is yet more to who we are. As later prophets of the Restoration have taught, at some point in our past this preexisting "intelligence" was "created" into a spirit body as a spirit daughter or son of God. President Joseph F. Smith and his counselors stated in 1909 that "man, as a spirit, was *begotten and born of heavenly parents,* and reared to maturity in the eternal mansions of the Father, prior to coming upon the earth in a temporal body."[42] Thus in a literal sense pertaining to our spirit bodies, God is not just our Creator but our Father. Knowing this through modern revelation, we can now understand Jesus' frequent references to our Heavenly Father as he intended them to be understood, with all the affection, concern, and kinship that exists between a child and a loving parent.[43]

Because we are daughters and sons of Deity with God as the Father of our spirits, an additional gem of revelation from the Prophet was needed to help us understand better our origin. It was articulated best by Eliza R. Snow, a plural wife of Joseph Smith, who wrote it in a poem, "My Father in Heaven" (now called "O My Father"), not long after the Prophet's death.

> I had learn'd to call thee father,
> Through thy spirit from on high;
> But until the key of knowledge
> Was restor'd, I knew not why.
> In the heav'ns are parents single?
> No, the thought makes reason stare;
> Truth is reason—truth eternal
> Tells me I've a mother there.[44]

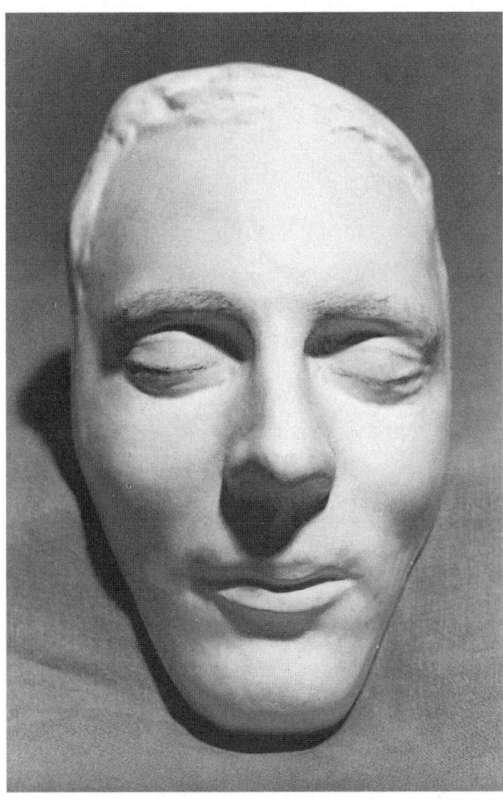

The Prophet Joseph Smith, death mask. It was common in the nineteenth century to make molds of the faces of deceased persons to preserve their image

We may become as God is. "What was the design of the Almighty in making man? It was to exalt him to be as God."[45]

That succinct statement tells us why God created our spirit bodies, why he created our physical bodies, and what our ultimate purpose is for being on earth. Joseph Smith taught that "all the spirits that God ever sent into this world are susceptible of enlargement." "God himself, . . . because he was greater, saw proper to institute laws whereby the rest could have a privilege to advance like himself."[46] Through laws, ordinances, and covenants, the Father makes available to his sons and daughters the opportunity to develop fully the divine qualities that we inherit from him.

In an act of profound unselfishness, he offers us all that he has (D&C 76:55; 84:38), which is "to inherit the same power [and] exaltation, until you ascend the throne of eternal power, same as those who are gone before,"[47] "enjoying the same rise, exaltation, and glory, until you arrive at the station of a God."[48]

Through Joseph Smith, the Lord challenges us: "To know God, learn to become Gods."[49] "You have got to learn how to be a God yourself and be a king and priest to God, same as all have done, by going from a small capacity to another, from grace to grace, until the resurrection, and sit in everlasting power as they who have gone before. . . . When you climb a ladder, you must begin at the bottom rung until you learn the last principle of the gospel. For it is a great thing to learn salvation beyond the grave."[50] Indeed, "it will take a long time after the grave to understand the whole."[51]

Again, a grand celestial process is at work in the cosmos, from eternity to eternity. A loving God provides blessing after blessing, advancement after advancement, and grace after grace for those who are willing to trust his plan and submit themselves to his kindness and wisdom, as those "who have gone before." To develop in faith the qualities that will make us like our Heavenly Father, we, his sons and daughters, have come as strangers to a fallen world, far from the celestial home of our origin, and subject to all the forces of confusion and sin that seek to divert us from our heritage. It is only through our Father's plan of happiness—brought to pass through Jesus Christ, his Only Begotten Son in the flesh—that we can know who we really are and how we can return to them. The Prophet Joseph Smith taught that "through the atonement of Christ and the resurrection and obedience in the gospel, we shall again be conformed to the image of his Son Jesus Christ. Then we shall have attained to the image, glory, and character of God."[52]

The Principles of Eternal Life

Joseph Smith acknowledged that these doctrines "are incomprehensible to some." Yet they are nonetheless "the first principles of the gospel."[53] They are "first principles" because they respond to the deepest human needs and answer the fundamental questions of human existence: "Who am I?" "Where did I come from?" "Why am I here?" "Where am I going?"

In unveiling God to humankind, the Prophet also unveiled humankind. He showed us that we are not the chance products of chemical reactions or accidents of physics. We are children of divine parents, eternal beings of the same species as God, who under his loving care and guidance are in training to prepare us for the eternities—to become like he is and to live the kind of life that he lives.

As we examine the gospel of Jesus Christ with unveiled eyes regarding our origin and our potential, we can see how the different aspects of the Restoration fit together to provide us with every needful blessing. Through the restoration of knowledge, priesthood, covenants, and keys, men and women are enabled to fulfill the purpose of their creation and assist those whom they love to do likewise. We now know, for example, why covenants in this life must be made in light of eternity to do what they were intended to do. We also know what the intended purpose of eternal marriage is, and why the eternal union of a man and a woman is the key to the grand celestial process in which each daughter and son of God is engaged.

This "is not all to be comprehended in this world."[54] But there is still much we can learn and much we can know. As "soon as we begin to understand the character of God, he begins to unfold the heavens to us."[55] And as we soften our hearts and allow ourselves to be taught the things of eternity through that unfolding, we will see things as they really are and obtain an even greater willingness to be instructed and an even greater love for truth. Joseph

Smith said concerning the learning of the things of God: "I want to see all, in all its bearings, and hug it to my bosom."[56] "This is good doctrine. It tastes good. I can taste the principles of eternal life, [and] so can you. They are given to me by the revelations of Jesus Christ, and I know you believe it."[57]

Notes

1. Andrew F. Ehat and Lyndon W. Cook, eds., *The Words of Joseph Smith: The Contemporary Accounts of the Nauvoo Discourses of the Prophet Joseph* (Provo, Utah: Religious Studies Center, Brigham Young University, 1980), 215; spelling and punctuation modernized in some quotations.

2. Joseph Smith diary, 8 February 1843; see Dean C. Jessee, ed., *The Papers of Joseph Smith,* 3 vols. (Salt Lake City: Deseret Book, 1989–97), vol. 3; spelling and punctuation modernized in some quotations.

3. "I told them I was but a man, and they must not expect me to be perfect; if they expected perfection from me, I should expect it from them; but if they would bear with my infirmities and the infirmities of the brethren, I would likewise bear with their infirmities." Ehat and Cook, *Words of Joseph Smith,* 132; see also 130, 369.

4. Ibid., 369.

5. Jessee, *Papers of Joseph Smith,* 1:175.

6. Ehat and Cook, *Words of Joseph Smith,* 363.

7. Ibid., 196.

8. Most of the Prophet's written legacy is collected in Joseph Smith, *History of The Church of Jesus Christ of Latter-day Saints,* ed. B. H. Roberts, 2d ed., rev., 7 vols. (Salt Lake City: Deseret Book, 1957). In this important work, which was compiled mostly after Joseph Smith's death, his diaries were supplemented with his letters, his other writings, transcripts of his sermons, and diary entries from others to fill gaps in his record. See Dean C. Jessee, "The Writing of Joseph Smith's History," *BYU Studies* 11, no. 4 (summer 1971): 439–73. Most of the important doctrinal material from Smith, *History of the Church* was collected in Joseph Smith, *Teachings of the Prophet Joseph Smith,* sel. Joseph Fielding Smith (Salt Lake City: Deseret Book, 1938).

9. The original diaries are collected in Jessee, *Papers of Joseph Smith,* vols. 2 and 3.

10. The Prophet's letters, those preserved in his own hand or dictated by him to scribes, are collected in Dean C. Jessee, ed., *The Personal Writings of Joseph Smith* (Salt Lake City: Deseret Book, 1984), 227–615.

11. It is not certain where or to what extent he may have used the assistance of other writers when preparing items for publication. See his comments in "To Subscribers," *Times and Seasons* 3, no. 9 (15 March 1842), 710.

12. President Rigdon's contributions to the Church diminished substantially during the Nauvoo years, and the Prophet was no longer able to rely on him as a spokesman, as reflected in D&C 124:103–4.

13. Ehat and Cook, *Words of Joseph Smith,* identified more than 170 sermons by Joseph Smith in Nauvoo in contemporary documents. Most transcripts are very fragmentary, but some are quite extensive. Some were recorded by persons with no official calling as scribes, such as Martha Jane Coray and James Burgess. But many were recorded by such official scribes as Willard Richards and William Clayton. Multiple transcripts of some discourses provide checks on accuracy.

14. Ehat and Cook, *Words of Joseph Smith,* 238.

15. William Rowley diary, 12 November 1843, ibid., 258.

16. Mercy R. Thompson, ibid., xx.

17. Ehat and Cook, *Words of Joseph Smith,* 343–44.

18. Ibid., 340.

19. See Ehat and Cook, *Words of Joseph Smith,* 340–62, 378–83; Donald Q. Cannon and Larry E. Dahl, *The Prophet Joseph Smith's King Follett Discourse: A Six-Column Comparison of Original Notes and Amalgamations* (Provo, Utah: Religious Studies Center, Brigham Young University, 1983); and Smith, *Teachings of the Prophet Joseph Smith,* 342–61, 369–76.

20. Ehat and Cook, *Words of Joseph Smith,* 214.

21. Ibid., 382.

22. Ibid., 378.

23. Ibid., 60.

24. "The Westminster Confession of Faith, 1647," 2.1, in Philip Schaff, *The Creeds of Christendom,* 4th ed., 3 vols. (New York: Harper, 1919), 3:606.

25. Ehat and Cook, *Words of Joseph Smith,* 64.

26. Ibid., 382.

27. Ibid., 245. President Heber C. Kimball taught, "The Holy Ghost is a man; he is one of the sons of our Father and our God," in *Journal of Discourses,* 26 vols. (London: Latter-day Saints' Book Depot, 1855–86), 5:179.

28. Ehat and Cook, *Words of Joseph Smith,* 357.

29. Ibid., 361.

30. Ibid., 344.

31. Ibid., 350.

32. Ibid., 382; emphasis added.

33. Ibid., 380.

34. Ibid., 378.

35. Ibid., 9.

36. Ibid., 351; see Cannon and Dahl, *Prophet Joseph Smith's King Follett Discourse,* 49.

37. Ehat and Cook, *Words of Joseph Smith,* 345.

38. Ibid., 359.

39. Ibid., 352.

40. Ibid., 346.

41. Ibid., 360.

42. First Presidency, "The Origin of Man," in Daniel H. Ludlow, ed., *Jesus Christ and His Gospel* (Salt Lake City: Deseret Book, 1994), 482; or in Daniel H. Ludlow, ed., *Encyclopedia of Mormonism,* 5 vols. (New York: Macmillan, 1992), 1668; emphasis added.

43. See Matt. 5:16, 45, 48; 6:1, 8, 14, 15, 26, 32; 7:11; 10:20, 29; 18:14; 23:9; Mark 11:25, 26; Luke 6:36; 11:13; 12:30; John 20:17.

44. *Times and Seasons* 6, no. 18 (15 November 1845): 1039; *Hymns of The Church of Jesus Christ of Latter-day Saints* (Salt Lake City: The Church of Jesus Christ of Latter-day Saints, 1985), no. 292.

45. Ehat and Cook, *Words of Joseph Smith,* 247.

46. Ibid., 360.

47. Ibid., 350.

48. Ibid., 345.

49. Ibid., 361.

50. Ibid., 350.

51. Ibid., 345.

52. Ibid., 231.

53. Ibid., 357.

54. Ibid., 358.

55. Ibid., 341.

56. Ibid., 381.

57. Ibid., 346.

Chapter 24

The Continuing Restoration

Like the Prophet Joseph Smith, we recognize the doctrine of the Restoration to be "good doctrine,"[1] and we too desire to embrace it and "hug it to [our] bosom."[2] We Latter-day Saints have much reason to be thankful, being among the most blessed of any who have ever lived on earth. In our time we enjoy the gospel's fulness—revealed in these last days to prepare the way for the coming of our Savior. The Church of Jesus Christ of Latter-day Saints is the Lord's church, having been built on the sure and indispensable foundation of true authority and true doctrine, both revealed from God. To our Father in Heaven and his beloved Son Jesus Christ we give all honor, praise, and love for the infinite goodness of their plan for our happiness and for their never-ending work to share its blessings with us. Through the witness of the Holy Ghost, we know that it is their work. It originates with them and not with men, and to them we freely give our worshipful praise and thanks.

It is not inappropriate for us to praise also the memory of the Prophet Joseph Smith, the prophet of the Restoration, the messenger of Christ who revealed Him to us and taught us His gospel. As Elder John Taylor wrote in words later canonized as scripture, "Joseph Smith, the Prophet and Seer of the Lord, has done more, save Jesus only, for the salvation of men in this world, than any other man that ever lived in it" (D&C 135:3). By reflecting both the character and the message of Jesus Christ, the Prophet Joseph Smith and his ministry of revelation have opened the way for us to know our Savior and to return to his presence. For his contributions as a servant in God's work "to bring to pass the immortality and eternal life of man" (Moses 1:39), we can freely exclaim, "Praise to the man who communed with Jehovah!"[3]

President Brigham Young said of Joseph Smith: "When I first heard him preach, he brought heaven and earth together. . . . He took heaven, figuratively speaking, and brought it down to earth; and he took the earth, brought it up, and opened up, in plainness and simplicity, the things of God."[4] On another occasion President Young said:

> I want to think of matters that will make my heart light, like the roe on the mountains—to reflect that the Lord Almighty has given me my birth on the land where He raised up a Prophet, and revealed the everlasting Gospel through him, and that I had the privilege of hearing it—of knowing and understanding it—of embracing and enjoying it. I feel like shouting hallelujah, all the time, when I think that I ever knew Joseph Smith, the Prophet whom the Lord raised up and ordained, and to whom He gave keys and power to build up the kingdom of God on earth and sustain it. These keys are committed to this people, and we have power to continue the work that Joseph commenced, until everything is prepared for the coming of the Son of Man. This is the business of the Latter-day Saints, and it is all the business we have on hand.[5]

Joseph Smith had a clear and perfect vision of what it would take to build Zion on earth in preparation for the Lord's coming and the Millennium. His untiring efforts to organize communities, build homes and other buildings, educate minds, and encourage collective industry and prosperity illustrate his interest in the Saints' temporal well-being and the spiritual blessings that would flow from it. But he also knew that the building of Zion involved the strengthening of human souls through spiritual learning, personal revelation, priesthood ordinances, and temple covenants.

The Prophet understood that these combined efforts would lead to the establishment of Zion. And he knew the significance of his role in that process, as well as that of the faithful Saints who worked with him to accomplish it. As he wrote in 1842, it would be a labor in behalf of all humanity that would involve the efforts of individuals on both sides of the veil:

The building up of Zion is a cause that has interested the people of God in every age. It is a theme upon which prophets, priests, and kings have dwelt with peculiar delight. They have looked forward with joyful anticipation to the day in which we live, and fired with heavenly and joyful anticipations they have sung, and written, and prophesied of this our day. But they died without the sight. We are the favored people that God has made choice of to bring about the latter-day glory. It is left for us to see, participate in, and help to roll forward the latter-day glory, "the dispensation of the fulness of times," when God will "gather together all things that are in heaven, and all things that are upon the earth, even in one" [Eph. 1:10], when the Saints of God will be gathered in one from every nation, and kindred, and people, and tongue, when the Jews will be gathered together into one, and the wicked will also be gathered together to be destroyed, as spoken of by the prophets. The spirit of God will also dwell with his people and be withdrawn from the rest of the nations. And all things, whether in heaven or on earth, will be in one, even in Christ.

The heavenly priesthood will unite with the earthly to bring about those great purposes. And whilst we are thus united in the one common cause to roll forth the kingdom of God, the heavenly priesthood are not idle spectators. The spirit of God will be showered down from above; it will dwell in our midst. The blessings of the Most High will rest upon our tabernacles, and our name will be handed down to future ages. Our children will rise up and call us blessed, and generations yet unborn will dwell with peculiar delight upon the scenes that we have passed through, the privations that we have endured, the untiring zeal that we have manifested, the insurmountable difficulties that we have overcome in laying the foundation of a work that brought about the glory and blessings which they will realize, a work that God and angels have contemplated with delight for generations past, that fired the souls of the ancient patriarchs and prophets, a work that is destined to bring about the destruction of the powers of darkness, the renovation of the earth, the glory of God, and the salvation of the human family.[6]

Joseph Smith knew that the Church would go on after him and build on what had been done in his time. We who live in a later generation, who harvest abundantly from the seeds planted in his day, gladly fulfill his prophecy: we do indeed call him and his noble contemporaries "blessed" and "dwell with peculiar delight" on the work they performed "in laying the foundation" for the blessings which we realize today.

The Prophet said that he was laying "a foundation that will revolutionize the whole world."[7] Yet he understood that after his time there would still be much to be done, and the work of the Restoration would continue. As long as the earth would stand, God's plan would be carried forth by others, and its effect on humanity would be enormous: "The standard of truth has been erected; no unhallowed hand can stop the work from progressing. Persecutions may rage, mobs may combine, armies may assemble, calumny may defame, but the truth of God will go forth boldly, nobly, and independent till it has penetrated every continent, visited every clime, swept every country, and sounded in every ear, till the purposes of God shall be accomplished and the great Jehovah shall say, 'The work is done.'"[8]

Through the ministry of Joseph Smith, the Lord revealed all the priesthood and keys that would be necessary to carry the Church forward to the time of Jesus' second coming. The sure foundation of doctrine was likewise revealed, with enough scripture and gospel knowledge to more than meet the needs of the latter-day Saints. But the work of the Restoration is a continuing process that will always require the service of men who hold the keys of apostolic authority, including the prophetic gifts that were so clearly manifested in the ministry of the Prophet Joseph Smith. He was not the last of the latter-day prophets but the first, and those who have succeeded him have carried on the Lord's work that he commenced, following the same course with the same vision and the same authority that he possessed. As Elder Spencer W. Kimball reminded us in 1960, "Never again will the sun go down. . . . Revelation is here to remain. Prophets will follow each other in a never-ending succession, and the secrets of the Lord will be revealed without measure."[9]

"This is the dispensation of the fulness of times. It is the greatest of all gospel dispensations, when all that was revealed in past generations has been revealed anew." So said another great successor to Joseph Smith, President Gordon B. Hinckley. "And from this time forth it will move forward to cover the earth, in the due time of the Lord, and touch the lives and hearts of good people everywhere. There is nothing like this work anywhere else on earth."[10]

As the kingdom of God rolls forth with the spread of the gospel message and the growth of the Lord's Church, we appreciate more than ever the foundation laid through the ministry of the Prophet Joseph Smith. We love him for his service, as we also love his successors who have been called of God to serve since the Restoration began. It is a continuing restoration because revelation remains the great hallmark of The Church of Jesus Christ of Latter-day Saints. And so it will continue as the Church prepares the world for the return of its Lord and Master, Jesus Christ. Perhaps these words of President Gordon B. Hinckley best express the spirit of hope and joy that Latter-day Saints everywhere feel as they contemplate the Lord's great work of the latter days: "How glorious is the past of this great cause. It is filled with heroism, courage, boldness, and faith. How wondrous is the present as we move forward to bless the lives of people wherever they will hearken to the message of the servants of the Lord. How magnificent will be the future as the Almighty rolls on His glorious work touching for good all who will accept and live His gospel. . . . I invite every one of you, wherever you may be as members of this Church, to stand on your feet and with a song in your heart move forward, living the gospel, loving the Lord, and building the kingdom. Together we shall stay the course and keep the faith, the Almighty being our strength."[11]

Notes

1. Andrew F. Ehat and Lyndon W. Cook, eds., *The Words of Joseph Smith: The Contemporary Accounts of the Nauvoo Discourses of the Prophet Joseph* (Provo, Utah: Religious Studies Center, Brigham Young University, 1980), 346, spelling modernized.

2. Ibid., 381.

3. *Hymns of The Church of Jesus Christ of Latter-day Saints* (Salt Lake City: The Church of Jesus Christ of Latter-day Saints, 1985), no. 27.

4. In *Journal of Discourses,* 26 vols. (London: Latter-day Saints' Book Depot, 1855–86), 5:332 (7 October 1857).

5. Ibid., 3:51 (6 October 1855).

6. *Times and Seasons* 3, no. 13 (2 May 1842): 776; grammar and punctuation modernized.

7. Ehat and Cook, *Words of Joseph Smith,* 367.

8. "Church History," *Times and Seasons* 3, no. 9 (1 March 1842): 709; punctuation modernized.

9. "To His Servants the Prophets," *Instructor,* August 1960, 256–57.

10. Remarks in Crawley, England, 26 August 1995; *Ensign,* August 1996, 60.

11. *Ensign,* November 1995, 72.

Scripture Index

PEARL OF GREAT PRICE

Moses

Subject Index